PRAISE FOR *THE SACRAMENT OF SAME-SEX MARRIAGE*

"USING THE VOICES AND EXPERIENCES OF LGBTQ MARRIED COUPLES who have connections to Catholicism, Bridget Burke Ravizza makes a strong case for the sacramentality of same-sex marriage. She argues that sacramentality is made concrete in the lifelong, covenanted, and life-giving relationships that make up the core of this volume. There is often pain in these stories as couples encounter hate and rejection from family and church, but there is also redemption in the ways these couples and those who love them model community and fidelity. This gem of a book reminds us that moral reflection is always enriched by attention to the many small details of everyday experience."—**Aline Kalbian**, author of *Sexing the Church: Gender, Power, and Ethics in Contemporary Catholicism*

"Burke Ravizza has written an excellent, exceptionally clear account of the sacramental nature of same-sex marriage. She deftly blends in-depth interviews of gay and lesbian couples with a nuanced engagement with Catholic sacramental and moral theology. This is a book for theologians, ministers, people in church on Sunday, and people who don't feel welcome in church on Sunday."—**David DeCosse**, author of *Created Freedom under the Sign of the Cross: A Catholic Public Theology for the United States*

"A landmark study! Centering the lived experiences of same-sex couples, *The Sacrament of Same-Sex Marriage* provides rich testimony for both the graces of married life and the disorienting harm of magisterial teachings. An essential reading for Catholic educators, Dr. Burke Ravizza's book will transform Catholic conversations about marriage."—**Emily Reimer-Barry**, author of *Reproductive Justice and the Catholic Church: Advancing Pragmatic Solidarity with Pregnant Women*

"In this inspiring study of 22 same-sex married couples, Burke Ravizza has undertaken what Francis calls 'listening with the ear of the heart' to give voice to the loving and fruitful sacramental character of their relationships. Her message for those who would erect ecclesial fences around the sacraments: love knows no borders and grace has no limits"—**Julie Clague,** coeditor, *Moral Theology for the Twenty-First Century*

"This book redefines the sacramental nature of marriage by providing ample testimony of the manifestations of grace in the union of gay and lesbian couples through the public commitment of marriage. Despite the ongoing tensions between the institutional Church, magisterial teaching, and the People of God, Burke Ravizza proposes a renewed hermeneutical lens that allows the witness of queer marriages to mediate the essence of God incarnated and imbued in the sacramental and quotidian realities of everyday life, challenging the institutionalization of sin that aims to control where, how, when, and through whom the essence of God is made manifest."—**Elsie Miranda,** Association of Theological Schools

The Sacrament of Same-Sex Marriage
An Inclusive Vision for the Catholic Church

Bridget Burke Ravizza

SHEED & WARD
Lanham • Boulder • New York • London

Acquisitions Editor: Richard Brown
Acquisitions Assistant: Victoria Shi
Sales and Marketing Inquiries: textbooks@rowman.com
Credits and acknowledgments for material borrowed from other sources, and reproduced with permission, appear on the appropriate pages within the text.
Published by Rowman & Littlefield
An imprint of The Rowman & Littlefield Publishing Group, Inc.
4501 Forbes Boulevard, Suite 200, Lanham, Maryland 20706
www.rowman.com

86-90 Paul Street, London EC2A 4NE

Copyright © 2024 by The Rowman & Littlefield Publishing Group, Inc.

All rights reserved. No part of this book may be reproduced in any form or by any electronic or mechanical means, including information storage and retrieval systems, without written permission from the publisher, except by a reviewer who may quote passages in a review.

British Library Cataloguing in Publication Information available

Library of Congress Cataloging-in-Publication Data

Names: Ravizza, Bridget Burke, author. Title: The sacrament of same-sex marriage : an inclusive vision for the Catholic Church / by Bridget Burke Ravizza. Description: [Lanham] : [Rowman & Littlefield Publishing Group], [2024] | Includes bibliographical references and index. | Summary: "Drawing on interviews with twenty-two same-sex, married couples, this book argues that the Catholic tradition should expand its definition of sacramental marriage to include same-sex couples. Stories from these couples illustrate that the church would benefit from a deeper commitment to practices of radical hospitality and sanctuary"-- Provided by publisher.
Identifiers: LCCN 2023052257 | ISBN 9781538182260 (cloth) | ISBN 9781538182277 (paperback) | ISBN 9781538182284 (epub)
Subjects: LCSH: Marriage--Religious aspects--Catholic Church. | Same-sex marriage--Religious aspects--Catholic Church.
Classification: LCC BX2250 .R37 2024 | DDC 265/.508664--dc23/eng/20240323
LC record available at https://lccn.loc.gov/2023052257

*For John and Clare
and
For Tim and Peter, two beloved brothers from other mothers*

Contents

Acknowledgments ix
Introduction xiii

CHAPTER 1: Marriage as Sacrament: Becoming One and
Growing in Holiness. 1

CHAPTER 2: Marriage as Sacrament: Grace Overflowing 31

CHAPTER 3: Family: Tension, Integration, and Belonging. 87

CHAPTER 4: Church: Tension, Integration, and Belonging 113

CHAPTER 5: Catholic Institutions: Tension, Integration, and
Belonging 147

Conclusion 181

Postscript on Blessings of Same-Sex Unions 193
Appendix: About the Participants 195

Bibliography 197
Index 205
About the Author 211

Acknowledgments

Truly a communal endeavor, this book depended on the generosity of many. My heart is full when I think of those who contributed, supported, prayed, and perseveringly encouraged over the years as this project grew from idea to final form.

While I can't name the people and parishes at the center of the project, please know of my profound gratitude for you. First of all, thank you to the twenty-two couples who told me your stories with touching vulnerability, courage, and grace. I deeply appreciate your trust in me. My greatest hope is that these pages honor your stories and your love.

To those who connected me to married couples for the study, thank you for your faith in the project. To those around the country who arranged and provided spaces in which to conduct interviews, thanks for your gracious hospitality.

To those who housed me and fed my body and spirit as I traveled around, thank you: Mara Brecht and Ben Kesling; Jim Keane; Reg Kim and Molly Sampson; Kristin Heyer and Mark Potter; Tom and Erin (Foley) Kozak; Dodie and Mike Ravizza—plus Heidi, Mitchell, and Molly—my San Jose fam; Peter Ravizza; and the Babcock clan—Paul, Christie, Grace, Molly, Meg, and the Mickster.

Thanks to treasured colleagues at St. Norbert College, especially my friends in Theology and Religious Studies. Thanks to those who read chapter drafts, helped me work through ideas, walked with me (literally and figuratively), and otherwise loved

Acknowledgments

me and held me accountable: Carrie Arnold, Christie Babcock, Tom Bolin, Mara Brecht, Clare Burke Ravizza, Karlyn Crowley, Deirdre Egan-Ryan, Debbie Faase, Howard Ebert, and Paul Wadell. Julie Donovan Massey—without our shared project, this one would not exist. You are a cherished friend and intellectual, spiritual, and euchre partner. To my ethics crew: David DeCosse, Karen Peterson-Iyer, Chris Vogt, and Kristin Heyer—thanks for the convos and laughs and for letting ol' Bronzie tag along with the bigwigs. (I miss you, Miss Lizzy Brinkmann.) Thanks to the Golden Girls for prayers, good vibes, and loon calls. To my house church spirit-family, you bring me hope, and I couldn't have made it through the pandemic years without you. And, to my CSJA group: breaking bread and sharing my heart with you fills me up and reminds me of what matters most.

I'm indebted to so many teachers and scholars whose work has shaped my own. Thank you for doing good, justice-focused theology and for sharing what you know. Special shout out to Professor Fred Parrella who taught Theology of Marriage at Santa Clara University, a course that first prompted me to consider the theological questions addressed in this book. And thanks to the LGBTQ students I've had the privilege of teaching and learning from over the years, whose own stories and friendship have taught me invaluable lessons of love, inclusion, and belonging.

Thanks to Richard Brown at Sheed & Ward for your enthusiastic, kind, and steady support as the manuscript took shape, and for generous readers who offered thoughtful feedback along the way.

To my family: Mike and Dodie, thanks for raising three beautiful sons and taking such good care of us all, especially CBR upon her return to California. Mom, you and Dad were my first and best teachers about unconditional love and hospitality. Thanks for creating a home where all were welcome. Christie Margaret, my sista!, you are my heart. Joey, years ago, you and Brendan expanded our little family, and you continue to widen our hearts—it's good

ACKNOWLEDGMENTS

to have you back in Wisconsin. Sweet Clare, thanks for your constant enthusiasm about this project and for helping to make it (and me) better along the way. I ardently love and admire you. Finally: Johnny, you are my sanctuary. Home is wherever I'm with you.

Introduction

An Invitation to Listen

We sat in Liam's office space on a May afternoon, the sun beating through the wall of windows, as Liam and Marty described their "beautiful" ceremony of holy union that had taken place twenty-one years prior. They told me about the effort to "strongly feature" both families, including Liam's dad, who walked him down the aisle; the vows proclaimed in front of a validly ordained Catholic priest (in a Protestant church); and the carefully chosen traditions, readings, and music (in retrospect, Liam jokingly noted, they probably "didn't have to do the litany of the saints for thirty minutes . . ."). Marty teared up as he explained that, on the morning of their holy union, Liam read the newspaper. "We'd already prepared the prayers of the faithful," Marty said, "but he's like, 'We need to add one.' He goes, 'There's this young kid in Montana who was gay bashed. Clinging to life. We don't know if he's going to live or die.' So, Matthew Shepard was killed the weekend of our holy union. You talk about the world at that point, that there could be so much hate. And so we prayed for him by name."

"Yeah," added Liam. "And then fast forward twenty years later, they're interring his ashes at the National Cathedral. And we go. And our kid is . . ."

"Our daughter's sitting between us," Marty said.

"There's twenty-eight hundred people in the cathedral for a kid who died twenty years ago," Liam described, when an old friend, who happened to be sitting in the same section, "came running up to us and she's like, 'I can't believe you're here. I can't believe you have a kid!'

Introduction

And she said, 'I first heard about him at your wedding. You prayed for him at your wedding. He was alive.'" Liam considers for a moment: "I don't know why I thought [we should pray for Matthew Shepard] that morning. The image they had. *The Post* had an image of a fence and they I think used the wording 'as if he were crucified' because they tied him to a fence with concertina wire with his arms out. And that's how the woman found him, thought he was a scarecrow, like tied. So that image immediately hit me as a Christian image of something done to someone. It wasn't all that deep or anything. It was a twenty-year-old boy who was crucified in Wyoming. That's what I thought about it. And he was alive and he was gay."

This multilayered story stirs my heart. I'm moved by its humanity: the messy intertwining of joy and grief—a beautiful celebration of married love and a boy beaten and dying. I'm moved by its Catholicity: the recognition of a cruciform body and the decision to honor that wounded body in the wedding liturgy—asking the church, the gathered body of Christ, to call Matthew Shepard by name, recognizing him as part of the communion of saints, though a stranger. When the community prayed for him, "he was alive," but not long after, he was not. He was one more name to be added to the litany of saints. Notice the bookends of the story: the wedding liturgy and the internment liturgy, twenty years later—Marty and Liam with their daughter sitting between them. United, through time, in the body of Christ. The story is both deeply human and Catholic. It is complicated and tragic, life-giving and joyful. It is challenging. And, I'd argue, there is a clear thread of the Holy Spirit moving through it.

This book is an invitation for you to listen to (or better, read) many such stories, an invitation to enter into them with an open mind and heart. They are the fruit of interviews I conducted with twenty-two married couples who have a meaningful relationship to the Catholic tradition. These couples also happen to be gay and lesbian rather than straight. My conversations with these couples are a follow-up to a research project that I conducted with a dear friend and colleague, Julie Massey, M.Div., resulting in *Project Holiness: Marriage as a Workshop for Everyday Saints*. For that endeavor, we surveyed hundreds of married couples who were active in Catholic parishes, and conducted interviews with fifty couples, as distinct couples and in focus groups.

Since historically much of what has been written about Catholic marriage has been top-down, often written by people who are not married themselves, Julie and I wanted to hear directly from married couples about how their faith impacts their marriage, and their marriage impacts their faith. We sought to think theologically about marriage from below, confident that these couples had something theologically enriching to share. Indeed, they did. Through their stories, we gained valuable insight on marriage as it relates to: authentic friendship; sex, generativity, and parenting; sacrament; mercy and service; suffering; and fidelity.

For that research, we relied on contacts within twenty Catholic parishes, who initially connected us to couples, and who often arranged interview space for us (and even provided snacks!). Hospitality abounded. I remember attending morning Mass at one parish, after which Julie and I were to conduct interviews, and a parishioner who knew why we were there asked us, "Are you including any same-sex couples in your research?" We answered no, adding quickly, "That'll be the next project," although we had no such project planned. Including same-sex couples was something we had discussed and decided against. It would complicate the already-challenging project on a number of levels, affecting, for example, how we would: recruit couples, find spaces to conduct interviews, focus questions and conversations, and determine a clear audience for the writing. It likely comes as no surprise that much of that complication is rooted in the fact that the Catholic magisterium currently does not recognize same-sex marriages as fitting their definition of sacramental marriage (more on that in the coming pages). The question posed to us—are you including same-sex couples?—nevertheless pricked at our consciences, and it was not the last time someone asked it.

After we completed *Project Holiness* and took a breath or two, a follow-up project with same-sex couples seemed both promising and necessary, particularly in light of debates about, and ultimately significant legal changes related to, marriage equality in the United States. Unfortunately, shifting work obligations meant that Julie was unable to collaborate, so I embarked on the project alone. This time around, in addition to hearing from same-sex couples about how their faith impacts their marriage and their marriage impacts their faith, I hoped to evaluate the position taken by the Congregation for the Doctrine of Faith in 2003,[1] and affirmed by Pope Francis in *Amoris Laetitia* in 2016, that "there are absolutely no grounds for considering homosexual unions to be in any way similar or even remotely analogous to God's plan for marriage and family." Indeed, I hope that encountering the stories collected in this book will help *you* to consider that position in a more informed way, and along with it, other magisterial teachings on same-sex relationships and family. Nevertheless, I invite you to encounter these couples and their experiences not primarily in a spirit of evaluation, but in a spirit of dialogue.[2]

Pope Francis beautifully and prolifically writes about the necessity and benefits of dialogue in the church and world. In *Fratelli Tutti*, he writes: "Approaching, speaking, listening, looking at, coming to know and understand one another, and to find common ground: all these things are summed up in the one word 'dialogue.' If we want to encounter and help one another, we have to dialogue."[3] Yes. We have to dialogue to encounter and help one another, to find common ground, to know and understand one another as members of one body of Christ. Crucially, genuine dialogue requires careful and humble listening. The Pope suggests:

> We need to practice the art of listening, which is more than simply hearing. Listening, in communication, is an openness of heart which makes possible that closeness without which genuine spiritual encounter cannot occur. Listening helps us to find the right gesture and word which shows that we are more than simply bystanders. Only through such respectful and compassionate listening can we enter on the paths of true growth and awaken a yearning for the Christian ideal: the desire to respond fully to God's love and to bring to fruition what [God] has sown in our lives.[4]

The moment is certainly ripe for intentional listening, as the Catholic church is in the midst of the Synod on Synodality that began in 2021. In this process, Pope Francis reminds us that we are called to be a listening and discerning church.

Introduction

I offer this book to the church as a small but hopefully meaningful contribution to ongoing dialogue about same-sex marriage and family, from a Catholic perspective. For me, this project provided an opportunity to practice "the art of listening." I strove to listen respectfully and compassionately to these gay and lesbian couples, with a commitment to honor what is good and true in their experiences of marriage and family, and to consider what the Church might learn from them. I understand that there are possible pitfalls in my gathering and sharing these stories of same-sex couples due to my heterosexual privilege and the limits of my experience. I'm a straight, cisgender, white woman—going on twenty-seven years married. My husband and I, both Catholic, were eager participants in the Sacrament of Matrimony. By virtue of our Catholicity and our heterosexuality, we were welcomed to bless our marriage in a Catholic church, surrounded by beloved family and friends. I recognize now, as I did those many years ago, that participating in the sacramental ritual was a privilege.

When I first embarked on this project, I knew it would be more challenging to find couples willing to participate than last time around. Julie and I connected to married couples through contacts at Catholic parishes and conducted most interviews at parish centers. The process was time-consuming, but fairly straightforward. This time around, I needed to work much harder—and more creatively—to connect to married couples and find spaces in which to speak to them. As noted above, I sought out same-sex, married couples who had *a meaningful connection to the Catholic tradition*. I defined that broadly for obvious reasons. I'm aware that many LGBTQ[5] persons have a strained or fractured relationship with the tradition, and I wanted to hear from folks with a variety of experiences. Hence, for a couple to participate in the study, it was not necessary for both or either of them to currently identify as Catholic or to be active in a Catholic parish. As the interviews came together, I ended up with a healthy mix: some folks identified as Catholic, some as formerly Catholic, some as non-Catholic. Some were actively practicing in a church community (either Catholic or Protestant), some were not, and some were searching for a welcoming community. But as couples, all claimed a meaningful connection to the Catholic tradition. In the appendix, I report couples' basic demographic information. You can see that interviewees were predominantly, though not exclusively, white and highly educated, which, admittedly, is a limitation of the study. I reflect on these narratives knowing that the church has much more to learn from couples representing diverse racial, ethnic, economic (and other) communities.

I cast my net widely and conducted in-person interviews with couples in Wisconsin, Chicagoland, Washington, DC, Philadelphia, New York City, Boston, San Diego, and the San Francisco Bay area. To find couples, I relied mostly on people who knew me, or people who trusted someone who knew me (or at least knew *of* me) and could vouch for the legitimacy of my project and my trustworthiness. Many were understandably wary of the project. One telling example is a pastor from a gay-friendly church in a major city on the east coast. I reached out to him because the church had been recommended by a couple of friends as a vibrant community and potential place to find couples for the study. I sent information about me and my study via email before calling him on the phone. When we spoke, the pastor immediately and emphatically told me no. He would not ask any couples to reach out to me to find out about the study. He told me that I was the second researcher who had contacted him in recent months, trying to connect to parishioners. He explained that people join that parish community for healing and nourishment rather than to be made subjects of study, and it was his job to protect them. I told him that I understood his position and appreciated his fidelity to his parishioners. Who could blame him or others for refusing to participate, in light of experienced harm and marginalization? Ultimately, however, twenty-two couples *did* agree to take a leap of faith and share their stories with me. I cannot thank them enough for their vulnerability, candor, and trust.

At the conclusion of interviews, I always asked: "Is there anything else you'd like to share? What else would you like the wider church to know about your marriage?" One woman, Maggie, quickly responded, "Well, just that we're here." She wants people to "reconcile the notion" that LGBTQ couples exist in the church, rather than pretending that "because it's not allowed, you know, [that] you can be gay but you can't act on it," same-sex couples don't exist. Maggie wants people not only to reckon with the fact that LGBTQ persons and couples are in the church—"we're here"—but to consider that the church is better for their presence. "We're adding value to the church, not taking away or causing any damage," Maggie said. "So let's just admit we're all here, contributing to the church. Do we want to formally acknowledge that? . . . [It] seems so short sighted to [ignore or downplay] how fully the gay, lesbian, queer community are active already in our church and have been for years and years." "Centuries," her wife added.

I relate this to a story that I heard from Dan, who at the time of our interview had been married to his husband, Jaime, for four and a half years; they'd been together for fourteen. Dan is now active in a gay-affirming and broadly welcoming parish, but for years was alienated from the Catholic church, "not really identifying as Catholic at all." He grew up "very involved with the church," living in a "small bubble" of Catholic families and attending Catholic schools. In high school and college, Dan "dealt with some serious depressions . . . all centered around coming out. It just didn't seem like a reality that could be." He described "growing up and having these feelings as a kid, and going to Catholic school and being taught: as you grow up, marry a woman. It just was this disconnect and I . . . just kind of repressed it, which led me to be very depressed." The seemingly irreconcilable disconnect between his gay identity and his Catholic identity brought Dan to "the point of being suicidal," both in high school and again in college.[6]

Dan was involved in the Newman Center in college and "had a very serious girlfriend" whom he met through the Center. "She was on a mission to get married, and I think I could see that." Since Dan believed he was gay, but was still struggling to come out, he broke off the relationship. He went to speak with a religious sister with whom he felt particularly close, and he came out to her. She immediately told him that he was not alone, and indicated other LGBTQ persons who were out and active in the parish—for example, a Bible study group leader and an older couple who came regularly to mass, one man pushing the other in a wheelchair. "She started mentioning all of these people." She seemed to want to normalize Dan's experience and show that he was not alone in the church,

Introduction

but Dan said, "Part of me got really angry at that. Because I was like, why is it hidden?"

Dan had "a similar conversation" with his parents when he came out. They talked with him about a neighbor who had died of AIDS, and other people in their various communities who were LGBTQ, including fellow church members. Dan explained, "So, it sounds a little funny, but it was a very eye-opening experience to me that, you know, I was kind of surrounded by gay people and I probably trained myself not to see it, and—rather than feeling welcome—I was kind of angry because I felt lost for so long and I felt like, why is this hidden?" While LGBTQ persons were hidden from Dan, what he most needed as a young, gay person was to have these members of the body of Christ held in the light. Had he known about their presence, perhaps he could have imagined a way forward for himself in the church. As it was, he got angry. He "pretty much stopped going to church with [his] family or through the Newman Center and drifted away from that circle of friends," "not really identifying as Catholic at all" for some years.

Today, Dan is alive, well, and married to a man; and he's reconnected with the church, though the relationship is not simple. Some of the reasons that LGBTQ persons were, and often continue to be, hidden in the church will be explored in this book. For now, it seems prudent to pause and consider Dan's recollection of that difficult time of life when he suffered from depression and suicidal thoughts. He told me: "In college, at that point, I came to this realization that if I'm willing to do something that drastic [that is, die by suicide], I might as well try living who I am and see what happens. I probably could phrase that much better. But I kind of learned to do that, and without any help from the church. And so it's still kind of hard to come back."

In the coming pages, you will read many stories about how queer persons in my study learned to *live who they are*, and how they negotiate their relationship with the Catholic church and tradition (as individuals and as couples). In turn, I hope you will contemplate what it means to "be church" when the people of God are diverse, and in that diversity, some feel "lost" and in need of being found, accepted, and appreciated within the body of Christ. What Maggie and Dan teach us is the value of recognizing and appreciating LGBTQ persons and couples in the church and the damage that's done when they remain hidden or on the margins. In sharing these stories with you, I hope to be part of an effort to move what is hidden into the light. Through this book, I invite you to come with an open heart on a journey of encounter, as the body of Christ continues to discern how the Holy Spirit is moving us, trusting that "Ours is a God of Surprises, who is always ahead of us."[7]

Moving forward, you should be aware that, in order to protect confidentiality, I use pseudonyms throughout, change the names of parishes, and do not identify specific locations by name. I've avoided including any information that would allow participants to be easily identified. Quotes are taken from recordings of interviews and have not been altered, other than being minimally cleaned up for clarity or changed to protect anonymity.

Here's what's ahead.

Chapters 1 and 2 focus on marriage as sacrament. In chapter 1, I highlight how these couples describe their relationships and marriages as sacramental, how they experience themselves as sacraments to each other. The couples discuss how their partner's love and care helps them more fully to know God's love for them. They explain how their wedding rituals bound them to one another before God and community, and how they live out their marital promises of unconditional love and fidelity daily and over the long haul. They reflect on the myriad ways their marriages function to make them better—that is, more authentically themselves, more virtuous, and ultimately closer to God.

In chapter 2, the discussion of sacrament continues, but focus shifts to how couples become sacrament to others—what I'm calling the outward-facing sacramental dimension of marriage. Their stories reveal marital love that is generative, spilling out and including others. Couples describe Christian attitudes and practices by which they live, bringing God's love into their homes and beyond—creating families grounded in love, practicing hospitality, and responsibly caring for others in need. Additionally, in chapters 1 and 2, we will see how spouses recognize and appreciate ordinary sacraments in their daily lives and homes, reflecting an expansive sacramental vision with deep roots in the Catholic theological tradition. Ultimately, in these first two chapters, I argue that these marriages are *de facto* sacramental and that the Catholic magisterium would do well to expand its definition of sacramental marriage to include same-sex couples.

In chapters 3 through 5, we'll hear stories of tension, integration, and belonging within the various communities of which these same-sex couples are a part. The chapters will focus on families, churches, and Catholic institutions, respectively. I hope listening to these experiences can help us understand what is at stake when queer persons and couples are outright rejected, treated unequally, or not fully integrated into families, church communities, and Catholic institutions. What becomes clear is that church teaching and its application often harms these couples, resulting in destruction of persons and rupture of families, churches, and Catholic institutions. On the other hand, the stories can help us better understand how gospel-motivated practices of radical hospitality and inclusion lead to the flourishing of persons, families, and communities.

I'll conclude with a theological reflection on the church's obligation to listen and respond to the stories of LGBTQ persons and couples in light of the sense of the faithful. I'll reassert my argument that these marriages are sacramental and in fact do fit the definition of marriage from a Catholic perspective insofar as they are lifelong, covenantal, and life-giving. I will suggest that the Catholic church would benefit from both pastoral and doctrinal change. Finally, I'll hold up *church as sanctuary* is a promising way to be church, taking to heart the testimony of these couples.

You will notice that a single couple's story begins each chapter, inviting us into that chapter's topic—sacrament (to one another), sacrament (outward-facing), and tension, integration and belonging in family, church, and Catholic institutions. Following the introductory story, the testimony of various couples will be woven throughout. Since there are many couples to keep track of, periodically I will provide reminders meant to help you keep track of couples as you move through the book. Now, let's get to the stories.

Introduction

Notes

1. Congregation for the Doctrine of Faith, Considerations Regarding Proposals to Give Legal Recognition to Unions Between Homosexual Persons, June 3, 2003, https://www.vatican.va/roman_curia/congregations/cfaith/documents/rc_con_cfaith_doc_20030731_homosexual-unions_en.html, sec. 4, quoted by Pope Francis in *Amoris Laetitia*, March 19 2016, https://www.vatican.va/content/dam/francesco/pdf/apost_exhortations/documents/papa-francesco_esortazione-ap_20160319_amoris-laetitia_en.pdf, sec. 251.

2. For a thorough and thoughtful examination of the ethics of encounter, see Marcus Mescher, *The Ethics of Encounter: Christian Neighbor Love as a Practice of Solidarity* (New York: Orbis Books, 2020).

3. Pope Francis, *Fratelli Tutti* October 3, 2020, https://www.vatican.va/content/francesco/en/encyclicals/documents/papa-francesco_20201003_enciclica-fratelli-tutti.html, sec. 198.

4. Pope Francis, *Evangelii Gaudium* November 24, 2013, https://www.vatican.va/content/francesco/en/apost_exhortations/documents/papa-francesco_esortazione-ap_20131124_evangelii-gaudium.html, sec. 171.

5. Throughout the book, I will use the acronym "LGBTQ" and the word "queer" (interchangeably) to describe persons who claim a sexual or gender identity that does not correspond to established binary notions of sexuality and gender, especially heterosexual norms. I know some use other acronyms, such as LGBTQIA+. Language develops, and there is not absolute consensus on these labels. Most fundamentally, I believe people should be able to name and identify themselves (and that others should respect those preferences). I hope my decision to use "LGBTQ" and "queer" honors the couples I interviewed.

6. Data shows that LGBTQ youth are more than four times as likely to attempt suicide than their peers. The Trevor Project (thetrevorproject.org) offers up-to-date, data-driven information on the mental health of LGBTQ young people and suicide risk and prevention. See "Facts About LGBTQ Youth Suicide," The Trevor Project, December 15, 2021, https://www.thetrevorproject.org/resources/article/facts-about-lgbtq-youth-suicide/.

7. Pope Francis and Austen Ivereigh, *Let Us Dream: The Path to a Better Future* (New York: Simon & Schuster, 2020), 93.

CHAPTER 1

Marriage as Sacrament

Becoming One and Growing in Holiness

"By 'sacrament' I mean any person, place, thing or event, any sight, sound, taste, touch or smell that causes us to notice the love that supports all that exists, that undergirds your being and mine and the being of everything about us. How many sacraments are there? The number is virtually infinite, as many as there are things in the universe . . . for all of you who are married, I hope that one of the deepest, richest, most profound experiences of the fundamental love which undergirds your being is your spouse."[1]—Michael Himes

Thinking of marriage as a sacrament is deeply rooted in the Catholic tradition, so it seems like a logical and meaningful place to begin our journey. Therefore, sacrament will be the focus and framework for chapters 1 and 2. In *Project Holiness*, Julie Massey and I discussed three dimensions of sacrament manifest in the lives of the couples we interviewed, and I will do the same in these chapters with the testimony from the couples in this study. As noted in the introduction, the three dimensions of sacrament are: spouses as sacraments to one another; spouses (and their families) as sacraments to others; and sacraments in daily married and family life. You will see that the three dimensions can be distinguished, yet inevitably overlap and thus cannot be neatly separated.

As noted in the introduction, in chapter 1, we'll consider how the married couples in my study are *sacrament to one another* in their daily care and ongoing fidelity, which is graced. In and through their covenantal love for one another, sealed in the wedding liturgy, these spouses grow ever closer to God. Couples as sacrament to one another = dimension one. In chapter 2, we'll see how these married couples are *sacraments to others* as their shared love overflows. Not surprisingly, such love often takes shape in loving, educating, and nurturing children. Beyond parenting, however, these spouses are sacraments to others in myriad ways, especially through expressions of Christian hospitality and care for the poor and vulnerable. Couples as sacraments to others = dimension two.

These first two dimensions of sacrament correspond to what magisterial teaching purports sacramental marriage is and what sacramentally married people *are* and *do*. According to a Catholic understanding of sacramental marriage, two baptized Christians pledge lifelong love and fidelity before the church community in the wedding liturgy, within which their relationship is celebrated and blessed. Empowered by the grace of Christ, the spouses henceforth live out that covenantal love with one another, simultaneously becoming a sign or icon of God's steadfast, gracious, and merciful love to and for others. Married couples become and work as one body within the wider Body of Christ, building up the good of the spouses and the common good.[2] Further, woven into chapters 1 and 2 will be testimony illustrating how spouses recognize and appreciate *ordinary sacraments* in their daily lives and homes. Applying an expansive sacramental vision with deep roots in the Catholic theological tradition, *quotidian, ordinary sacraments* = dimension three.

At the conclusion of chapter 2, we'll spend some time theologically wrestling with official Catholic teaching on the Sacrament of Matrimony in light of the experience of these couples—whose marriages, by their own accounts, are deeply sacramental—with the help of relevant work of some contemporary theologians. The testimony of the couples, you will see, problematizes current magisterial teaching, which limits participation in the Sacrament of Matrimony to opposite-sex couples. In short, same-sex couples are denied the sacrament outright. And so we'll dig into and evaluate the reasons why the magisterium officially excludes same-sex couples from participation in the sacrament and the definition of marriage itself. Ultimately, I will argue that the church would do well to expand its understanding of marriage as sacrament to fully include same-sex couples. But first I invite you to listen to how couples reflect with great conviction and profundity on their marriages as sacramental.

Excitement was in the air as I walked in the door. Megan and Mary had just added a new member to their household—an adorable puppy, bouncing around the front room. After a proper introduction to the pup, we settled in at the kitchen counter to begin our conversation. At the time we spoke, the couple had been happily married for four years[3] and together for fourteen. They described their marriage as wonderful and a calling from God. Facing Mary, Megan said, "It definitely feels, like by the Spirit, I feel like you are for me. And that I am in a space where I am supposed to be." "I really always felt like that," Mary affirmed. Nevertheless, there was a moment early on in their budding relationship, in 2005, when Mary and Megan resisted their bond and at one point "tried to give each other up for Lent."

The two met in college—Megan a senior, and Mary a junior. They quickly became "the best of friends." Not long after, they "realized that things were more than friendship." Megan connected to Mary through campus ministry, and thought " . . . whoa, this woman is just, like, the cat's meow. Look at how she is just so wise and so filled with the spirit!" Looking at Mary, she said, "You were the best human that I'd ever met. All I wanted to do was be with you from the beginning. I wanted to be with you because you made me happy and you were interesting, and obviously I was attracted to you. *That* I realized more and more." In turn, Mary reminded Megan why she fell in love with her: "You were just so interesting and wonderful and so generous and giving . . . [I was drawn to] the way that I saw your spirit sort of come into the world, so generously and openly, with joy but also vulnerability. I had never experienced that in someone before. And I thought you were super interesting. And you were like a year older, so you knew how to register for classes." They laughed. Mary described their relationship as "super organic and very inevitable." Organic and inevitable in retrospect, but far from easy at the beginning.

Megan said, "I came out to Mary, telling her that I think I have these feelings for her at the beginning of the second semester of my senior year . . . And I think [she] said, 'Whoops.'" *Whoops*. They had become "intertwined," yet did not know how to process their intense and increasingly romantic feelings for one another. Megan continued: "It was really very hard and very confusing for a long time. And then I think even when we were together, we spent the first eight months trying to decide how we were going to stop being together, which when I think about it makes me want to cry. It was super sad because it was so great and so wonderful, and I think our relationship is really great and wonderful, and it was really sad not to be able to enjoy it or share it with anyone." They hid their relationship from others, and they struggled.

"When Megan graduated from college, I was still left because I was a year younger," Mary explained. "I felt like I lost half my blood. I felt like I was half, like half of my soul was gone and I didn't understand that. And I beat myself up about that a lot like, 'Geez, get over yourself. Move on. You have other friends. You have a great life. You really like school.' But it was just very confusing about why it was so hard for me."

"You weren't at the point where you [could admit]: I think I'm in love with her," Megan responded.

"No, because I didn't have a schema for that. I didn't know any gay people in high school. There were no out people," Mary said. "[I was] just really naive. *Really* naive. I just had no exposure. You know, I came from a super homogenous place—school and town and church—and there wasn't that much in the media, and I was pretty religious and so it never really crossed my mind, you know." Therefore, when her feelings developed for Megan, she had no adequate frame of reference for understanding them.

Megan was attracted to girls before she met Mary. She "definitely worried about it," though she dated boys in high school because it made her "feel normal." Being with Mary was the first time she was honest about her sexuality. She said that her relationship with Mary gave her "the courage to think about it and talk about it."

Both young women were conflicted. As faithful and practicing Catholics, they strategized together and decided to try to give each other up for Lent. Mary explained, they were "trying to integrate faith and practice and what we were taught Lent was about: returning to God and, you know, getting rid of things that cause you harm." They were attempting to faithfully respond to what Catholic teaching asserts: that their more-than-friendship relationship was sinful and harming them. "It was awful. It was so destructive. Just theologically. I mean, it was terrible. It was terrible in all ways. And we sort of laugh about it now." Looking at Megan, "But you're also crying a little bit." Teary-eyed, Megan said, "Well, you know we laugh about it for sure. But sometimes when you pause . . ."

"When you think about it, it was like, *Good God, you know?*" Mary said. "And that was totally a moment when no one else knew what we were going through. You know we hid it from everybody. And so here we're struggling through Lent, thinking that maybe we'll be strong enough, partly so that I could have a job, because we felt like I wouldn't have a career or I didn't have a future in ministry if we would continue forward." Mary hoped to pursue ministry upon graduation. She has in fact worked as a minister "in a couple of different settings, mostly Catholic or predominantly Catholic settings," and is currently a chaplain. But she worried as a college student that such work would be an impossibility if she stayed in a relationship with Megan.

The two also worried at that point about their families and how they'd respond. Megan, in particular, feared her family's reaction because both her mother and grandmother worked within Catholic settings. Mary said, "We could not imagine a world in which it was going to be possible to have our families and to not be abandoned or to not have to hurt them so badly that we wouldn't be able to make it." In light of these multilayered concerns—related to church teaching, work, and family—giving each other up for Lent seemed like a logical move: "it was like, well here the Church has given us this time in the liturgical cycle, in the community, in which to try our best to do this right."

In the 1986 "Letter to the Bishops of the Catholic Church on the Pastoral Care of Homosexual Persons," the Congregation for the Doctrine of Faith writes: "What, then, are homosexual persons to do who seek to follow the Lord? Fundamentally, they are called to enact the will of God in their life by joining whatever sufferings and difficulties they experience in virtue of their condition to the sacrifice of the Lord's Cross. That Cross, for the believer, is a fruitful sacrifice since from that death comes life and redemption. While any call to carry the cross or to understand Christian suffering in this way will predictably be met with bitter ridicule by some, it should be remembered that this is the way to eternal life for all who follow Christ" (sec.12).[4] Yet, Mary and Megan's experience (and the stories of others like them) calls us to consider whether it is fair and just to ask some Christians—namely, those who do not have an opposite-sex orientation—to practice celibacy for life, without the possibility of entering into a married partnership in which they may express their sexuality in moral and life-giving ways, as heterosexual persons are able to do. Why must this community carry this cross when others in the Christian community need not?

For Megan and Mary, striving to do what was right from the perspective of magisterial teaching was not limited to the season of Lent. Megan said, "I think that I spent that year after college making a plan that you were just going to be my friend and that I was going to figure out how not to be gay and not be in love with you, and that you were always going to still be my person." But (obviously—you already know the ending) the planning for platonic friendship and the practice of Lenten sacrificial offering did not ultimately result in the dissolution of the relationship. Looking back on the experience, Mary noted, "Even in that, you know, it wasn't true for me. That was what I felt imposed on me from outside. That was not my internal truth. And I knew that's why it was so fraught, because there was this tension of *she is for me* and I'm being asked to give it up and I'm going to have to let it go or sacrifice it because that's what a Christian does."

"At that time we were so much more stuck in the rules or structure of the Catholic church, for sure," adds Megan. She suggested that they also suffered from "internalized homophobia." But even so, even in "that Lent moment," they both knew that they were *for* each other. They ultimately followed what they trusted was their internal truth, what the Catholic tradition describes as one's conscience, one's "secret core" and "sanctuary."[5] Vatican II's *Gaudium et Spes* helpfully emphasizes the dignity of moral conscience:

> Deep within their consciences men and women discover a law which they have not laid upon themselves and which they must obey. Its voice,

ever calling them to love and to do what is good and to avoid evil, tells them inwardly at the right moment: do this, shun that. For they have in their hearts a law inscribed by God whose voice echoes in their depths. Their dignity rests in observing this law, and by it they will be judged. (.16)

Catholic teaching upholds the primacy of conscience, which suggests that we are morally obligated to follow what we believe to be right and fitting under the circumstances we're in, what we believe to be good and loving.[6] From this perspective, perhaps ironically, Mary and Megan's Lenten practice did what it was meant to do: it allowed them to step back and prayerfully discern what is true and what really matters. While they entered into their Lenten "fast" for different reasons, the spiritual discipline ultimately helped them choose what for them was loving and life-giving.

Many of the couples in the study, like Megan and Mary, went through an extended, and often excruciating, process of discernment during which they attempted to reconcile their religious and gay identities. In the case of this couple, what moved them toward an acceptance of their sexual orientation and their relationship was the support of others and an extended break from the Catholic church.[7] They began to speak with trusted mentors first. Mary said, "It was all of our female, faith-filled mentors. It was campus ministers, it was spiritual directors, it was pastoral figures. . . . we sort of finally got the gumption to say, 'Our life is blowing up, what do you think of this and what do we do? ['Are we going to hell?' Megan chimed in.] What does the future look like? Is this possible?" Mary believes it was those conversations that gave her "courage to keep moving forward and to stop denying what was happening and to stop fighting it." She said, "I feel like I knew. I feel like we knew." Looking at Megan, she continued, "I mean you were saying this before, for a really long time [we knew] that we were good together and we were okay, and that God loved us and everything was going to be all right."

"I was a little worried about the 'God loved us' sometimes," Megan inserted.

"Okay, I was too. But a little less so. There was just so much doubt. And it took a really long time to be able to stand in faith and truth rather than the doubt. And it wasn't until we could, for me especially, start talking to other people, talking to our friends. Oh my gosh, those were awful conversations. People were like, *we thought you were going to tell us that you were dying or you had cancer.* It was so hard. It was like the whole world was going to crash in."

"Oh yeah," Megan said. "My body. I mean I feel a little tense right now, but I remember coming out to [a good friend] and my legs were just so achy because they had been shaking and so tense that whole day and . . ." ["Physical stress," Mary said.] "Physical stress of having to have that conversation," Megan concurred.

Their burden significantly lifted once they began sharing their truths, doubts, and worries with "super-important" people they trusted, though the process was emotionally and physically taxing. Through these conversations, they were reassured that they were okay. That they *would be* okay. And that God loved them. One conversation that struck Mary in particular was one she had during that fraught Lenten journey—"it might have been in the middle of Lent or when Lent was done." After listening to Mary and Megan's story, a friend said, "You know what you should do next year? You should be really good to each other, and you should love each other really well. Wouldn't that be something?" *Wouldn't that be something?* It pointed Mary in a new direction to have "somebody else sort of flip [their Lenten practice] on its head." These early coming-out conversations with wise and trusted female mentors and friends, "Catholic people, people of faith," ultimately helped them to "stand in faith and truth rather than the doubt."

This language of careful discernment in order to "stand in faith and truth" surely illustrates the conscience at work. Mary and Megan knew the Catholic teaching (that same-sex relationships are immoral) and gave it the benefit of the doubt (or due diligence). They attempted to do what is right according to that teaching, almost desperately so. They reflected on the teaching in light of their lived experience, in which denying their relationship made them miserable and affirming it made them feel happy and whole.[8] They prayed. They sought the counsel of wise members of the body of Christ. And they came to a conclusion they believe to be prudent in their circumstances. Courageously, they trusted the voice that echoed in their depths and together followed the path where God led.[9]

I want to be careful here. My intent is not to invite scrutiny on the decision this couple came to as a result of their discernment, but rather reflect on the language and process they describe in light of Catholic teaching on conscience. I fully understand that the conscience can be misinformed and clouded by sin, inhibiting our ability to authentically hear and respond to the good to which God calls us. In coming chapters, the magisterial assertion that same-sex activity and relationships are sinful will be critically assessed. For now, it is important to emphasize that Catholic teaching on the primacy of conscience suggests that one is *morally obligated* to follow one's conscience, even if doing so means going against church teaching. At the same time, giving due diligence to church teaching is a key part of the process of informing one's conscience. The ability to come to a right decision (one that is good and loving) largely depends on one's *capacity* to recognize the good and one's ability to engage in a thoroughgoing *process* of discernment.

In the end, Mary and Megan believe that embracing their romantic partnership and ultimately sealing it in marriage has (contrary to what magisterial teaching suggests) brought them closer to God. "I feel like when we were falling in love at some point, I remember thinking," Mary recalls, "this is a sliver of how God must love someone so much, like me. Like I remember a new depth of awareness of unconditional love. Of just deep, vast, wide admiration and joy and honor. And at that time, that was a spiritual thing for me because I felt like being with Megan opened me up to something Divine that I had not realized in this life. And I feel like that's a sacrament."

Mary's description of her relationship with Megan as sacrament took my breath away. I paused in order to take it in. *A sliver of how God must love someone so much, like me. A new depth of awareness of unconditional love. Deep, vast, wide admiration and joy and honor.* Megan opened Mary up to this knowledge of God. She allowed her to experience and recognize God's profound love and delight in her. This, indeed, is sacrament. For this reason, I offer Mary and Megan's story as an entree for thinking about these same-sex marriages as sacramental.

United in God: Becoming One in Community

To be fair, the language of sacrament did not resonate with every person with whom I spoke. For example, one man said, "I don't really think about our marriage in that way [meaning, as a sacrament]. I mean, I just think: We're together. We've always been together. We're going to stay together." He described the lifelong fidelity that one would associate with sacramental marriage, but was not terribly attached or attracted to the language of sacrament. However, the vast majority of participants *adamantly* categorized their marriage as sacramental. When asked, "Do you think of your marriage as a sacrament? And if so what does that mean to you?," a more typical response was something closer to the following: "Yes. Yes. Yes. Yes. Yes." And "Absolutely."

Many used the language of sacrament to describe their wedding ritual and how it shaped their identity as married partners. For example, Liam recalls their wedding day as "one of the most grace-filled days of [his] life." He described the sacramental nature of his marriage to Marty: "We stand in love with each other in a public way. You know. That's what we did at our wedding. We stood in love with each other in a public way. And we invited God and the community into our relationship." Note that Liam begins by saying they stand (present tense) today in love before the community, and roots that reality in their wedding liturgy, when they stood (past tense) in love before God and the community and made promises. Who they are as a couple now is informed by what happened on their wedding day. "I had a very real experience of love manifested through the community that had come there for us, and through each other. Yeah, so I don't doubt for a moment that God was at the heart of it all. I definitely believe it was sacramental. But I also believe that as the result of the incarnation, all of creation is sacramental. So that's good enough for me."

Liam described how Marty "affects grace" in their married life as they continue to live out their wedding vows. He looked tenderly at Marty and said, "What would my life be without you? Like, c'mon! That's not an imaginable thing to me." For me, this sentiment conjures up the one body imagery that is so central to a Christian theology of marriage, rooted in the Book of Genesis where the two become one flesh (or body). While such one body imagery may seem abstract, Liam's acknowledgment that life without Marty is "not an imaginable thing" makes it concrete. You may also recall how Mary described her separation from Megan: "I felt like I lost half my blood. I felt like I was half, like half of my soul was gone." What is this if not one body imagery? The language implies deep union, a union sealed in the wedding liturgy. To tear such a union asunder, it follows, would do tremendous harm to persons. And yet isn't this what current magisterial teaching on same-sex relationships requires—a turning away from such unions—when it presents celibacy as the only moral choice for gay persons? The testimony of couples such as Marty and Liam and Mary and Megan can help us more fully reckon with the repercussions of such teaching on flesh-and-blood persons.

William and Mateo also thoughtfully described the theological import of their wedding liturgy and the sacramental nature of their marriage. They were "going on two years" as a married couple, and together for seven, when we spoke. The two have a shared intellectual interest in theology and liturgy, which is apparent in their reflections. Both were raised in the Catholic tradition; today Mateo identifies as Catholic, though William is estranged from the Catholic church. The couple were married in an Episcopal church by an Episcopal priest. In creating a marriage liturgy that was "familiar, but also unique," they used the Episcopal blessing of same-sex unions as their main resource, incorporating elements of different liturgies and integrating family and cultural traditions. Mateo noted that the people who attended seemed "surprised at how familiar it looked from a religious Catholic perspective."

"I remember when we were planning the wedding," Mateo said, "what immediately stood out to me in terms of what I wanted the liturgy to mean for us, and for whoever was open to receiving it this way, was I wanted people to perceive the link between what we were doing in our vows to each other—marrying each other—and the eucharist. And that's why it was important for me from the beginning that our marriage would take place in the context of the eucharist . . . on the basis of my relationship with Will and my relationship to the tradition. I felt that the only way to be married for us would be to do so in a eucharistic way and in a eucharistic kind of environment."[10]

"What that meant for me . . . [was that] fundamentally what we were doing was embodying a kind of relationship, a kind of union that is only possible because of the union that we have with God in Christ." [T]he eucharist, as the sacrifice of the mass, . . . represent[s] God's wanting to be completely for us and completely with us and completely at one with us. And that being realized in the sacrament itself seemed to me related, if not identical, to what we are performing as two people getting married. . . . I felt like it was kind of an act of hope and acknowledgment and recognition and aspiration toward the kind of union that is given to us in the eucharist and given to us in Christ, embodied in our own particular way." Mateo makes a theologically profound point here: the eucharist reminds us that God is *completely for us and completely with us*. And a marriage that is celebrated within a eucharistic liturgy aspires to embody that same kind of complete, generous, everlasting love.

Mateo believes that the "gestures" of the wedding liturgy "actually make present and bring into a reality among us this ultimate reality, which is God's love for us in Christ. And if we can participate in that in some way by the relationship we bear to each other, the fidelity we practice to reach toward each other, then it's sacramental." In this way, married couples become icons of God's unconditional love. Adding to this, William said, "I feel like the sense of the sacramentality of our marriage is that the marriage is a joining of two people with the ultimate goal of becoming better people and becoming closer to God."

Like Liam above, Mateo emphasized the essential aspect of *community* in the wedding liturgy, "acknowledging that we were made from, came out of, and [are] supported by community, by our families and our friends. [Acknowledging] that what we were doing together was the creation of family and community and that it required the participation and assent of the assembled, those who loved and supported us. And *that* I think is another dimension of how I feel our marriage is sacramental." He suggested that while Catholics generally understand that "the sacramentality of marriage consists in the way it reflects the union of Christ and the church . . . that doesn't mean anything unless you are conscious of the ways in which the church is the community and the body of Christ is community."

I heard from other couples, too, about the importance of the eucharist and the eucharistic community (in the tradition, both are the body of Christ) for the marriage ritual. Kevin and Timothy, for example, highlighted the eucharist when reflecting on their marriage as sacramental. They were five and a half years together when we spoke, and four years married. They also wed in an Episcopal church. Kevin grew up evangelical Christian and Timothy entered the Catholic church as a high schooler, though both men now are active in the Episcopalian church. They centered their marriage liturgy around the eucharist, and Kevin likened the sacrament of the eucharist to their marriage. He said, "The bread is not just bread. It is bread, and it's another thing. I feel like our marriage [is like that]." Looking at Timothy, "You are fully you. I am fully me. And there is this other thing that is us. And so that's where I see it as sacramental. I think there is something to promises and trying to live into those promises. And forgiving and dealing with all the ups and downs. Better or worse, sick, poor, all of those things. That sense of it wasn't just a document that we signed . . . We often say to each other: 'I'm here. I'm not going anywhere.' Like, we're here in the ups and downs. So I think there is a sacramental side" to the marriage.

I was particularly moved when Kevin said, "The priest holds up the eucharist, the host. It's the idea of like, everyone see, there's something special here. We see our marriage and our lives . . . it's almost like we want to raise it up for our fourteen-year-old selves and say, 'See here! There is something good.' We often talk about how our younger selves would just be out of their minds looking at us today, [having] no understanding of the love that could be had." *See here. There's something special. Something good. Unimaginable love.*

Timothy said their marriage is sacramental "if by sacrament we mean a making visible of God's work in the world . . . I find God in my marriage more than anywhere else. And certainly these days more than in any kind of institutional church." He described the God present in their marriage not as "the classical hypermasculine, grumpy God" but as "selflessness, among other things." He added, "In terms of living into a fullness of myself and my life and what's possible, it has been in our marriage that I have found the capacity to do that most." Timothy straightforwardly identifies the sacramental nature of their relationship: in their marriage, they find God and grow into fullness of self and life.

Whether or not couples centered their wedding liturgy around the eucharist—some explicitly indicated that they would have if they could have—couples emphasized the importance of having loved ones gather to witness, to recognize the *something good and special* that was their union. For example, Christina and Emma have been together since 2006 when they met in college, but did not think they'd get married until they decided to become parents. We talked in their living room as their toddler, newly awakened from an afternoon nap, walked around and periodically chimed into the conversation. They describe themselves as "*really* Catholic," and they realized they wanted to marry before having a child, marking their union with a ritual that was sacramental.[11] "We asked an Episcopal priest to marry us, and we had great joy in creating the liturgy and the experience of just celebrating our lives together with all the people we weaved in our lives."

Emma talked about their marriage broadly as "revealing God's grace, specifically the love of God. You have faith, and the grace comes." But "having an event, a celebration, family and friends gathered to acknowledge and to see, I guess that's another thing to add on to [what's] sacramental. It's not just *you* seeing and experiencing it, but it's a community that sees it, and when you're seen in their eyes—your validity, your worth, your relationship, the joy, the grace that they experience . . . you know, so many people at weddings do experience that. And a lot of people who went to ours said they felt so uplifted and joyful. So to see our reflection in their eyes and to be received as we are was pivotal . . . That public witness made a difference." The wedding ritual enabled their loved ones to "get on board supporting the level of seriousness and commitment [that marriage brings]."

Community was also at the heart of Sarah and Katie's wedding. They planned an entire weekend to celebrate their marriage commitment. The two met through the L'Arche community,[12] an experience that profoundly shapes their way of relating to one another and being in the world. One core value they share is community. For their wedding, it was important for them to bring loved ones together, so they "rented part of a retreat center, run by a bunch of hippies." Some people came and stayed for the full weekend, sleeping in cabins and tents, and others came for the wedding day, which took place "in the middle of a cedar grove on a creek."

Sarah is Lutheran and Katie is Catholic, and they relished the freedom they had to build a wedding celebration "from the ground up" that reflected their values. Katie said, "L'Arche was a big part of it—probably half the crowd—and then other friends and family." They had a commitment ceremony that included meaningful readings, music, and vows that had been "crafted" from a "mishmash" of examples until they "felt authentic" and reflected what they "were willing to commit to." During the ceremony, "We had a blessing where we sat in chairs in the middle. It was in a big circle. We sat in the chairs and people could just come up and offer a prayer or a blessing or a hope."

The ceremony, which Katie described as "the most beautiful thing on earth," was followed by: "dinner theater where we told the story of our relationship" (a play that included a tap dance routine!); a potluck of favorite foods that friends brought; and a bonfire with s'mores. It was "just a beautiful celebration of the community we were a part of." In fact, for each person that came, Sarah and Katie hung a picture of them around the tents, with a story of how they knew them. Truly, it was a celebration, both of the couple and of the community gathered.

Every year on their anniversary, Katie and Sarah "read through the whole thing, reenact the whole ceremony. We reread the vows and we sing all the songs, the two of us [It's not clear whether this includes tap dancing]. And every year I get emotional and a little teary when we do the vows. This is what we said yes to." Sarah said, "I do believe there is something that happens between the space of two people that is holy and sacred—it's romantic relationships, but it's friendships, it's community relationships. There is something sacred between two people that doesn't exist on its own and I think that's something of God showing up." *The holy and sacred space between people where God shows up.* That's sacrament.

Theologian Michael Lawler describes the covenantal love that is at the heart of sacramental marriage. It is more than romantic love, much more than simple affection. Rather, modeled on the covenantal love in scripture that exists between God-and-the-people of Israel and Christ-and-the-Church respectively; it is marked by fidelity, service, and giving-way.[13] Lawler explains: "A couple entering any marriage say to one another, before the society in which they live, 'I love you and I give myself to and for you.' A Christian couple entering a specifically sacramental marriage say that, too, but they also say more. They say, 'I love you as Christ loves his church, steadfastly and faithfully.'"[14] This marriage therefore is not only human covenant, but religious covenant. This marriage "is more than law and obligations and rights; it is also grace."[15] It is a Christ event.

Growing in Holiness and Wholeness: Covenantal Love and Fidelity

Magisterial teaching professes a universal call to holiness. In the words of Vatican II's *Lumen Gentium*, " . . . all the faithful of Christ of whatever rank or status, are called to the fullness of the Christian life and to the perfection of charity."[16] In other words, we are all called to sainthood, though we have different callings. Many are called to marriage as a way to live out discipleship, as their path to holiness. In and through their daily lives, the logic goes, spouses are sanctified—they become more and more virtuous; they flourish as human beings in friendship with God. William put it beautifully above: "Marriage is a joining of two people with the ultimate goal of becoming better people and becoming closer to God." That's the ideal, anyway, though most of us who are married do this imperfectly. When we reflect on how spouses are sacraments to one another in their daily care and ongoing fidelity, we begin to see how these couples make one another better, bringing each other more fully to life and closer to God.

Val and Margaret worship in a gay-affirming church. When we spoke, they'd been together for thirty-two years, and married eleven. Val said, "When the announcement was said [in the parish] that we were going to get married, the whole community put their hands up and blessed us. And that felt, in a sense, the conveyance of the sacrament. It was a demonstration that the whole community was saying, 'We're behind you.' And while it was evident that day, it was something we felt right from the start here [at the parish]: affirming us as a couple, recognizing us in that way. And I think that the sacramental part of marriage is when we regard it as a holy union. It wasn't a matter of convenience. It was because we wanted to make our lives holier. And I felt . . . that Margaret was my compass. That I would be a better person by being with her. That I could be better together than being on my own." She looks to Margaret, her compass, as a "guide of right and wrong," Val said, "because she is the most honorable person I've ever known."

In turn, Margaret said, "I think [the marriage] brings me closer to God because I feel like in Val's love for me, unconditional, that she truly is the presence of God in my life. I have a better understanding of who God is because of her, and how God loves me . . . And I'm a better person because her generosity is boundless, and I try to imitate it."

Val is appreciative of the fact that she and Margaret have "been able to support each other in difficult times. It really has been an incredible balance. I mean, when I'm off, Margaret's there to kind of buoy me up and ground me. And I do the same for her. So we have relied on that anchor for each other. But whenever we do that, we always [ask]: so what's the source of this? And it's God. God is our source . . . because it isn't that *we're* doing it. It's that we're reaching into our deepest selves to find out how to figure this out, or how to do it. One of the prayers that we read often is the prayer of Thomas Merton.[17] *Lord, I have no idea where I'm going. I don't see the [road] ahead of me.* And it's something that we pray because we know that God is guiding us. I think that's kind of the grounding of our relationship, that we know God is guiding us. If we get off the path and are getting too petty or selfish or whatever, it is there to course-correct and we don't get too far off."

"The mantra in our lives is: providence never fails," Margaret added.

The two do not take their marriage relationship for granted. Val explains, "We tell each other that we love each other and we appreciate each other. That we're grateful for each other." She notes that they "pay attention to when things escalate" and attend to problems when things feel "out of sync." "We don't ignore each other . . . when she is upset or when I'm upset, we pay attention to that. We value harmony. And I don't think we sacrifice how we are feeling for harmony. But we work to achieve it."

Looking at Val, Margaret added, "What you said previously about appreciating each other. We say thank you to each other all the time. Thank you for dinner. Thank you for doing the dishes. Thank you for making the bed.[18] And I don't think it comes from a place of, *I'm always supposed to say thank you*. It's that I really appreciate it." Such daily gratitude, openly expressed, serves to sustain their marriage. As does "talking about things that are bothering" them. Val agreed, noting, "We have good tools to be in relationship. I think we fight fairly. We are fair with each other. And we also think of the other first." They often end up laughing at the end of an argument. Margaret said: "You have to take it seriously if there is something that needs to be discussed. But at the end of the day, we're still going to be together. And we're going to be laughing about this, so we just need to get from here to there."

Daily gratitude, openly expressed. A willingness to think of the other first, even when angry, and to work to achieve harmony. Keeping a sense of humor. Trusting that God's grace will help move them from pettiness to generosity and will guide a path forward. Believing that no matter what, at the end of the day, they'll still be together. All of these are practices of marital fidelity.

Catholic ethicist James Keenan explains that practicing fidelity in any loving relationship requires more than simply refusing to walk out on or abandon it. More importantly, he suggests, fidelity requires defending and sustaining those relationships.[19] Active, daily efforts to defend and sustain their relationship are powerfully illustrated by Val and Margaret, along with so many other couples in my study. Keenan argues, moreover, that from a Catholic perspective, the virtue of fidelity should be informed by mercy. He defines mercy as "the willingness to enter into the chaos of another so as to respond to their need."[20] Fidelity in marriage requires, then, a willingness to enter into the chaos of one's spouse, into the chaos of a shared life. This is the no-matter-whatness of covenantal marriage. And it is far from easy to practice over the long haul.

Kevin and Timothy spoke candidly about their fidelity to one another and their partnership. "We value commitment," Kevin said. "Like, we're gonna get through hard stuff. We're in it. And so there's a sense of [we can do] the hard bits. We're there." Timothy expanded on the importance of facing "the hard bits" through "honesty and transparency." He said, "Part of my experience has been learning to vocalize what I think of as almost shameful fears, things that I shouldn't be thinking because they're just so silly, or whatever. At first I was very hesitant to name them for fear they would generally sound crazy. But I've come to understand that, if I don't, they fester and then they lead to more complicated sorts of situations. So it's just been a willingness to take on the hard, hard conversations when they come up, rather than sort of push them down and hope they'll go away or get better without really being dealt with." Timothy has vocalized his fears to Kevin, who has shown steadfast understanding and support in the face of them. In fact, the two have willingly shared their vulnerabilities with one another—sexual and emotional—and that sharing has made them and their relationship stronger.

Timothy explained that he's had panic attacks for years, "mostly having to do with gay stuff in different shapes and forms. So, I had this long period of time where I was convinced I was going to contract HIV. And so most of my panics were around HIV phobias, and they were not fun. But even after . . . getting over most of those things, I still get panicky with some regularity. But not only have I noticed—but most of our good friends have noticed—that [being] married has reduced all of that stuff dramatically. I mean the duration of them, the frequency of them. It's really remarkable. I still struggle with it, and it still happens from time to time, but this sense of health that comes from our relationship" has made a significant difference. Having a devoted partner in Kevin, one willing to enter into his chaos and love him through it, has brought stability and healing to Timothy.

The couple spoke beautifully about how their relationship brings each of them to authenticity. Kevin praises the "deep commitment to goodness" and "ridiculous, incredible integrity" he witnesses in Timothy. "An integrity not just in honesty and doing the right thing, but wholeness. When I'm with him, he is who he is. And the selfish thing I love about that is that [it] allows me to come out and be more who I am. Which I think is an amazing thing." Kevin celebrates the "joy in seeing [Timothy] and then myself become more of who we actually are. As children we have this beautiful sense of self and it just gets buried and beaten up. So one of the joys I have is seeing the fullness of who he is, like busting through the walls that have been built around him, and then *I enjoy*. I've never been more myself than when I am with him." These married partners surely are discovering their true selves, their best selves, in and through their relationship, including the difficult aspects of it.

In a similar vein, Maggie discussed a challenging time in her life—and therefore in her marriage to Jane—when she was struggling with anxiety and depression. When we spoke, she and Jane had been married for three years, together for seventeen. She said, "I had a rough spell, and I wouldn't have had the strength to go through that period had we not had this commitment *to be with each other for the rest of our lives*. I had a memory of Jane saying that to me in a community, I remember our vows, I remember us exchanging those vows. And I would draw on that memory when I was really struggling. I wasn't struggling about being with Jane. I was struggling to be me, but there was a sense of comfort and security that [the wedding ritual] did happen. I'm married. We're together. And it's going to be okay."

Relatedly, Mark and Tom, who'd been married two and a half years, addressed vulnerability and authenticity in marriage during their interview. Tom suggested that one of the "most important challenges in a marriage is that sense of daring to allow the other person to know you. You can say that with God, too. But I think especially in a marriage relationship, it's: Can I let Mark see this about me? Can I let him know that this [is the] kind of person [I am]—nasty, ill-tempered, impatient, fearful . . ."

"Keep going," Mark said, making us all laugh.

"Can I let him see those things about me, or do I have to try to hide those from him?" Tom continued, undeterred by the sarcasm. "And I mean it's not always that kind of negative thing. But I think that's where he's special. He's the only person that I show those things to. That's partly a conscious choice, but it's also just a function of, he's the only person close enough to me to see them, and for me to reveal that. I think that's one of the things I'm learning: not to be guarded about everything. You know there is a sense in which self-protection is not a bad thing. But there's also a sense in which it can stop you from entering into a kind of closeness that you long for." Fidelity creates the context for the vulnerability that results in deeper unity, which is "built up through time." *The one-body connection, strengthened through time.* "Okay, I revealed that part and it was okay. He didn't run away and now I can let him see this other thing about me too. That's fidelity: that sense of counting on that and being faithful in accepting what the other person is showing you, but also . . . your willingness to show more."

Emma described fidelity in her relationship with Christina in a similar way. "The commitment definitely gives me a lot of trust in order to be who I am, in order to trust in the future of us, and I think the longer we are together, the more moments we have that are vulnerable, flare up moments that we then mend, [when] it's like, *Oh yeah, we've done this before.* The next time it happens, it's like, *No, no, no. Just push through and we're going to be fine because we've [gotten through] all these other moments. Just trust.*" Looking at Christina, she said, "I think you are trustworthy and it gives a lot of safety and courage in the relationship." In turn, Christina said, "There's a lot of peace, consolation, challenge, invitation when you love me because [I wonder], Can I really go deeper? I can because [of who] you are . . . It's not easy to cry sometimes, and sometimes laughing is a defense mechanism, but it's easy with you. I think the vulnerability piece is easier with you . . . because of the practice we've had."

Through the repeated practices of revelation and acceptance, through the brokenness and mending, authenticity grows. And the oneness between the spouses deepens. Confidence that both partners are "all-in," willing to wade in and move through the chaos, provides the safe context for these challenging but fruitful practices. At times, it is a small gesture or reminder of love that helps to sustain a relationship. Joseph and Matt have had a lot of practice loving one another, mutually offering small gestures of love. They'd been together thirty-nine years when we spoke, and married for four. Matt said, "Sometimes we'll be laying in bed and falling asleep and Joseph will say, 'You old man, I really love you.' I mean, through all of this. It's so very tender."

Joseph laughed a little. "I don't think I usually put 'old man' in front of it, but I do say it every night as we get into bed. I don't deny what you just said."

"I think before we go to sleep at night, give a little kiss and a hug. That's been really important," Matt said.

"Those little things. Sometimes a surprise," Joseph added. "The other day I came home and I brought him an orchid." Such small gestures of love are powerful.

Sarah and Katie likewise have a cherished night-time ritual. They consistently go to bed at the same time, and enjoy "chatting and sharing highs and lows every night." Katie said, "It has to be dark when we're in bed. The lights have to be out—that's the rule."

"I think the highs and lows every night is pretty important," Sarah agreed. It's something the couple looks forward to on a daily basis. "Yeah. It's really sharing highs and lows *and* notable events because it's a recap of the whole day. Everything you need to know about my day. And it's usually after we've had dinner together and chatted all day, so yeah, we do have a pretty good life!" They told me there are "maybe two nights a year" when they don't go to bed at the same time because they "delight in each other" and they count on this ritual—"if it didn't happen, it would be sad."

Indeed, as the old song says, *little things mean a lot*. Saying thank you. Offering a hug, kiss, and an "I love you" (with or without the "old man" attached). Surprising your spouse with flowers. Turning the lights out for a daily recap. All of these small gestures and rituals matter and, in these cases, are clearly expressions of marital fidelity.

Couples also offered testimony of what might be called larger expressions of fidelity.[21] I think, for example, of spouses who supported each other in: getting sober and maintaining sobriety; managing rejection from family and negotiating difficult family relationships; coping with job insecurity or loss because of marital status; dealing with ongoing anxiety or mental health conditions; surviving harassment and violence due to sexual identity; and/or, parenting children who were particularly challenging.

Tony and Pete are one couple who spoke meaningfully about fidelity in their married life. When we spoke, they'd been married eleven years and together for sixteen. Tony said, "I love having someone that I can count on, that I can rely on, who has my back." Pete said, "I like that I have somebody to call when something good or something bad happens, you know? That I don't have to worry. We're together a long time. So I know what to expect [today and] tomorrow. I know everything is predictable, which I like. [It makes me] comfortable." It's clear that Tony and Pete are secure in the constancy of each other and their relationship.

Tony told a powerful story of Pete's fidelity to him, through Pete's fidelity to Tony's mother: "You know, we've been together for a very long time, and as in any relationship, it's rocky at times. You have to figure out how two totally different people come together. When we moved [across the country from family], within a year my mom had to move in with us because we thought she'd be done in six months. And she was with us for six years. I saw Pete in a whole different light during that time. He adored my mom. But I think he adored my mom because he loved me. My mom took a lot of work, especially toward the end. And there was never a time that I thought, *I can't ask*. You know, I was trying to work two jobs at the time, and he was there constantly. I knew, yes, he loved my mom, but he loved my mom because he loved me. I know Pete loves me because he will do things. Like especially with my mom, right? I knew it because he [cared for her] without ever complaining. I mean, toward the end he was staying up all night long to be with my mom. And I knew that was for me."

"I was the one that told you it was time for her to go somewhere," Pete said.

Tony nodded and explained: "Because I had promised my mom I would never put her anywhere. She would stay with us. The last few days, it was horrible. And hospice said, we have this bed at this beautiful place. Thank God my mom in a moment said, 'Yes, I'll go.' That made it easier for me. Yeah. But it was tough, and he stuck it out. And to be very honest, I think a lot of people would have said, 'This is not what I signed up for. Like, she needs to go five years ago!' I mean, I really believe that. And he did not. I often say that, of course, my mother loved me unconditionally, but I think she liked Pete more than she liked me. I mean, he would sit in with her and they would be laughing hysterically, and I would be the one that would have to go in and say, 'No Mom, you need to do this and this.' Whereas Pete would just go in and . . . they would talk, and they would laugh."

"And if she wanted ice cream for dinner, she got ice cream," Pete said.

"Where I was saying, '*Excuse me*, she's got diabetes.' And he's saying to me, 'For God's sake, she's got three months to live. You want ice cream? Have it all-the-day-long. Who cares?"

Hearing Tony and Pete tell this story in real-time, bantering back and forth (as they did the whole interview through), was a gift. Although the story is centered around the terminal illness and death of Tony's mother, we were all laughing. The telling of the story was tender. Sad, yes, but also sweet. It is a story of care and perseverance. Pete rose to the challenge: *He was there constantly. He stuck it out.* And he did so with generosity, humor, and grace. Pete shows how love looks in the form of fidelity.

Another vivid example of fidelity comes from Michael and Brian, who are grateful for the "complete feeling of love and security" that marks their marriage. At the time of our interview, they'd been together for eleven and a half years and married for nearly five. They share similar values, communicate easily and well, are adept at forgiveness, and "know how to have a good time." The two enjoy simple pleasures, like playing cards "everywhere [they] go"—they've had a continuous gin rummy game going for years. They hold dear their friendship, which they describe as the center of their marriage. Michael said, "You know we spend as much time together [as possible]. We talk on the phone four times a day. This is just after I leave the house with him at 10:00 and then we're back together at the gym at 5:30. We just want to talk all the time and catch each other up on what's going on in the day, and have lunch together even though we're not in the same place. 'Let's talk on the phone,' you know. And I think that companionship is something that we most love about our marriage." Nodding his head, Brian explained that when he travels for work, they talk every day, recapping their days. "But then three or four days into it, it's like, 'Oh, hurry up! Come home! I can't wait to see you!' The house is not the same when you're by yourself, you know? So we enjoy being in each other's company. I mean, we certainly know when it's time for someone to experience something with their own friends or whatever. But [our relationship] always seems easy."

As close as their married friendship is, it is far from closed off; rather it expands to include others. Michael explains, "Our marriage is more than just us, right? It's our families, it's our communities, it's the people that we live around and with. And we're so fortunate. We have such close families, on both ends. Me with Brian's whole family—parents, nieces, nephews, siblings, cousins—and vice versa. You know, everyone is very much in it together and I think *that's* our marriage too. It's our ability to love everything that encompasses each other." Michael and Brian described being accountable both to one another and to their wider circles. For them, fidelity goes far beyond sexual fidelity. Brian said, "Fidelity is promising to [do something] and following through with it, knowing that that person is counting on you. And it's not hard."

In response, Michael said to Brian, "I think we learned a lot in our first years of marriage. Like we had an amazing, blissful period through our wedding and then [looking at Brian], your family got sick. The dynamic shifted. It wasn't about us, you know what I mean?" In just a few years, Brian's father and brother each became ill and died. They also happened to be Brian's partners in a family business, which meant that Brian's emotional and professional worlds were in turmoil. Michael continued, "When things get really hard and you have to rely on each other for support in different ways, you start to understand what a lot of these tenets mean. They take on new meaning. And, as I mentioned before, our marriage is more than just the two of us, our marriage [includes] our families and the people around us. I think that was a really pivotal moment when I understood that my fidelity to our marriage is also, like, to his family and vice versa. I think that was very enlightening for the maturity of our marriage."

"I know what you mean, I think," Brian replied. "To expound on that, Michael spent the night with my dad in the hospital the day before he died. We all left and went home and he was the only one there. And they were talking and carrying on . . . Michael was spending the last dying moment with this guy. And they had a good relationship. A really good relationship." Brian continued, "[During the hospital stay], what I saw was, and [addressing Michael] you saw it too, was my mom watching my dad die. We're all sitting in the hospital room and just waiting and talking, and you're realizing that this is the culmination of their marriage. You know, soon it will be over. And just noticing the devotion and the fidelity that she had to him and vice versa. It was a teaching moment for anyone watching because—Michael and I both picked up on that—you know, you can have fun, and the sex is fun, and all that kind of stuff. But spending your life and being devoted to one person in the end like that. It's so powerful. It has so much meaning. I'm sure life is hard in between—they tell us that, and we all experience it. Some couples experience infidelity, but the ones that remain devoted and have that fidelity, you just notice that. You can see that in the couples. And I noticed it especially at that point. Like wow. She spent her whole life with this guy, and he with her, and now it's coming to an end. But the love and devotion that was there at that moment was a teaching moment. So, you know, that's what I want for myself in the end. I think, you know, we're building that and working toward that as we go through life here. You want to trust, to know that that person is just for you. And they're there for you no matter what. Nothing can shake that. And so I can see, over time, that protecting the fidelity that a couple has for one another: it's like gold." *Fidelity, precious like gold.*

    The couples in this chapter understand and appreciate God's profound love for them in and through their partners—they are sacraments to one another. The promises they made before God and community—to become one, to love and care for each other for a lifetime—inspires daily efforts to lovingly attend to their spouse and their relationship. The couples testify to the innumerable ways that their spouse makes them better—more authentically themselves, more virtuous, and closer to God. Their stories illustrate sacramental-married-friendship-in-community that reflects God's grace and brings about flourishing. In them, I believe, we witness a Christ-event.

Notes

1. Michael J. Himes, "Finding God in All Things: A Sacramental Worldview and Its Effects," in *Becoming Beholders: Cultivating Sacramental Imagination and Action in College Classrooms*, ed. Karen E. Eifler and Thomas M. Landy (Collegeville, MN: Liturgical Press, 2014), 13. © 2014 by Order of Saint Benedict. Used with permission.

Himes is far from alone in understanding sacrament in this broad way. For two additional examples, especially as it relates to family life, see Angela Alaimo O'Donnell, "Everyday Sacraments: Final Lessons of Love," *America Magazine*, November 25, 2014, https://www.americamagazine.org/issue/everyday-sacraments and Andres Dubus, "Epilogue: Sacraments," in *Signatures of Grace: Catholic Writers on the Sacraments*, ed. Thomas Grady and Paula Huston (Eugene, OR: Wipf & Stock, 2001), 220–32.

2. See Pope Francis, *Amoris Laetitia*, March 19, 2016, https://www.vatican.va/content/dam/francesco/pdf/apost_exhortations/documents/papa-francesco_esortazione-ap_20160319_amoris-laetitia_en.pdf, especially chapters 3 through 5. Also see United States Conference of Catholic Bishops, "Marriage: Love and Life in the Divine Plan," November 17, 2009, https://www.usccb.org/topics/marriage-and-family-life-ministries/marriage-love-and-life-divine-plan.

3. Three years prior, they'd had a civil union.

4. See Congregation for the Doctrine of Faith, "Letter to the Bishops of the Catholic Church on the Pastoral Care of Homosexual Persons," October 1, 1986, https://www.vatican.va/roman_curia/congregations/cfaith/documents/rc_con_cfaith_doc_19861001_homosexual-persons_en.html.

5. Second Vatican Council, *Gaudium et Spes*, December 7, 1965, https://www.vatican.va/archive/hist_councils/ii_vatican_council/documents/vat-ii_const_19651207_gaudium-et-spes_en.html, sec. 16.

6. In *Amoris Laetitia*, sec. 37, Pope Francis emphasizes the importance of making room in married and family life for "the consciences of the faithful, who very often respond as best they can to the Gospel amid their limitations and are capable of carrying out their own discernment in complex situations. We [read: the Magisterium] have been called to form consciences, not to replace them."

7. Unfortunately, too often LGBTQ persons and couples don't return to the Catholic church after taking a necessary break—the break is permanent. We should pause to mourn the people we've lost and take concrete steps to counter the inhospitality so many experience. More on that in chapter 4.

8. Here I grant that what is actually good for people, what leads to genuine flourishing, is not necessarily what makes them *feel* happy. The Christian tradition teaches that Christians are called to and designed for holiness, for a state of being in right relationship with God and others—a state of flourishing. Sometimes moving toward that flourishing requires that we do what does *not* feel good, what may in fact require suffering and sacrifice.

9. For a helpful collection of readings on conscience, see Charles Curran's edited volume, *Conscience: Readings in Moral Theology No. 14* (New York: Paulist Press, 2004). Also helpful is the chapter on "Conscience and Discernment" in Michael Lawler and Todd

Chapter 1

Salzman's *Introduction to Catholic Theological Ethics: Foundations and Applications* (New York: Orbis Books, 2019), 198–219.

10. See the reasoning presented in the Catechism of the Catholic Church for "normally" rooting the celebration of marriage within a eucharistic liturgy (#1621–1624). You will see remarkable parallels to Will and Mateo's description of the theological import of their own wedding liturgy and what the catechism describes. *Catechism of the Catholic Church*, 1993, https://www.vatican.va/archive/ENG0015/_INDEX.HTM.

11. Christina and Emma were not alone in the conviction that they should be married before raising children. For example, Gianna and Kathy, together since 1991, insisted there "should be a joining of beings" before having children. Gianna said, "[Sacramental marriage] is a joining of two people under God. And there's the power and responsibility that that brings with it to stay together, to weather life's storms, to look to each other. To become one in the eyes of God. God is the only one who creates and the only one who joins." This kind of commitment ideally provides a stable environment for the nurturing and education of children.

12. L'Arche is an international organization (active in thirty-eight countries) of people with and without intellectual disabilities who live, work, pray, and play together in community. You can learn more about the history and mission of L'Arche at larcheusa.org.

13. See Michael Lawler, "Marriage in the Bible," in *Perspectives on Marriage: A Reader, Second Edition*, ed. Kieran Scott and Michael Warren (New York: Oxford University Press, 2001), 7–28.

14. Michael G. Lawler, "Marriage and the Sacrament of Marriage," in *Christian Marriage and Family*, ed. Michael G. Lawler and William P. Roberts (Collegeville, MN: Liturgical Press, 1996), 35.

15. Lawler, "Marriage and the Sacrament of Marriage," 35. On sacramental marriage as a Christ event, see also Michael G. Lawler, "Faith, Contract, and Sacrament in Christian Marriage: A Theological Approach," in *Christian Marriage and Family*, ed. Michael G. Lawler and William P. Roberts (Collegeville, MN: Liturgical Press, 1996), 38–58.

16. Second Vatican Council, *Lumen Gentium*, November 21, 1964, https://www.vatican.va/archive/hist_councils/ii_vatican_council/documents/vat-ii_const_19641121_lumen-gentium_en.html, sec. 40.

17. You can find "The Merton Prayer" in Thomas Merton's *Thoughts in Solitude* (New York: Farrar, Straus and Giroux, 1999).

18. In December 2021, Pope Francis urged couples to remember three key words in married life: please, thanks, and sorry. See Nicole Winfield, "Pope's 3 Key Words for a Marriage: 'Please, Thanks, Sorry,'" *AP News*, December 26, 2021, https://apnews.com/article/pope-francis-lifestyle-religion-relationships-couples-23c81169982e50c35d1c1fc7bfef8cbc. In a general audience in 2015, the Pope argued that he would write the words "please," "thank you," and "sorry" "on the door of every family home" because "they contain great strength: the strength of protecting the home, even through a thousand difficulties and trials." And "when they are lacking, cracks gradually open up that can even lead it to collapse." See Nancy Ward, "Pope Francis: Three Key Words: Please, Thank You, Sorry," *JOY Alive in Our Hearts*, May 13, 2015, https://joyalive.net/pope-francis-three-key-words-please-thank-you-sorry/.

19. James Keenan, "Virtue Ethics and Sexual Ethics," *Louvain Studies* 30, no. 3 (Fall 2005): 195.

20. Ibid., 192.

21. By "larger" expressions of fidelity, I do not mean to imply that they are necessarily more meaningful or significant in maintaining the relationship, I simply want to differentiate them from the smaller gestures just discussed. Perhaps "grand" gestures of fidelity might be more appropriate.

CHAPTER 2

Marriage as Sacrament
Grace Overflowing

IN THIS CHAPTER, I INVITE YOU TO LISTEN TO COUPLES REFLECT ON their efforts to live out Christian discipleship as married partners, thereby becoming *sacraments to others*. I invite you to consider how these married relationships are both gospel-inspired and life-giving as couples live out virtues such as hospitality, love of neighbor (particularly the most vulnerable neighbor), and solidarity. The testimony of these spouses reveals how their marital love overflows and widens to include others: the second dimension of sacrament. We will also see more examples of *ordinary sacraments* in daily married and family life and home (for example, practices of table fellowship), the third dimension of sacrament.

At the end of this chapter, we will evaluate magisterial teaching on sacramental marriage in light of the experience of these couples (as presented in chapters 1 and 2) along with relevant theological work that can inform and deepen our perspective.

"We met on retreat because we're good Catholic boys," Liam said. The retreat was sponsored by Dignity, which is where Liam "found a church home" as an "out gay man" in the early nineties.[1] When they met, Marty was "drawn" to Liam "because he understood. We were both steeped in our Catholic upbringing, we had deep values, we both wanted [a relationship] in contrast to the stereotype of gay relationships—the one-night stands. We wanted what our parents had."

Chapter 2

Four and a half years into their relationship, they got married. "We've done a good job of building a life from early on. We both realized we were stronger together. We were better people as a result of being in relationship with each other. We brought out better parts, stronger parts . . . of each other than we did individually," Marty explained. The story of their wedding, during which they prayed for Matthew Shepard, began the introduction to this book.

In addition to committing to one another for life, they got involved in ministry through Dignity, helping other couples prepare for holy unions. In an odd way, they felt like pioneers. "It was just so crazy that doing the most traditional thing—marrying the person you love and promising to live a life together—could also be one of the most radical things we could do. It's like, I'm not doing anything different than what people have been doing as long as there's been people. Why is this radical? This is pretty traditional," Liam said.

At that time, Liam and Marty referred to their marriage as a holy union rather than a marriage because that was the language that Dignity was using.[2] "It would be another ten years before we could legally marry. It wasn't until we could legally marry that I would call Liam my husband," Marty said. "It took ten years of unthinking because he was always my partner. I used the word 'partner' because I'm like, *No, I'm not allowed. That term* [husband] *has a specific meaning and I'm not allowed to appropriate that for myself.* And once I could legally marry it was a big shift. *No, he really is my husband.* And it took me a while because even during that time, figuring out how to come out at work, the climate was changing during [that] whole twenty years of our relationship."

"During [the legal debates about marriage equality], there was lots of conversation around, you know, this is a horrible thing and it's going to destroy the institution of marriage. I don't understand how me marrying the person I love is going to impact straight folks' ability to marry the people they want to love," Marty said. "So yeah, we called it holy union back then because it didn't feel like we were allowed to call it marriage. We still used the word 'wedding,' though, because [it didn't seem to have] the same legal, theological overtones as marriage, as one of the seven sacraments. But we were also very clear that it's the couple who's standing before God that confers the sacrament to each other. That grace comes not because of the priest—he's there to witness it, but he doesn't cause it. And so we were very aware that we are the ones who are calling down God's blessing. That we are making the sacrament happen, and we're sharing it in the context of the people we love."

"Language matters a lot," Liam said. "I am going to claim the language [of marriage]. When it was a new frontier, when semantics were being sorted out, I was more ambiguous, or at the end of the day [didn't] care what you call it as long as the reality behind it is conferred. But now having lived it, I would be more insistent. No. What we have is at its core, at its essence, the same thing. [You only] have to use two different words because you're trying to say they're different realities. I would have a harder time with that now."[3]

Certainly, Liam and Marty experience the oneness that sacramental marriage implies—such unity is suggested in Liam's comment to Marty that was highlighted in chapter 1: "What would my life be without you? Like, c'mon! That's not an imaginable thing to me." Liam told a story about how much his nieces and nephews associate Marty and him as a pair: "My nephew Jimmy, when he was four, he was looking for Marty and he said to my father, 'Liam-and-Marty, Liam-and-Marty' like he didn't know us apart. And my father giggled and said, 'That's right, Jimmy. Whenever you see one, you see the other!'"

Now, Liam and Marty are adamant about claiming the language of sacramental marriage and family to name the reality of their identity and life. They've adopted and raised two children, and "to deny that the four of us are a family . . . that's absurd to me," Liam said. "It's just so far from my experience." Marty added: "We had to explain it to our kids at one point that some people don't think two men should be a family. And their reaction to that was fear about what it meant for the four of us. They intuitively understand that our marriage was the key to build[ing] a family. And when they thought our marriage was under external forces that were against us, they worried about their own self as part of the family. To me, the logic of that is exactly correct. There's a marriage between two adults who choose love and then the family gets built on that block." In fact, this logic reflects the way that the magisterium affirms healthy marriages for the well-being of church and society; committed married couples are "the block" upon which families rest, and thriving families are the bedrock of thriving communities.[4] Accordingly, supporting marriages and families benefits the common good.

Liam and Marty reflected on what it means to be family. "When you're part of it, in a context of being loved and held and celebrated and having a place in it, all that's really great," Liam suggested. "Yeah," affirmed Marty. "It's a deeper belonging. And I think we had to fight for it every step along the way, to claim our relationship, to claim our right to be a family, and so we don't take it for granted. We don't just presume. There's a deep valuing that goes with knowing that there's folks who would deny our relationship to begin with, who would tell us, 'You have no right to love each other. You don't have a right to be together.' And then you know there's another group that would look in on the four of us and say, 'You have no right, that somehow you're stealing something by calling yourself a family.' Yeah, it's in reaction to that. What makes family is a heart connection. It's not blood. It can be blood. But there's a heart belonging that I claim you as mine." *Being loved, held, and celebrated. Having a heart connection. Knowing you are claimed by another, you are a part of the whole.* For Marty and Liam, that's family.

In their wedding vows, Liam and Marty "promise[d] to make [their] home a place of love and welcome." From the beginning of their marriage, they've been committed to hospitality. "We're going to open our home, and we're going to open our hearts," Liam said, "We're going to try to create a community. You know the Catholic overlay is that it's almost always around the meal. That's a formula that works. Have some wine. Have a good meal. Life is good. And Marty's really been able to create those kinds of environments." Marty noted, "The dining room has always been the most significant room in our home because we know that life happens at the table." Marty praised Liam for connecting easily and "intuitively" with people and bringing them into their lives. He told me that as an introvert, he largely credits Liam, an extrovert, for their "very rich life," steeped in community. "Community is critical," Marty stressed. "Yes, we have our individual relationship, but if it's just the two of us, we don't have the strength of the tribe. We don't have this larger net. We don't have the communion of saints, living and dead. We become so much richer when we're all in it together." Their home has been, and continues to be, a place of welcome.

"From early on" the couple talked about becoming parents. They finally moved forward with the adoption process after about a decade of talking about it. What prompted them to take the step was the purchase of a big house in need of renovation, and the events that surrounded it. Liam explained, "It had been a rooming house and a crack house and it was in pretty rough shape." Liam and Marty were showing the house to a good friend and her son, who is their godson: "We're walking through, it's scary," Liam describes, "we get to the top floor and [their godson] says, '*Just you two* are going to live here?' And it was like, *Wow*. And then my nephew Jimmy said something very similar: 'This place is scary, but a lot of people can eat in the dining room and can sit in the family room'—however he said it. *This house could feel a lot fuller.* Yeah. So little guys who love you, call you to your own sense of self." The two boys called Liam and Marty to ever-greater hospitality, prompting them to see their vocational path: the house was meant to be filled with their children.

Marty and Liam signed up for parenting classes, which was a required part of discernment in the adoption process. "By the third class we knew we were going to be dads because it was so clear [that] we had been so blessed. We had so much to give and so much had been given to us. We had a deep relationship with each other. We had a circle of support. We had material wealth. You know, for us, to not find some way to give this back would be wrong. It became obvious that making a home for kids that needed homes, that was the right way for us," Marty explained. They adopted two children out of the foster care system—Marcus and Kayla, a biological brother and sister. Liam said, "I don't have any doubt in my mind that we were destined to be their parents. And they were destined to be our kids. The woman who did the matching at the foster care agency, I think she's a genius or a holy woman or something. She just had a sense about it, and she was dealing with an organization that was pretty homophobic and racist as well. She's a black woman and had to sort of mediate through all that sort of stuff [Marty and Liam's children are black; they are both white] and focus on the kids and what was good for them."

"Parenting has stretched me in a way that nothing else compares to," Marty said. "It takes it to an even deeper level to open your heart up to two children who are vulnerable, who need to be cared for, who've been traumatized, who need love. It stretched me in ways I never would have imagined, taking me to places of pain but joy as well. And it's changed us because we shared that journey together. We really relied on each other to make it through."

Kayla and Marcus joined Marty and Liam at the same time, at the ages of nine and seven. The children were different from one another. "Kayla, she was a handful. She was loud and pushy and needed to be reined in a bit. Marcus needed to be brought out more. He was more shy and retiring and when he expressed anything, it was usually anger, and so helping him find joy was more difficult to do," Liam said. The couple spent time "paying attention to their emotional life," so they could meet each child's specific needs. One shared need was for stability and routines, which Marty and Liam worked to provide. "So, [when they first came to us] they had no morning routines," Marty said. "They didn't know that you get up and you make your bed and you wash your face and brush your teeth. I'd make little checklists for them before they would come downstairs. When they lived in foster care, they didn't have their own toothbrushes. Underwear was in a communal drawer. The most basic routines that I had grown up with—you just assume every kid knows how to brush their teeth—they didn't have that. And so wherever we could build structure and tradition helped us build family." Marty and Liam created family traditions (and simultaneously "built family") around holidays and "seasons of the church," and, not surprisingly, around the family table.

"Two weeks ago, Kayla, who is now twenty-two and home from college, living at home, has her friend, Sasha, who's her same age, sit down with us," Marty said. "It's the night of our men's meditation group, so we always start with a meal together. Table fellowship is how you build community. And so Kayla will often join in with us, and because Sasha was here, Sasha joined us. So I made a shrimp and pasta dish, and Sasha's like, 'I've never had this before.' And we're like, 'You haven't had shrimp?'

And she's in her twenties. 'No. I've never sat at a table with people that talk and eat together.' And Kayla just sort of rolls her eyes, and she was like, 'That's what I grew up with. It's kinda overrated.'"

"Yet she brings stragglers to dinner every time we have dinner together!" Liam said.

"Yeah. We knew that time [over shared meals] is when we become a family. That's where we shared our journey of the week. Our kids who came through foster care had physical hunger, but deep emotional and spiritual hunger as well. And so we knew that [family dinner] was the primary time as a family where you nourished each other on those different levels," Marty said. They focused on such rituals both at home and at church, which provided normalcy and stability for the children. "We became a family in November. Well, it was in October when we first met our kids. And so making a Halloween cake, decorating the house, getting costumes became the vehicle by which we started doing these things. Then Thanksgiving was a family celebration and big dinner and then Advent and Christmas—stockings and trees and decorating the front door," Marty explained. Those seasons that mark each year "helped us cultivate traditions for kids who didn't have any when they joined us."

Liam prompted Marty to tell me a story about when their daughter was sixteen. Marty obliged, saying: "So she's in the middle of high school and at this point in her life when she's . . . getting crappy [fast] food, and I'm trying to get them to eat healthy whenever they can. And so it's just her and I in the kitchen, and I'm making dinner one night. It's actually one of her favorites—salmon and asparagus and rice. And I said, 'Kayla, you have to promise me that when you become a parent and have to feed kids of your own, that this is how you're going to feed them—good, healthy food.' And she's like, 'I'll never admit this, but I'm going to do it all. I'm gonna do everything you did.' I'm like, 'You're going to cook like this?' And she goes, 'No. I'm going to make us sit down at dinner time and I'm going to help them with their homework, and I'm going to . . .' Yeah. That was pretty cool. That was cool. At sixteen I got that. What every parent hopes for."

"She'd deny it today," Liam said.

"Yeah. She totally would," replied Marty, with a chuckle.

Chapter 2

"But they understood too that mealtime was all of that. Even now they delight in traditions. As much as they complain about decorating the Christmas tree, they want to be a part of it," Liam said. And, of course, Kayla is consistently bringing the "stragglers" home for dinner. Those of us formed within a sacramental tradition that centers around the eucharist will easily see—and likely resonate with—these stories of shared family meals as they connect to eucharistic practices. I'm struck by the powerful Christian imagery of the building of family around a shared meal. Utilizing language from the Catholic tradition, I'd suggest that Liam and Marty have created a *domestic church* that experiences, celebrates, and deepens communion through table fellowship (and other cherished family rituals and traditions). This mimics what we do when we gather at a eucharistic liturgy—we participate in the shared meal and become ever more profoundly one (baptized) family in Christ. Chapter 4 will focus on experiences of same-sex couples in church communities and will consider how those experiences might help us think more deeply about what it means to be the body of Christ. But I'd note here how Marty and Liam's rootedness in the Catholic faith helped them name the sacraments-of-the-ordinary in their home and recognize how those rituals brought them into deeper communion.

I offer Marty and Liam's testimony as an entree for thinking about how the couples in my study are sacraments *to others*, as their love overflows—to children, to extended families, to others in their communities. As briefly noted in the last chapter, the layers of sacrament are inseparable in the Catholic understanding of marriage. I hope you are coming to see how they manifest and overlap in the lives of these spouses.

"Pretty blissful." That's how Katie described her marriage to Sarah.

"Pretty blissful," Sarah repeated.

"Well, it's a little different now because we have a fourteen-year-old. She's kinda moody," Katie said, laughing.

"Everything's new because she's been with us two months. Previous to that, I mean our day-to-day life was pretty awesome," Sarah explained. When I spoke to them, Katie and Sarah were adjusting to having their adopted daughter, Ivy, in their home. She came to them out of the foster care system.

During our conversation, Sarah and Katie talked at length about discernment; it's a thread that's run through their adult life. They share Christian faith, though Sarah is active in the ECLA tradition, while Katie is Catholic (with tension). As noted in chapter 1, the couple's shared experience at L'Arche shapes their understanding of themselves and their responsibilities in the world. Their Christian faith is a stance of trust in God and a belief that "whatever this life is, it's bigger than us, and it's about how you treat people. A commitment to look beyond yourself and your own needs. That's something we both, on our good days, try to see and practice," Katie said. "It is bigger than us, so we can trust something bigger than us as we kind of stumble along in this life. Which we do."

Reflecting on her attempts to trust and follow where God is leading her, Katie said, "I feel like there've been so many moments where I'm like, *I don't want to go that way. It's kind of scary*. You know I remember distinctly sitting on my bed at L'Arche . . . I was like, *Oh my God, I think I like a woman but I'm not supposed to. But I think it's okay. But if I go this way, it's going to shatter all these other pieces of my life. But I am going to trust.* And even with this kid [their adopted daughter], it's just gonna create all kinds of chaos for our life. Our life is so beautiful and simple, just blissful, but that's not actually what life is meant [to be]. All these big moments in life, I would be clinging desperately to *stay here*, but felt called toward something a little different. Trusting that it was okay to go in that [new] direction has made all the difference."

The couple learned at L'Arche that life is not about being comfortable. In that community, they learned that "the good stuff" is often found "when we're being vulnerable and maybe a little broken down," Katie said. "What feels like getting broken apart is sometimes just being broken open," Sarah said. They discovered that meaning comes in and through "seeing beauty in the chaos and embracing that." "And recognizing that vulnerability is not a weakness," Sarah added. So much of what Katie and Sarah revealed in our conversation was an attitude and practice of giving-way out of love for the other, even when difficult. Worth noting again here is James Keenan's definition of mercy as the willingness to enter into the chaos of another in order to meet their needs. Sarah said,

"There's something about the Lutheran tradition that's big on the daily dying and rising—your baptismal journey of daily dying and rising—and that's kind of what marriage is. Every day you kind of die to yourself and rise in relationship . . . there's great challenge in that, and great joy in that."[5]

Sarah described hitting a "rough patch" with Ivy after "a pretty good" first three weeks. The rough patch coincided with an educational series at church about stewardship, and "it was interesting [to look at the whole adoption] experience through the lens of stewardship," she said. "We tithe ten percent [of our earnings], and this experience with this fourteen-year-old is tithing the rest of our lives. Like we have an overabundance of love. We have an overabundance of time and commitment and life and so looking at sharing life with a fourteen-year-old is tithing the rest of our lives. Not just our money, but our energy, our talents, the things we have to share with the world." And "there's some level of sacrifice involved . . . it's going to hurt a little sometimes. [Yet] you can also come back to a place of joy." Coming back to a place of joy following sacrifice sounds a lot like resurrection.

This framework of stewardship reminds me of what Liam said about feeling an obligation to share the many gifts they'd been given with children: "To not find some way to give this back would be wrong." Sarah and Katie discussed a variety of ways they might bring a child into their lives. They decided to pursue foster adoption because "there are enough kids in the world who need a home" and it "fit" with their shared values. Sarah said, "We went to this training and this woman got up and talked about the story of a family who brought in a sixteen- or seventeen-year-old. It's just some little random story, and we went out for lunch [afterward] and we're both like, *When she was talking I was thinking maybe we should be open to a teenager*. Like, we're both thinking the same thing. Yeah. Okay. We can be open to a teenager."

"When it came down to it, we had this option of a nine-year-old who had way less trauma and just seemed easier," Katie explained. The social worker described her as a "typical" kid. "Whereas there's this fourteen-year-old, who was in an orphanage and has all these wounds and, I don't know, we're both like . . ."

"She's going to be fine," Sarah said.

"We just kept coming back to: we don't really know anything about teenagers or trauma, but we think that's our kid. Yeah, it's kind of painful, but, yeah."

"She's a good kid," Sarah added. "She's a teenager, but . . ."

"It just kind of happened," Katie said. "And that's like all the best things in my life. I never could have even imagined or asked for or planned [it] in any way." Indeed, God is a God of surprises. And Sarah and Katie continually choose to follow through the "next door" that God opens, trusting that—even in challenges and chaos—they're headed toward "the good stuff."

Christina and Emma, introduced in chapter 1, also exemplify an outward-facing Christian marriage that includes parenting. "We're committed to being true to each other. And that's realigning our lives to what's true." For them, what's true is a life centered on "companionship with Jesus." Emma said, "We really measure decisions based on our understanding of Jesus and our relationship with Jesus and the way we walk with Jesus. That's a lens [through which] we look at the world." "Like that beautiful image of what marriage is like: two people holding hands, but they're not looking at each other . . . ," Christina said, " . . . [they're] facing the world, on mission, together."

The shared mission of this couple is shaped by "a sense of global solidarity." Emma said, "Look, we don't embody it all the time, but it keeps us accountable, attempting to live it out. Being aware of the world [when] making decisions about where we live and how we live, with our impact on others and the ways we want to build relationships with others— whether it be through nonprofit affiliation, the boards that [Christina] serve[s] on . . . how we spend our weekends, what we read. Yeah. All of that. How we choose to participate in consumerism or not. Our commitment to downward mobility. You know, like lessening the gap . . . we're not navel gazing. It keeps the world at the center of us and it keeps us moving into the world a little bit."

The couple finds "deep joy" in simple pleasures like family walks, bike rides, "going on adventures," and spending time with good friends. In fact, when we spoke in their home, they were busy packing up for a weekend camping trip with their daughter, niece, and nephew. Christina and Emma believe it is "really important" to carve out "sabbath time" in their busy lives and to "offer [the] hospitality that they've received from people to other folks." Their conversations about becoming parents revolved around hospitality and "how we share our life with people."

Initially, they thought about fostering. "But we don't have a two bedroom," Christina explained, and the high cost of living in their area meant that "they couldn't move into one. And that's a real limit." The couple were on a list to welcome an "in-betweener," "like the sixteen- to nineteen-year-olds who just, they didn't need a family, they just needed *somebody*, but none of that ever worked out, which we thought was weird.[6] So we were open, open, open, open, open. And then as far as a child goes, a few of our friends were toying around with fostering to adopt or actually doing it, and we were like, *Hey, we should do that*. But because of the limitation [related to their living space], we couldn't." The couple ended up pursuing pregnancy aided by technology and were successful. They hope to have a few more children.

Christina suggested that official Catholic teaching is "so limited in the way [it] considers procreation.[7] Even the science behind it. Come on, people. God is trying to show God's brilliance through a myriad of ways and a diversity of realities and life. And is it too much for us?" She proposes that we consider that new ways of conceiving children via reproductive technologies may, in fact, "elevat[e] the goodness of creation. . . . We can't think that we're better than God. Like here is *the* definition [of procreation]. And because [the magisterium] just can't deal with our lived experience—*this doesn't make sense*—it's like trying to fit our lived experience in the square. Now, I actually think [our experience] expands the square, and I'm okay with that. That square was so finite. That's the irony."

"Why are we such a threat?" Emma wondered aloud.

When asked what their daughter, Joy, has brought to their lives, Emma responded, "How much time do you have?" She described Joy as one of the "really sweet, beautiful surprises" of their marriage. Emma said, "I didn't know [parenthood] was going to be so great. Joy is pretty awesome!" The couple told me excitedly about Joy's baptism. "I love everything that baptism represents," Emma said. "I mean, it's the best rite. It's grace. I mean all sacraments are grace, right? But, it's rebirth. New life. New creation. It's hospitality and welcome to a church, or to a community of faith. It's acknowledging that somebody is worthy before they even do anything to earn it. I love that God's initiating and [we] say yes. [We're] saying yes for those who cannot yet say yes and helping them grow into that affirmation of their own life and worth. And I love that it symbolizes the call to join in Jesus's mission."

"I mean the mission can't be controlled," Emma continued. "All of it. It's like everything to me. And then, more concretely, to raise up a child in the faith that has meant a lot to us, and to help her understand her life in the context of Jesus's story—hope and love and forgiveness and redemption. Just like our wedding was an affirmation of a beautiful community . . . a really beautiful symbol. And I guess you put that in contrast to what the magisterium teaches and it's a beautiful little symbol of resistance, too." Christina explained that their robust understanding of church gives them "the ability to claim" their daughter's full membership in the body of Christ and to "wish that for other people too. *This is our church. This is our community.*"

Christina and Emma said yes to each other in marriage. They were "open, open, open, open, open" to children. They said yes to the birth of their daughter and yes to her baptism—yes to rooting her in their faith tradition. Yes to their responsibilities to family and community. From their perspective, God initiated, and they responded. Theirs is a vocational story of marital love that overflows. Theirs is a story of the *really sweet, beautiful surprises of marriage*. It's a story of sacramental grace at work.

Michael and Brian, whose marital-familial fidelity was highlighted in chapter 1, talked with each other about having kids. They even filled out adoption forms at one point. But those plans were put on hold when Brian's family got sick. "Yeah. Then my dad got sick and my brother got sick, and I've spent the last four years dealing with that, and then they both died. And now here we are." A couple years following their deaths, the couple was asking, "Where did we leave off?" in their discussion about becoming parents. But "there's been a lot of water under the bridge," Brian said. "My brother had two boys and a wife. And the kids, they were ten and twelve, and now they're twelve and fourteen, and we've sort of stepped in to be the surrogate[s]. My sister-in-law had me down the other day. She's like, 'I found him smoking pot. You gotta talk to him!' I gotta go do some dirty work, you know, and pick up where the father left off. And Michael's done it as well. And the two boys look at us and one said to me, 'You're the closest thing we have to a dad.' [Brian's eyes welled up with tears.] That still gets to me. So that's what we've been doing. We sort of tabled our own kids. Now we're taking care of these other kids. They live in [another state] so we have to fly back and forth."

"They're all getting along. You know, it's pretty amazing how everybody is," Brian said. "Pushing ahead. I mean, it was tough. My mom lost her son and her husband. These guys lost their grandfather and their dad. I lost my business partners. I mean, it ran really deep. The whole thing did. So the idea is to give these kids little extras. Extra attention. There are other nieces and nephews, but [all of this] got us looking at the role we wanted to play [in their lives]. Sometimes life throws you a curveball. We wanted to be parents, and maybe where—at least for the current time—our energy needs to be is with these kids whose dad left too soon. They really need father figures like us to be there, more than just a typical uncle, and really to help fill-in in emotional, financial ways. They may need more to become the people that we all want them to be. . . . We're putting on a hat that was tossed at us. And we're proudly taking that on." Sorrow over the loss of beloved family members *ran really deep*. So does the generosity of these uncles-turned-surrogate-fathers, proudly stepping into their new roles, as needed. Michael and Brian are putting on "the hat that was tossed" to them—putting their own children on hold, but not their parenting.

Of course, not all of the couples in the study want to be or are parents. They nevertheless are procreative or generative insofar as they support the flourishing of others in need. Megan and Mary, for example, don't feel a "deep desire" for kids of their own. Megan said, "It takes a village to raise kids, and there aren't enough villagers out there. And we've gotten really good at becoming [villagers]." She and Mary "really like being the people who can come in and help when help is needed . . . I really appreciate being able to be the village. To be able to help. And I think that is really hard to do when you have kids."

Likewise, Liz and Abigail decided against having children of their own. They have a "no kids, no pets" agreement. At the same time, being of service to others is a shared core value. "Part of the 'no kids, no pets' allows us to be available to anybody else. It's much easier to drop anything. Have people stay with us. Go places. Go to the hospital in the middle of the night," Liz said.

"It's also the work that we do to support a whole bunch of people [in the community]. [That work] is just made much easier by the fact that we're not supporting children," Abigail said. She works in education, and Liz works directly with an at-risk population. "We support each other in finding careers that are of service, regardless of what the salary is," Liz added. They also spend "a crazy amount of time" volunteering at their parish, for example, or writing emails for LGBTQ causes. "Whatever the case, it's all part of the service," and, from their perspective, not having children or pets frees up time to serve.

The two were married for four years, together for eleven, at the time of our interview. Liz and Abigail are both Catholic and understand their marriage as sacramental. Abigail said that part of why she knew Liz "was the person who I was going to marry [was] because we both thought of marriage as a sacrament, and that means a lifetime commitment. Unless somebody dies or there's something really heinous like abuse, you stay with me and figure it out. Probably the reason I was thinking I wouldn't [ever] get married was, well, nobody else is going to think of marriage that way. And what's going to happen if they think of it differently than I do? I'm not willing to take that risk."

When she found Liz, who was also interested in "inviting God into the relationship," she knew she found something different and took a risk on her, on *them*. Their shared Catholic faith was "the basis [of] something really powerful and meaningful. It was a value system and whatever, but it's just a way of being in the world." Liz said, "We live out the sacrament in the way that we treat each other, and the representation of our relationship is indicative of how we believe we should treat all people." Simply put, their married love is the model for how they love others.

Moreover, Abigail said, "Catholic social justice teaching is pretty much the basis of everything we do on a daily basis." She explains that the focus of her Catholicism growing up was "always on . . . helping people. For lack of a better term, it was like, How do you help other people? How do you give service to other people? . . . Sort of like social justice-y. There was a lot of focus on poverty. What are we doing for the poor?" As adults and life-partners, Abigail and Liz share this sense of responsibility to care for the poor and vulnerable, understanding it as inherent to their Catholic faith and grounding all that they do. Clearly, their Catholicism is essential in shaping their combined *way of being in the world*, which is outward facing.

Tom and Mark are also excellent examples of marital generativity beyond a narrow focus on procreativity. Mark told me that very early on in their relationship, Tom announced that he had something important to tell him. "I could tell he was a little tortured about what he was about to say. It's like, *Okay, what's he going to say? Will this be a deal breaker?* And he said, 'I make too much money.' And I'm thinking, *Who can make too much money?*" Tom proceeded to explain to Mark how he decided to spend his paycheck every month. He regularly sent hundreds of dollars each month to some missionaries, annually supported several charities, and was supporting a young Turkish man at the University of Cracow. Mark said, "This was a young man Tom had met through a family he knew in Istanbul" who practiced his English with Tom and they became friends. At some point, the man "confided in Tom that he wasn't sure where, or if, he was going to be able to go to university, given [his] financial situation. . . . this young Muslim man, smart, you know, personality plus, who would not have had an opportunity to do something important to match his talents. And for Tom it was just, *I can do this.* So, if I'm remembering correctly, [looking at Tom], you went home, looked at your budget, shifted a few things, and decided how you could free up three hundred and fifty dollars a month, which in Cracow gets you a lot." Tom's support enabled the young man to earn an international relations degree. Mark and Tom attended his graduation together, at which he was a featured speaker. "He's a star, you know," Mark said. "And when he walked up to his podium to give this talk, I thought, *Where would he have been otherwise without Tom making that possible?"*

Tom has made a point to live simply in order to share what he has with others. He said, "I don't even know what people spend money on [Hence his statement: 'I make too much money.']. I just don't understand that . . . Choosing not to spend money on whatever it is—that I'm not going out to eat, I guess, or [have] expensive hobbies—I have the resources to be hospitable and be welcoming. It's not just how I spend my money. It's also that sense of learning to welcome others, of learning to accept people as they are. Greg Boyle says, *You know God is so busy being delighted with the way we do things that He has no time to be disappointed.*[8] I can have that attitude with the people I interact with . . . I can only be welcoming to the degree that I learned to sort of get rid of all that other judgey stuff."

I have the resources to be hospitable and be welcoming. What's striking in Tom's description of hospitality is that it requires more than financial resources. It requires spiritual and emotional ones as well. Hospitality requires a particular *attitude* of welcoming without judgment, of delighting in another in an unconditional way in order to make them feel worthy and loved.[9] Indeed, Tom has practiced hospitality in remarkable ways, and since they've been married, he and Mark have extended hospitality together. Mark said, "When I started spending time at Tom's house, there were a couple of rooms upstairs and the doors would be closed all the time. So I asked, 'Are there people living here?' He told me the story of a young man who had gone to college until a few years back. He had been in a foster home." The young man, Phillip, had gone to a very good high school and on to college with the support of his foster parents, but "the connection there disintegrated." "Tom got a call one day from a friend who was on staff at [the college] and she said, 'I have a young man who's going to go into a nosedive pretty soon. He's not going to stay here, but he has nothing. He has nowhere to go. No one.'"

"He continues to see his mother, but she suffers from some kind of mental illness," Tom inserted.

"[The friend at the college] asked Tom, 'Could you help me find a place for him to stay?' So Tom said, 'Well, he comes here.'" Phillip moved in with Tom. He " . . . sort of stayed [isolated] in his room for a while. I mean months," explained Mark.

"It was a long time before he would even have dinner with me," Tom said.

"So what I found out was that one of those closed doors was where this guy Phillip lived. I got this backstory and it was like . . . *Will there be no situation where I don't discover, oh, somebody's surviving because Tom did something?*" Mark said.

Phillip tried another college, but "the college life wasn't a match for him," and he entered the Marines. "He's been in now for a year, doing very well. He will send letters back to both of us and basically says, 'I know I have a home, and that's made all the difference,'" Mark said. "And I'm sure Tom would basically say, 'What? It's a room.'" Tom is so practiced in generosity and hospitality that it is second nature to him. That's how virtue works. An important part of this story is that Phillip's room remains *his* room, even though he is out of the house. He has a key and a home to which he can (and does) return. He has a family, with no conditions attached.

"I don't know anyone else who would be a partner in those kinds of relationships," Tom suggested. "When Phillip writes to us, he never says, 'Tom, you provided a home for me.' He says, 'You Two have provided a home for me.' That's what he always says. And I think that's where we are now. It's that sense [that] we have common values about what it means to extend hospitality to welcome the stranger. It doesn't mean becoming Catholic Workers and it doesn't mean moving to [a developing country] together."

"It doesn't *have* to mean that. Right," said Mark.

"But it means when the door opens, when you get that phone call that says, 'Do you know anybody who can take this guy?' You say, *Yes!* And we share that sense of: that's the way we ought to live. I mean, it's a combination of that's the way God works, by offering us things we didn't expect and saying, *Well, here you go. You want to do it, or not?* And in that sense it's our joy to say, *Yes, yes we'll do that. Yes, we can do that. I've never had a Marine in my house before, but that's okay, we can do that.*" Again, we hear about the God of Surprises, calling couples to love and serve in unexpected ways and, in response, their willingness to enthusiastically say yes.

One of the first things that Tom sent to Mark—they met online—was a paragraph that sums up who they want to be to each other and, as a pair, to others. Tom recited it from memory during our interview: "It's by Henri-Frederic Amiel, a Swiss theologian, and it's, 'Life is short and we do not have much time to gladden the hearts of those who make the journey with us. So be swift to love, make haste to be kind.'" "So for me," Mark said, "That's what ends up happening. And for Tom and me to be in a place where we can take that seriously and nod to it, I know that's what my life is moving toward, being swift to love and to be kind."

Once or twice a month, Mark and Tom bring the eucharist to a small group of folks in a senior home. The couple first attends the morning service at their Episcopal church, where Tom takes notes on the homily, and then the two head over to the senior home for a "home eucharist." It includes the readings, summary of the sermon, and distribution of the eucharist. Tom is a musician, so he also brings copies of a couple of hymns so they can all sing together. "We both value that a great deal," Tom said. "Having eucharist with six other people when you know their names and you know something about them. In some ways, it's more meaningful than the church of three hundred people. Even if they don't have priests and they don't bless it right there while you're watching . . . when we get up and pass the peace, we pass the peace to everyone there and we call them by name." Tom appreciates "doing that together." It's one way that Mark and Tom are able to gladden the hearts of those who journey with them.

Tom remarked on the importance of the eucharist in his spiritual life several times during our conversation. I asked him why receiving the eucharist is so meaningful to him. He said, "[It's] that sense of centering, that sense of recall. These are the things that matter. This is what it's all about. It's about self-giving love. And I can never be reminded too often of that. It's not about you. It's not about the things you do. It's about your willingness to let that self-giving love into your life and to let it change you. It's just being reminded of that."

Indeed, it is a eucharistic sense that life is *all about self-giving love* that seems to animate the couples highlighted in this chapter, along with others in my study. They know that life is not about themselves alone, but about "something bigger" in which they participate—they are responsible: to children, to community, to those most in need, to those hungry for food and love and belonging. They are open, listening, and willing to be called and changed by a God who invites them to give themselves away—both within their marriage and beyond it. And they are bearing good fruit. Again, in these marriages, we witness a Christ-event.

Digging In: A Reconsideration of Magisterial Teaching

"If there is the danger of running amok in the messiness of bodily experience and the ambiguity of claims to the work of the Spirit in human lives, there is certainly much more danger in proceeding as though God were not at work in bodily experience and the Holy Spirit were not active in human lives here and now."—Luke Timothy Johnson[10]

The testimony above (that is, presented in chapters 1 and 2) problematizes the position taken by the Congregation for the Doctrine of Faith in 2003[11] and affirmed by Pope Francis in *Amoris Laetitia* in 2016 that "there are absolutely no grounds for considering homosexual unions to be in any way similar or even remotely analogous to God's plan for marriage and family." As seen, these couples describe their marriages as sacramental and their marital commitment as life-long, life-giving, and centered in God. When they recounted their wedding rituals and vows, such an understanding of marriage was front and center. Further, we see how their shared, lived commitment to those vows animates their commitment to move beyond themselves to care for family and community, especially those most in need. In fact, the perspectives and experiences of these couples—including their theological understanding of their marriages—were strikingly similar to the opposite-sex couples that Julie Massey and I interviewed for *Project Holiness*, couples we held up as examples of sacramental marriage and virtue.

And yet.

As noted above (and as widely known, even outside of Catholic circles), same-sex couples are not welcome to participate in the Sacrament of Matrimony according to magisterial teaching.¹² In fact, in March 2021 the Congregation for the Doctrine of Faith (CDF) released a document indicating that Catholic pastors are not permitted to bless same-sex unions, for fear that doing so would imply that such unions are equivalent to heterosexual marriage and because the church "cannot bless sin." The statement was received with dismay by many same-sex couples, LGBTQ persons, and their families and allies.¹³ The CDF's explicit emphasis on same-sex unions as sinful contrasts the tone of Pope Francis's *Amoris Laetitia*, which emphasizes mercy, conscience, and pastoral care in particular situations and warns that moral laws should not be used as "stones to throw at people's lives."¹⁴ Since the CDF's statement, Belgian and German bishops have voted to formally bless same-sex unions (while stopping short of calling these relationships marriages). To date, Pope Francis has neither explicitly condoned or vetoed those local determinations, while aware of them. In any case, the CDF's 2021 statement presents nothing *new*, but reiterates long-standing Catholic teaching on marriage and the sinfulness of homosexual relationships.

I assume that Pope Francis and even the most traditional church leaders would acknowledge and affirm the presence of grace in: the way the Christian couples in my study love and care for one another, bringing each other to holiness and virtue; the ways that they bring life to others and practice the corporeal and spiritual works of mercy in home and community; the ways that they celebrate and honor ordinary sacraments in their daily lives and homes. With what evidence could the presence of sanctifying grace in their lives possibly be denied? And if these three dimensions of grace indeed are affirmed in their shared lives, on what basis are the couples *not* sacramentally married, and wherein lies the sin? To answer those questions, we must dig deeper into magisterial teaching. Exactly what are the reasons that these relationships fail to meet the definition of sacramental marriage and are deemed sinful?

Let's briefly unpack the teaching. In a nutshell, the Catholic magisterium defines marriage as strictly between a man and a woman. To be married sacramentally in the church, a couple both needs to *reflect heterosexual complementarity* and *be open to procreation*.¹⁵ Heterosexual or male-female complementarity is assumed to be "inherent within God's creative design" and thus necessary for marriage and, more broadly, for any genital sexual activity to be moral.[16] Male-female (or heterosexual) complementarity is most basically the idea that men and women are equal but different by God's design, created by God to fit together—or, stated differently, to complement one another—in order to flourish and create family.[17] This complementarity is not merely biological, but also social and psychological; the "fit" includes sex, gender, and sexual orientation. As planned or ordered by God, the argument goes, "[t]he purpose of sexual desire is to draw man and woman together in the bond of marriage, a bond that is directed toward two inseparable ends: the expression of marital love and the procreation and education of children."[18]

Therefore, the US Conference of Catholic bishops suggest in *Ministry to Persons with a Homosexual Inclination: Guidelines for Pastoral Care* that "[a]ny sexual act that takes place outside the bond of marriage does not fulfill the proper ends of human sexuality. Such an act is not directed toward the expression of marital love with an openness to new life," and is thus "disordered" and "morally wrong."[19]

And so, while it may be granted that graced-goodness exists in the lives of the same-sex couples in my study, while it may be acknowledged

> **A WORD ABOUT DISORDER**
> The language of "disorder" as it relates to homosexual persons and relationships has been widely criticized because it is often heard and received as implying some sort of brokenness or defect of the person. Indeed, participants in my study referenced claims about "disorder" in church teaching specifically, telling me that they feel hurt by it and strongly disagree with it. To be clear, the language of disorder reflects a natural law approach to sexual ethics, suggesting that heterosexual persons are properly ordered to one another and thus to the proper ends of sex—heterosexual marital love and family. On the other hand, homosexual persons are oriented toward persons of the same sex and thus considered disordered because "acting in accord with such an inclination simply cannot contribute to the true good of the person."[a]

The USCCB specifies that "it is crucially important to understand that saying a person has a particular inclination that is disordered is not to say that the person as a whole is disordered. Nor does it mean that one has been rejected by God or the Church. Sometimes the Church is misinterpreted or misrepresented as teaching that persons with homosexual inclinations are objectively disordered, as if everything about them were disordered or rendered morally defective by this inclination."[b]

Whether or not hearing "disorder" as a personal judgment and rejection is in fact a "misinterpretation" or "misrepresentation" of church teaching, if continued use of the language of "disorder" as it relates to sexual orientation confuses and harms LGBTQ persons and/or contributes to prejudice toward them, it is a good pastoral move to avoid it altogether. Whether the claim that "acting in accord with such an inclination cannot contribute to the true good of the person" is convincing in light of the experience of LGBTQ persons is another valid question, and one that is addressed in this work and others.

Theologians David Matzko McCarthy and David Gushee, for example, emphasize the fact that the inclinations of homosexual persons are not any more disordered than heterosexual persons in a world marked by sin. We all, no matter our sexual orientation, need our desires to be "tutored in holiness."[c] McCarthy argues: "A consistent position would hold that all homosexual acts, like all heterosexual acts, are not alike. Some acts are ordered to God and the goods of common life, others are not. The orientation itself is not disordered, but it can be misdirected. Both chastity and steadfast fidelity in marriage are our typical means of ordering desires."[d]

To say that our desires need to be "ordered" or "tutored in holiness" is to argue that all humans need to learn how to integrate our desires so that we act upon them in ways that make us and our relationships (including our relationship with God) better. If we do not learn how to order our desires, we become captive to them and they can damage us and our relationships—consider for example, sexual addictions, sexual violence, and the sexual commodification of persons. McCarthy notes that virtues such as chastity and fidelity help us direct our natural desires so that we act upon them in ways that lead to flourishing.[e] This focus on virtues allows us to be ethically consistent by focusing on the ways that *all* human sexual inclinations need to be directed by virtue rather than speaking of nonheterosexual inclinations being disordered in some particular way.

Relatedly, David Gushee writes: "Traditionalists often speak as if heterosexual people's sexuality is innocent while gay and lesbian people's sexuality is broken/damaged/sinful. Revisionists often speak as if everyone's sexuality is innocent." He instead suggests that, in light of universal human frailty and brokenness, "no one's sexuality is innocent.... Everyone's sexuality needs to be morally disciplined and ordered."[f] Therefore, Gushee argues, all Christians, no matter sexual orientation, should be held to *the same* covenantal-marital ethic.

I appreciate this emphasis on the need for *all of us* to integrate our sexual desires in ways that make ourselves, others, and our relationships flourish.[g] We see in chapters 1 and 2 how marriage is a powerful context in which queer persons *are* in fact integrating their sexual desires in healthy ways that lead to flourishing. Their testimony stands in contrast to the church's current teaching on "disorder," which asserts that acting on same-sex inclinations thwarts flourishing.

NOTES

[a] USCCB, "Ministry to Persons," 6.

[b] Ibid.

[c] David Matzko McCarthy, "Homosexuality and the Practices of Marriage," *Modern Theology* 13, no. 3 (July 1997): 393.

[d] Ibid., 393–94.

[e] See the work of theologians Margaret Farley, James Keenan, and Karen Peterson-Iyer to consider additional virtues—beyond the chastity and fidelity

noted by McCarthy—that contribute to ethical sex (such as justice, equality, and mutuality). While space does not allow me to develop this here, I'd note that while I agree we all need to order our sexual desires, I think we'd do well theologically to begin with and emphasize the *goodness* of our bodies and erotic desires—and their potential to bring us into communion with others and God—as opposed to starting with and focusing on our embodied potential for sin. The language of disorder certainly does the latter, with an unjust focus on queer persons.

[f] David Gushee, *Changing Our Mind*, third edition (Canton, MS: David Crumm Media, LLC, 2017), 97. He names this recognition of universal brokenness a "Genesis 3 perspective," noting that the fall affects everyone's sexuality.

[g] I think a virtue or value approach to sexual ethics—geared toward human flourishing and attentive to concrete experience—is preferable to a traditional sexual ethic for a number of reasons, not the least of which is that it includes both straight and queer persons. Karen Peterson-Iyer's feminist approach to sexual ethics in *Revisioning Sexual Ethics* is particularly helpful.

that these Christian couples bring one another closer to God insofar as they build up virtue in one another and love their neighbors, they do not meet the definition of marriage because they do not reflect male-female complementarity and cannot naturally procreate. Further, assuming the couples are sexually active, from this perspective they are habitually sinning by engaging in immoral and disordered sex. Moreover, if they choose to use reproductive technologies to have children, they are sinning by separating the procreative meaning of the sex act from the unitive meaning. If they adopt children into their same-sex household, they are depriving those children of their "right" to be parented by a mother and father (who reflect male-female complementarity).[20]

Many scholars have thoughtfully and critically interrogated magisterial teaching on sex and marriage, using agreed-upon sources of Christian theology—scripture, tradition, reason, and experience.[21] I understand this study on same-sex married couples to be a limited (but hopefully meaningful) contribution to a wider conversation about same-sex marriage from a theological-ethical perspective. Since the crux of the magisterial argument against same-sex marriage hinges on male-female complementarity and procreation, below I draw on the relevant work of a handful of theologians and the testimony of the couples in my study to discuss briefly these components. I hope to highlight some of the overarching theological questions at hand in conversations related to complementarity and procreation without getting too far into the weeds, so to speak. For more detail, you can delve into the work of some of the scholars I mention here (and others—see the bibliography).

Rethinking Male-Female Complementarity: It's Complicated
In recent Catholic church documents, male-female complementarity is presented as *a given* in God's plan for creation and therefore essential both for any moral sexual relationship and for marriage. Church leaders ground this perspective in scripture, especially the creation stories that appear in Genesis, and natural law theology, whereby Christians reasonably reflect on "the intrinsic order of creation" and attempt to live according to that order.[22] But according to some scholars, this view of male-female complementarity based in scripture and natural law is not as readily apparent as the magisterium suggests.

Scripture: Experience, Power, and Interpretation
Catholic and mainline Protestant traditions do not take a literal approach to scripture. Instead, scholars apply historical-critical tools to interpret the Bible, attempting to determine who likely wrote the texts, for what audience, in what time period and location, and so forth. The Bible is more like a little library than a single book with one consistent perspective; it's a collection of many texts written by different people in diverse historical and cultural contexts. Therefore, scholars do exegesis in order to unearth knowledge about what the texts meant in their original contexts. We are then better able to figure out, in community, what the texts might mean for us today. We do not simply pluck out passages from their original contexts and apply them blindly to our own, as if our reality is the same as biblical times.[23] Rather, we do interpretive work. Determining what the biblical texts mean for us today requires that we put them in conversation with tradition, reason, and experience.

Thankfully, many biblical scholars and theologians have done (and are doing) this work with the passages in scripture that relate to same-sex activity and marriage. You can easily find scholarly work to help contextualize the handful of biblical passages that deal with same-sex activity.[24] I am not going to delve into that work in any detail here; I'm really just scratching the surface. I would like to highlight an overarching approach to interpretation taken by two scholars that I find particularly compelling and thought-provoking. I will then return to discuss the creation stories in Genesis, which are used by the magisterium to support male-female complementarity and will discuss an alternative way of thinking about those stories.

Luke Timothy Johnson, New Testament scholar, focuses on rereading and reinterpreting scripture in light of human experience. He acknowledges that scripture does indeed contain passages that condemn same-sex acts. But he also notes how often we reject commands in scripture based on what we know and believe today. For example, we disregard commands and dietary restrictions that exist in the holiness codes of the Hebrew Scriptures, that forbid believers from eating shellfish or mixing certain fabrics in clothing. More significantly, we reject passages in scripture that justify slavery (e.g., "Slaves obey your masters as is fitting in the Lord" Col 3). Johnson claims that contemporary Christians who want to support same-sex relationships as covenantal and life-giving are in a similar situation as abolitionists in nineteenth-century America; in that context, scripture was being used by those in power to justify inequality as God-ordained, and on the other hand used by those who sought justice and equality for all persons as made in the image of God.

Johnson notes that what changed people's minds on slavery was human testimony and direct personal contact with those who were enslaved. "Once the experience of their full humanity and the evil of their bondage reached a stage of critical consciousness, the nation never turned back to slavery and never read the bible in the same way again."[25] It was experience—human encounter and testimony—that transformed the hearts and minds of believers and made them reinterpret scripture. Johnson notes that such rethinking of scripture in light of experience can be seen at various key moments in Christian history. For example, something similar happened in the early Church when encounters with Gentiles prompted Jewish-Christians to reinterpret scripture (for example, by setting aside food restrictions and circumcision requirements for full belonging), inspired by the Spirit of the risen Christ.[26]

Christian ethicist David Gushee makes a similar argument in *Changing Our Mind*. He describes "transformative encounters" that cause biblical "paradigm leaps," such as the one that occurred as a result of contact with newly converted Gentiles in the early church. He cites several helpful historical examples of paradigm leaps, in which one long-held way of interpreting scripture on an issue was let go of for another. Gushee's examples include slavery, women's roles, and Christian attitudes and behaviors toward Jews. It is a regrettable fact that for centuries the Christian tradition interpreted the Bible in ways that justified the conquest and enslavement of indigenous persons, the moral inferiority and unequal status of women, and contempt for Jewish persons. Thankfully, our interpretation of the Bible on these issues changed. We made paradigm leaps that were far from easy or comfortable and that often led to division within the church, especially at first. But transformative encounters with persons demanded these new understandings. The abolitionist movement, the feminist movement, and the Holocaust made Christians think differently about what it means to follow the Spirit of Christ, and in turn they engaged scripture differently.

Gushee writes: "Some of us believe that in our time an older, destructive paradigm based on a particular way of connecting the biblical dots has not survived the transformative encounters we are having with LGBTQ fellow Christians, encounters in which we experience regular and astonishing reminders of God's presence."[27] I'm reminded of Maggie's words, noted in this book's introduction: "We're here. . . . We're adding value to the church." So . . . how are we being changed by these encounters? How are we transformed by our relationships with our LGBTQ brothers and sisters and their testimony—of faith, joy, and suffering? How are we informed and altered by what we know (via science and story) about their lives?

Let's take a brief turn to the creation stories in Genesis, which are at the forefront of arguments about male-female complementarity as God's fixed design for creation.[28] Gushee makes a couple of important interpretive suggestions for these creation texts. First, he argues (along with many others) that we should approach these origin stories as *theological accounts* "rather than scientific descriptions of the world as we find it."[29] We should not look to ancient texts to teach us about science—that's not what they are supposed to do. Most Christians have already accepted this as it relates to evolution; we are able to integrate scientific consensus about evolution with faith convictions that God created the world and continues to sustain it. In a similar way, Gushee argues, we "face the challenge of integrating contemporary scientific findings about gender and sexual orientation into our theological story of the world God made."[30] I will highlight the work of theologians doing such integration below.

Before I do, I'd like to emphasize a warning that Gushee raises in *Changing Our Mind*. He rightly points out how problematic arguments about "God's purported design in creation" have been in Christian history. He cites ways that creation narratives have been "used and abused," including: the use of "dominion" language to harmfully treat the earth according to its instrumental value rather than its intrinsic value; the use of creation stories to justify women's secondary status and moral inferiority; the use of "curse of Ham" language to justify the slavery of persons of African descent; and the manipulation of "orders of creation" language in the German Christian context to link concepts of blood, soil, race, and nation.[31] Biblical interpretation does not happen in a vacuum, but in particular contexts marked by power. Intentionally or not, biblical interpretation has been and continues to be a means of maintaining power, as these examples illustrate. This seems particularly dangerous when claims about *God's design* and *God's order* and *God's plan of creation* are made in ways that divide people and assign power and roles accordingly (and/or divide people from the rest of the created world). We need to tread very carefully.[32]

A relevant and helpful interpretation of the creation narrative in Genesis appears in womanist theologian Kelly Brown Douglas's "Contested Marriage/Loving Relationality." In this essay, Douglas suggests that the experience of enslaved-married-persons under the rule of slavery in America has something important to teach the church about its responsibility to acknowledge and support the marriages of same-sex couples today. She points out that within "a white racist society defined by slavocracy," the marriages of enslaved persons were "a contested reality" and the "sacredness of their intimate relationships" were disrespected and denied by those with social, political, and ecclesial power.³³ In short, "[marriage] was simply not a right granted to a brutally marginalized, hypersexualized people."³⁴ Douglas argues that the experience of married couples who were enslaved "suggests the theological foundation for discerning the church's response to same-sex marriages—*loving relationality*."³⁵ She writes:

> Any appreciation for what it means for human beings to be created in the image of God and thereby to reflect that image must begin with the imperative to engage in loving relationality with one another. The Genesis creation narrative puts it thus: 'So God created humankind in [God's] image, in the image of God [God] created them' (Genesis 1:27). What is made clear in this creation account is that human beings are not meant to live a solitary existence, but to live relationally. In this regard, the emphasis is not on the biological creation of male and female but on the existential creation of human relationship. Essentially, made clear in the creation of male and female is that the fullness of one's humanity is to be found in relationship. The model for this relationship is God's very Self as attested to by the claim that humans are *imago Dei*.³⁶

Note that Douglas's interpretation does not emphasize a natural, sexual binary necessary for marriage to be morally legitimate today, but rather the natural sociality of all human beings and the theological conviction that humans are made in the image of God. Douglas proceeds to reflect on the import of being made in the image of a specifically trinitarian God who *is* loving, mutual, reciprocal relationship. We have here a compelling reading of the creation stories that is theological, not scientific—one that emphasizes *loving relationality* at the heart of existence, central to God's design of creation. Douglas concludes: "What the church must affirm is what many enslaved men and women apparently understood: the sacredness of loving relationality. The theological imperative of human creation is not for men and women to conform categorically to social/historical contrivances of marriage, but for them to adhere to what it means to be *imago Dei*." The church, she argues, "must encourage and provide a protected space for those relationships that mirror the mutuality and reciprocity of a trinitarian God" because what is at stake is "not the biological/gendered form of a committed intimate union," but its "relational character."[37]

Douglas's Genesis reflection connects to a "simple message" for the church that one interviewee, Frances, offered during our conversation. She said: "This is who we are and this is how God created us. And our love is life-giving." Frances notes that Christians are taught to "look at the fruits of the Spirit—if they're present in a relationship, then it's of God. So show me where it's not. And then we can talk about some of these teachings. But if our relationship gives us those gifts, and gives the community those gifts, then don't dare say it's not of God."

Nature: Experience, Power, and Interpretation

Theologian Susannah Cornwall's compelling work takes up Gushee's noted "challenge of integrating contemporary scientific findings about gender and sexual orientation into our theological story of the world God made." Cornwall interrogates traditional sexual ethics, giving particular attention to reason (science) and experience, especially the experience of intersex and trans persons who exist outside a binary, two-sex model of humanity.[38] She argues that we would do well to move beyond a sexual ethic that centers on male-female complementarity because it does not do justice to what we know to be "natural" from scientific observation (of sexual and gender diversity) and from the experience of diverse members of the body of Christ—both legitimate sources of God's revelation.[39] She notes that while a binary, two-sex model of humanity is sometimes presented as "just obvious" or "observable fact," such a model has not been historically or culturally universal and "is something we have been trained to see, often because of preexisting commitments to a binary gender system."[40] The presence of intersexuality in the natural world, for example, problematizes assumptions about a narrow two-sex model. She writes: "Intersex exists in many other animal species as well as in humans. In fact, theologians who appeal to a natural law-type 'self-evident' binary sex system often end up appealing to other evidence—notably, the scriptural witness—for warrant, precisely *because* the two-sex system isn't incontrovertibly evident from nature."[41]

I agree with Cornwall's assertion that the experience of intersex persons—outside the sexual binary—is important not only for intersex persons but "for all people who care about what bodies signify and about the integrity of embodied existence."[42] She makes a powerful theological claim that Christians are called to take seriously others' experience, "especially bodily experience, since Christianity is an incarnational religion."[43] That bears repeating. We should take bodily experience seriously *because Christianity is an incarnational religion*. Further—and this is crucial—the bodily experiences of the majority (for example, those who are male or female, those who are cisgender, those who are heterosexual) are not the only ones that matter and are not the only ones that are *true*. With reference to intersex bodies and the challenge they bring to male-female complementarity, Cornwall simply states: "maleness and femaleness are not the only 'true' experiences of embodiment just because they are the most frequent."[44]

Catholic sexual ethicists Todd Salzman and Michael Lawler develop this line of argument as it relates to human dignity and acts between homosexual persons. In building their argument, they point out up front that the magisterium grants that sexual orientation is "a *deep-seated* dimension of one's personality [or nature]" and recognizes "its *relative stability* in a person."[45] They emphasize the important fact that official Catholic teaching acknowledges that heterosexual orientation is not universal in nature and that sexual orientation is something that is stable, or at least relatively stable, in persons.[46] Salzman and Lawler proceed to lay out the following case, which is worth quoting at length:

> Sexual orientation is predominantly heterosexual, homosexual, or bisexual. This natural, socially, and experientially revealed reality may be obscured by the statistical preponderance of heterosexual orientation, but it is in no way negated by the statistical preponderance. We are in complete agreement with the CDF when it teaches that 'there can be no true promotion of man's [and woman's] dignity unless the essential order of his [and her] nature is respected.' We disagree with the CDF, however, on its exclusively heterosexual interpretation of that 'essential order of [human] nature.'

Humans have no access to pure, unembellished nature. Nature reveals to their attention, understanding and judgment, only its naked fact. Everything beyond that fact is the result of interpretation by attentive, intelligent, and responsible persons; we experience nature only as rationally interpreted and socially constructed. Our sexual anthropology, then, recognizes sexual orientation as an intrinsic dimension of human nature, and what is accepted as natural sexual activity will vary depending on whether a person's orientation is homosexual or heterosexual. Homosexual acts are natural for people with a homosexual orientation, heterosexual acts are natural for people with a heterosexual orientation. They are natural because they reflect the person's fundamental human nature as interpreted by right reason [natural law]. To be ethical, we stipulate, every sexual act, homosexual or heterosexual, must be not only natural but also free, just, loving, and respectful of the human dignity and flourishing of both partners.[47]

You can see parallels to Cornwall's argument: what is ethically important is not simply what occurs most frequently—as though majority rules and determines what is true, good, and just—but rather what we determine to be moral *by reason* based on what we observe in nature. Salzman and Lawler thus conclude that ethical sex is sex that reflects one's orientation and is marked by virtue, respecting human dignity and the flourishing of both partners.[48] They suggest we move toward a sexual ethic that integrates orientation into how we think about complementarity: "the needed complementarity for a truly human sex act is *holistic complementarity* that unites people bodily, affectively, spiritually, and personally under the umbrella of a person's sexual orientation."[49] This compelling shift is toward a person-centered, virtue-based sexual/marital ethic that equally applies to all, whether straight or queer.[50] It moves us beyond a notion of complementarity that sees "penis and vagina, biological genitalia [as] the foundational requirement for the personal meaning of marital sex acts."[51]

Further, Salzman and Lawler argue that many same-sex couples, such as the ones in my study, *de facto* reflect a holistic complementarity that leads to their flourishing. The testimony of married partners presented in chapters 1 and 2 bears this out. Susannah Cornwall rightly asserts that, "[a]lthough humans indeed need to exist in relationship in order to fill out their humanity, this relationship is *not* fulfilling only or specifically as it connects men and women (or males and females)."[52] This corresponds nicely to Douglas's theological emphasis on the inherent propensity of *all* human persons for loving relationality that leads to flourishing. Cornwall suggests that "whilst gender is important as a repository for identity through which difference and diversity are expressed, it is not the most fundamental thing about being human, nor the only thing in which difference inheres." There are other ways—beyond the male/female-gender-sex binary—that human beings differ from each other, fit together, balance each other out, and complement one another that result in flourishing persons and relationships. To be sure, being a "good fit" for one another in the married life is about more than stereotypical gender characteristics[53] and opposite-sex genitals. The couples in my study attest to that.

Couples on Complementarity
When conducting our study on opposite-sex couples, Julie Massey and I were struck, but not surprised, by the fact that the language of "male-female complementarity" was not typically present when couples described their marriage. In fact, only one of the fifty couples we interviewed referred directly to male-female complementarity as important when describing their relationship. With the single exception, we simply did not hear husbands spontaneously discuss the femininity of their wives as important or necessary for their flourishing as men or the success of their marriages or families. Nor did we hear wives discuss fitting well with, or being completed by, the masculine characteristics of their husbands. While the language of male-female complementarity is in the forefront of current magisterial documents, it was not central (or generally present at all) in the descriptions of marriage by the opposite-sex couples we interviewed. Nor, anecdotally, does it appear in casual conversations that I have with heterosexual, Catholic married couples in my everyday life, even those very actively practicing their faith. Instead, in the *Project Holiness* study, couples talked about particular virtues (such as patience, generosity, and kindness) they admire and appreciate in their spouse—virtues

that make them, their marriage, their families, and their world better. The language of complementarity was personal and particular, and not typically gendered. Complementarity in these conversations sounded more like being "a good team," sharing core values, and balancing each other out in terms of personality traits and diverse expressions of care within marriage and family.

This kind of complementarity-talk likewise spontaneously appeared in my conversations with same-sex married couples.[54] Allow me to offer a handful of examples to amplify the stories already included in chapters one and two, which broadly illustrate the holistic complementary within these marriages.

When we spoke, Nicholas and Gabe had been together for thirty-two years. They proclaimed marriage vows to one another in their church one year into their relationship, and were legally married when that became possible. When asked what he most loves and appreciates about his spouse, Nicholas said of Gabe, "He's the opposite from me. He is very active, very outspoken, I'm shy. He's very spontaneous. I'm not. So I like that he's the exact opposite. He complements me in many ways, and initiates a lot of things."

Gabe nodded. "That's the first thing that came to mind when you asked the question . . . I always told [Nicholas] that I think together we were bigger because we complemented each other and actually grew as a result of that union." Notice the language of being each other's complement that both use. They appreciate the ways they differ from one another, what those differences bring out in them, and how their partnership helps them grow.

"Because he likes things that I don't, it actually forces me to do things that I normally would not do, and vice versa," Gabe continued. "He's very intellectual and I like being able to have intellectual conversations. We can achieve [more] by being together. There's a lot of [complementarity] but there's also commonality." Gabe speaks not only about how they complement each other as opposites-becoming-more-together, but also about the commonalities they share, making them compatible.

William and Mateo also talked about commonalities and differences that make their relationship flourish.[55] William said, "We have many of the same values and interests and so we're very similar . . . we have really good conversations." He names their shared roots in Catholicism and overlapping intellectual interests as similarities. At the same time, William notes that different cultural backgrounds resulted in "slightly different worldviews" that require negotiation, and that "different things make us anxious." "Different things upset us, but I find that in many cases those are sort of complementary" insofar as "he can comfort me in those things, and the reverse is true as well. There is a similarity in values and also a slightly different worldview. It really helps us to support each other."

"Yeah, I agree," said Mateo. "I think we fit together in terms of a lot of those checks and balances, which are just . . . I mean, you grow into each other in a relationship but you can't really control some of those baseline personality traits, and we just came together and fit together in a really great, organic way." He agreed that they are "anxious about" and "moved by" different things, "but there's a lot of overlap in terms of values." *A great, organic fit—similarities and complementary differences.*

Sofia and Frances, married since 2007, also described the complementary nature of their relationship. Sofia said, "For me, [with Frances], we round each other out. We balance each other nicely and I think, in that sense, we challenge each other to grow. What I love about Frances is that she is very laid back and incredibly inclusive. She's just very generous and humble."

"What I appreciate about Sofia is her generosity and her energy. [Frances laughs.] We're opposites that way. I always say she's like the Energizer Bunny in her desire to reach out to those on the margins."

The pair enjoy "simple things" such as cooking a meal together, being outside in the garden, connecting with people in the neighborhood, going for walks, and talking. They share a love for music and justice, and their church community is important to them. "We complement one another very well in terms of our spirituality," Sofia said. She described how their relationship has developed. "In the beginning, there was just this excitement around loving someone who shared your passions and shared your dreams and shared your hopes. I remember we would sit together and plan our lives, which by the way, turned out nothing like we planned [shared laughter], but there are moments! But to be able to dream together and to know there is someone walking beside you that is equally inspired by life, that's equally passionate about life. In the beginning, there's all that energy, and of course sexual energy—all of that went into the relationship. Then as we've grown and matured, what I think keeps me going or gives me life in a different way is that we challenge each other to grow. Frances puts up a mirror to me, and I don't always like that." Sofia explained how they do the challenging work of intimacy well—honestly illuminating parts of one another in need of development and supporting each other in personal growth.

Frances powerfully stated: "Being together, and our connection, our relationship . . . brought me alive in such a beautiful way. Our love for one another was something that was just really pure and honest and true. We worked at continuing that . . . we've always worked at it. So for me it was like, wow, I can love somebody. And even in the difficult times we can find our way forward in a healthy, happy way." Again, with this couple, we hear lovely descriptions of complementarity—rounding each other out, balancing each other nicely, connecting deeply (including sexually), challenging each other to grow amidst differences, and sharing values and spirituality.

Tony and Pete, whose story of caring for Tony's mother was highlighted in chapter 1, delightfully talked about their complementary partnership. "He's the total opposite of me," Tony said. "Pete has this reputation of being the life of the party. So everyone wants to be around him. That's not so with me. I'm not going to make you laugh all the day long. Pete will make you laugh all the day long."

"And you won't make anybody laugh for a minute," Pete responded.

"No! That's not me. It really isn't. That's great to have that kind of difference, right? He supports me. We are so comfortable together. We have routines in life." Pete has a very emotionally challenging job, so Tony keeps their lives organized and things running smoothly at home. "I'm the one who tells us: *This is what we're doing, and this is when we're doing it. Make sure your suitcase is packed because we're leaving tomorrow.* Also in the house I make sure all of it gets done because I realize that at work he is dealing with stuff that most of us don't want to even hear about. And so he comes home and he knows that I'll take care of it, and that's how we do it. He's the total opposite of me, there's no doubt about that."

Both men remarked on how comfortable they are with one another and how fully they rely on each other for support—that support takes different shapes based on personalities and needs. In our conversation, I appreciated what a practical look Tony provided into what mutual care and joy looks like for them on a daily basis. *That's how we do it.* "I know when Pete comes in the door, he's going to be happy. Even if he's had a shitty day." When he walks in the door, Tony said, he "wants to make you smile and wants to make you laugh. We have a great life together." Reliance on their complementarity, appreciation of their personality differences and their balanced roles in daily life, contributes to a great life together.

Kevin and Timothy also spoke about their differences in their married relationship. In particular, they reflected on how exploring those differences has led to integration, authenticity, and depth of life. Timothy told me that he is a planner, while Kevin is not. Timothy has learned to appreciate Kevin's "zest for life" and adventurous spirit—"let's just go out there into the world and explore and find out what's there. I've found over the years that that's pulled me out of a certain part of my shell and made me feel more alive." Because of Kevin's spontaneity, Timothy "take[s] life a whole lot less seriously."

"You know what I find funny . . ." Timothy adds, "is that we look at the most obvious day-to-day things in completely different ways. I just get so much joy out of the quirky, strange things that he thinks are normal." One concrete example Timothy shared about their differences relates to order in their home. Timothy likes things "more organized" than Kevin, which he admits can become "obsessive," so when they moved into a shared apartment, they had to manage expectations, alter habits, and compromise. Timothy told me that his one-time earnest effort to "tidy up" the space they designated for Kevin's things did *not* go over well.

But "on a much more serious note, it really is about getting outside myself," Timothy stated. "I found that in our marriage I cannot hide emotions or thoughts in the way I was formed to in different contexts.

So it's forced me to not just be more honest . . . but to actually understand why I see something in a certain way or think about something in a certain way, and just to talk about it. We had communication challenges early on, but as we've gotten better about these things, there really aren't any areas we can't talk about. There are some that we talk about better than others. But it's a whole other way of being for me. I grew up in a family where you just didn't talk about stuff. It was very much on the surface. That was my dad's philosophy. So we've been learning a whole new way of being."

"For me it wasn't my family so much that blocked conversation, but it was being closeted for so long," Timothy added. "I always set up an apparatus around me to block people from seeing me. . . . There was a real sense of [needing] to hide who I am in order to survive. In marriage, you just can't do that." This reminds me of what Sofia said about Frances holding up a mirror to her. *You can't hide in a marriage* (at least if the marriage and the spouses are going to be healthy). Kevin appreciates that his marriage "pulls" him out of his ingrained practice of blocking his true self, helping him become more "integrated." It is often through the exploration of differences that partners learn "a whole new [and better] way of being."

Bernadette and Anne are another couple who explicitly talked about complementarity in their relationship. They'd been together as a couple for twenty-nine years at the time of our interview and married for two and a half years. They met as Catholic Workers. Looking at Bernadette, Anne said, "You're still as adorable as the day that I met you." Turning to me, she continued, "Within the first couple of days [of knowing Bernadette], I was overwhelmed by her sense of compassion and kindness." Anne said she was "totally smitten within a couple of weeks." The two shared similar economic and religious backgrounds as well as a deep commitment to justice. "It seemed we just really clicked as friends and then I just fell and fell and fell." She'd been in a previous relationship with a woman who was Jewish and an atheist. A couple of years after that break up, Anne explained, "I remember specifically thinking: *What if I ever find somebody that I loved that could also deal with this whole side of me, [the one] in this odd, alternative lifestyle of a real commitment to God and the poor and all that?* So [finding Bernadette was] like a double bonus."

Bernadette said, "If I had been attracted to women, it wasn't conscious up until that time [when she met Anne], or acknowledged, and I was already into my thirties."

"I heard from Bernadette's sisters that Bernadette had guys flocking to her her entire life. It's really pretty comical. I think it's funny how many guys were out there waiting for her," Anne said with a smile. But despite all the interest in her, Bernadette said, "I never met anyone that interesting or that I really felt I connected to on certain levels." She contemplated becoming a religious sister, but decided to pursue "a life of service with community" as a Catholic Worker. "Then enter Anne."

"In the beginning I went from total confusion, to [asking]: What is this relationship? What does this mean?" Bernadette said. She recollects "having a lot of baggage" and "not even realizing internalized homophobia" telling her "how wrong it was and all that." She began "very consciously working that out" with Anne and with a counselor. In the meantime, Anne supported Bernadette's process. "I could not figure out why I was connecting with her and why I felt so close and I couldn't find a category," Bernadette explained. "I would literally say: *She doesn't feel like a sister. It's not that kind of relationship. She's not like my cousins. She's not like . . . What is she?* It took me a while to say, Oh my God."

In her confusion, Bernadette decided to go to Guatemala for a month to think things through and to learn Spanish. "I knew I had to get away. I just could not make sense of it. It was overwhelming."

"I was praying every day that she'd have a conversion!" Anne chimed in.

Long story short: Bernadette surprisingly met an amazing man in Guatemala—one who finally *was* interesting and with whom she connected. "It was blowing my mind," she said. But as they got closer, Bernadette explained, "I realized . . . I really can't let myself go into this because my heart was already with Anne and I couldn't imagine. My thought was: even though we were never together, it felt like a betrayal already, even though I had committed nothing. It became clear that I had to go back and at least explore what this meant. We got together and have been together ever since."

Bernadette loves "a million things" about Anne. From the start, they bonded in their work for justice, and Bernadette appreciates Anne's "compassion, standing up for the rights of others." She loves that Anne is strong and assertive and full of adventure and humor. She loves that she is "very, very, very fun loving." Since Bernadette is "more intense" and somber, Anne can "get me out of that" because she's "a lot of fun."

In turn, Anne is clearly still smitten with Bernadette, whom she described as "completely driven toward justice, completely driven toward getting involved. She is the brainchild of everything we've ever done. And I am like the detail lackey."

"Stop!" Bernadette interjected.

"It's so true," Anne insisted. "She literally is the heart of the community and the person who draws people in. She has the ideas and the vision—visionary is the word I was looking for. She has all the ideas all the time and I'm just kind of plodding along and get stuck in the day to day. But she's genuinely visionary."

"None of the visions would take shape if it weren't for Anne, so we make a good team."

"I would say I think we are complementary despite the lack of a Y chromosome," Anne responded. "And I believe I would have never in a million years stuck with the Catholic Worker without Bernadette. The fact that we've done this as a team, as a partnership, is the single reason I'm still here. [The Catholic Worker] is really likable and I'm really happy with it, but given [that] the nature of the beast is living in community with random people, [it] has its challenges. Having another person who is similarly committed" is what has enabled Anne to persevere.

In addition to working side-by-side these many years as Catholic Workers, Anne and Bernadette fostered and adopted two boys. Negotiating the foster care system was extremely difficult, and their children brought their share of particular challenges, but raising children was another meaningful and often joyful project the couple handled in partnership.

Parenthood teaches couples a great deal both about their individual strengths and how to work as a team. At one point in our conversation, Marty and Liam reflected in detail about the practical complementarity in their day-to-day parenting. Marty said, "He was the morning dad. I was the afternoon dad . . . [W]hen we adopted our kids, we both initially thought we would work full time. Within three months I went to part-time so I could be done at two every afternoon. Get them from school, do the whole afternoon homework routine and whatever extracurricular activities. Something we've always said is there is a strength in same-sex relationships. We have so many straight friends where because of these defined roles of what a woman is, [assumptions that] a woman is responsible for everything in the house and taking care of the kids . . . and dads, you know . . . they're babysitting the kids. [People say,] 'Isn't that a wonderful thing?!'"

"Look how good he is with the kids!," Liam chimed in.

"Yes!," Marty replied. "It's like, *they're his own kids*! So, as a gay couple, we always divided the challenges according to our strengths. I was the afternoon dad. He was the morning dad. I was a school teacher, so helping them do homework [was my responsibility], and I'm the one who cooks. Creating a home, having a meal together, having a sense of routine and liturgy in the home—prayers, customs, tradition—all these things were important. And those were my strengths . . . When they were in an emotional crisis, they go to Liam. Liam is Papa. I'm Dad. Anyway, given the nature of this, I do think there is a benefit that comes from not having assigned tasks, assigned roles before you even step into a relationship, but having to define them as you live through it."

Studies affirm the truth in what Marty suggests here: married relationships do benefit from dividing tasks and roles according to interests and gifts rather than gender. In a 2020 opinion piece in the *New York Times*, "How to Make Your Marriage Gayer," marriage historian Stephanie Coontz draws on research to make a case that heterosexual couples would have happier and more satisfying marriages if they learned some lessons from same-sex couples.[56] Coontz notes that "[S]haring domestic tasks has become an increasingly important component of marital stability, and lack of sharing an increasingly powerful predictor of conflict."

Yet in opposite-sex marriages, studies continue to show that—because of gender stereotypes that are internalized and enforced—women do the bulk of the housework, childcare, and cognitive and emotional labor, even when both spouses work outside the home.[57] The burden on women often leads to resentment and discontent. On the other hand, same-sex couples cannot easily fall back on gendered notions of who does what, and so typically divide responsibilities more equally, according to gifts, interests, and time-availability. As a result, they report greater happiness and relationship satisfaction. As we increasingly emphasize the equality of men and women as well as persons outside of the gender-sex-binary, learning from the expansive, practical complementarity of same-sex couples like the ones in my study can serve all married couples well.

We can deepen our critical analysis of magisterial teaching on gender and marriage by engaging the work of Catholic ethicist Cristina Traina. In "How Gendered Is Marriage?," she highlights the ways that the teaching relies on cultural norms of masculinity and femininity, norms that "change with culture over geography and time."[58] She disputes the notion that the theologies of gender within magisterial documents on marriage "truly express universal, eternal experiences of marriage and gender."[59] In other words, she suggests that claims about gender complementarity in marriage are limited and at least partially socially constructed, so we should be wary when they are presented as natural and true for all by God's design.

Traina illustrates the elasticity of gender, drawing especially on Darcy Lockman's *All the Rage: Mothers, Fathers, and the Myth of Equal Partnership*. She discusses studies related to gender and parenting/caretaking that challenge the idea that women are natural caretakers in a way that men are not. "The key news is that caretaking is a human, not a gendered, trait; nearly any human being can acquire it" through practice, Traina notes. "The bad news is that we write social scripts of gender into children so unconsciously and early that they are hard to arrest, so that people arrive at adulthood with brains and habits already primed for cultural masculinity or feminine caretaking."[60] From infancy and through early childhood and adolescence—when peer gender-policing dominates, children learn to associate masculinity with aggression and femininity with nurturance.

Behavior in accordance with these norms becomes "second-nature to most of us" and shapes marriage and parenting.

Traina argues that resisting these gendered norms would be good for marriages and families. Overemphasis on binary gender differences as "natural," Traina argues, "is bad for children because it narrows the parenting resources they receive, bad for women because it saddles them with a second shift that men do not perform, and bad for men because it distances them from their partner and children. Redescribing child-rearing traits as parental rather than feminine would help to relieve these unhealthy patterns."[61] Relationships that challenge these unhealthy patterns surely have something important to teach us. What these same-sex couples tell us about the complementarity within their marriages, and how it leads to their flourishing and the flourishing of their families and communities, matters.

Ultimately, Traina suggests that "a just and lasting theology of marriage will need to bypass gender altogether, embracing a vision of complementarity that emerges from the gifts and choices particular partners bring to their shared, faithful vocation."[62] Paying attention to the experience of the married, same-sex couples in my study—and others like them—fleshes out such a vision. As one man in my study simply put it about his relationship of thirty-two years: "We each have our gifts and they have fallen together naturally in terms of what we each do best." *That's complementarity.*

Rethinking Procreativity and Parenting
I'd suggest that rethinking procreativity and parenting is more straightforward than rethinking heterosexual complementarity, though they are clearly related, since obviously it does require an egg and a sperm to conceive. It is a strength of Catholic teaching to emphasize the tight connection between sex and procreativity insofar as sex often results in conception, and vulnerable children who are brought into this world are owed love and care. Stable parenting and family life are undoubtedly good for children, which is part of why the Catholic tradition links marriage and procreation: it's a matter of justice for children.

One can grant that logic, of course, and also acknowledge that not all heterosexual married couples have children. Some marry past menopause, some face infertility, and some choose not to have children.[63] It is clear in official Catholic teaching that heterosexual couples who are unable to conceive are not somehow *less married* than those who can and do. In "Marriage: Love and Life in the Divine Plan," the USCCB emphasizes that procreation is essential in the official Catholic understanding of marriage: married partners are a communion of persons whose love overflows to children and thus—following *Humanae Vitae*—couples ought to be open to conception in each and every sex act. Yet the bishops acknowledge that "some marriages will not result in procreation due to infertility, even though the couple is capable of the natural act by which procreation takes place." They note that infertility often comes as a surprise, "and can be a source of deep disappointment, anxiety, and even great suffering for a husband and wife. When such tragedy affects a marriage, a couple may be tempted to think that their union is not complete or truly blessed. This is not true. The marital union of a man and a woman is a distinctive communion of persons. An infertile couple continues to manifest this attribute."[64]

That bears repeating: heterosexual married couples who are unable to naturally conceive remain "a distinctive communion of persons." While children are described in Catholic teaching as the "crowning glory" of marriage,[65] the tradition also acknowledges that "[s]pouses to whom God has not granted children can nevertheless have a conjugal life full of meaning, in both human and Christian terms. Their marriage can radiate a fruitfulness of charity, of hospitality, and of sacrifice."[66] In "Marriage: Love and Life in the Divine Plan," the bishops go on to discuss ways that couples "continue to be life-affirming" beyond their child-bearing years "by staying involved in the lives of young people, and especially their grandchildren, as spiritual mentors, teachers, and wisdom figures. They can also continue to be nurturing through the exercise of care for those who are needy, disabled, or pushed to the margins of society, and by their support for or participation in works of charity and justice."[67] The notion of what it means to be generative and life-affirming is expansive here.

CHAPTER 2

There is room already in the tradition for couples to be sacramentally married while unable to naturally conceive children, to be a sacred communion of persons whose love overflows into community without the physical ability to conceive through intercourse. The same-sex couples described above—who are "open, open, open" to children, who adopt and nurture children in need, providing security and family—also radiate fruitfulness. The same-sex couples who are not parents themselves but who provide hospitality in their homes, become "the village" for other children, and care for vulnerable persons in the wider community are also "life-affirming" in their practice of charity and justice. Further, as you heard in their testimony, the couples' generativity is not separate from but rather flows from their married love. It stems from gratitude for the "bliss" and "abundance" they experience together that seemingly demands to be shared. It is an extension of their married vocation, an affirmative response to the God of surprises who calls them to more, and then to more. It seems reasonable to affirm that the fruitfulness exhibited by these same-sex couples reflects "a conjugal life full of meaning" in a way that parallels opposite-sex, infertile married couples. A lack of male-female genital/heterosexual complementarity need not undermine this moral claim. Official Catholic teaching has not adequately integrated the experience and testimony of so many same-sex married couples on this matter.[68]

It also falls on the magisterium to provide more compelling and updated evidence for its continued assertion that it is unjust for children to be raised by same-sex household parents because it deprives them of the mothering and fathering (rooted in male-female complementarity) that they deserve by right and that is necessary for their flourishing.[69] In a widely cited 2003 document, the CDF stated that allowing children to be adopted into same-sex households actually *does violence* to them.[70] The statement has never been retracted and the magisterium continues to oppose fostering and adoption by same-sex couples, despite established and growing research showing that children who grow up in homes with same-sex parents are typically well-adjusted and have comparable outcomes to children raised in opposite-sex households. A recent meta-analysis of sociological studies concluded: "Research on child well-being in same-gender-parent families finds that parents' sexual orientation is not related to children's psychological and social well-being, academic achievements, delinquency and romantic outcomes, and physical well-being. Family instability rather than family structure is related to poor outcomes for children."[71] *Family instability rather than family structure is related to poor outcomes for children.*

I hope the testimony of same-sex couples presented in this book can contribute to a richer conversation within the church about same-sex parenting. These stories run counter to the narrative that children are somehow harmed or treated unjustly by being nurtured and educated by same-sex couples. Instead, we hear about couples choosing the stability of lifelong, covenantal partnerships and providing family ties, routine, tradition, love, and joy to children. These stories add evidence to the growing body of research undermining the notion that male-female, heterosexual complementarity is the only kind of complementarity that can create balance and stability in parenting.

Conclusion

The stories from the same-sex couples in my study contribute to a contemporary theological conversation about sacramental marriage from a Catholic perspective. As we've seen, their married, covenantal partnerships result in proper love of self as created and cherished by God as well as growth in virtue. The love between these spouses overflows to love of others, to care for children and other vulnerable persons in need of support and inclusion. These couples build families and communities that are stable and marked by virtue—contributing to the common good, to church and society. They recognize and celebrate experiences of grace in their daily lives. In sum, they exhibit all three dimensions of sacrament. *De facto*, they are sacramental. Moreover, their marriages reflect holistic complementarity.

The magisterial claim that "there are absolutely no grounds for considering homosexual unions to be in any way similar or even remotely analogous to God's plan for marriage and family" fails to convince in light of the experience of these same-sex, married couples.[72] Rather, I'd argue that the magisterium should consider expanding its definition of sacramental marriage to include them.

Notes

1. As described in their mission statement: "DignityUSA works for respect and justice for people of all sexual orientations, genders, and gender identities—especially gay, lesbian, bisexual, and transgender persons—in the Catholic Church and the world through education, advocacy, and support." In local chapters across the United States, they "worship openly with other LGBTQI and supportive Catholics, socialize, share personal and spiritual concerns, and work together on educational and justice issues." See dignityusa.org.

2. "Dignity used holy union. I think there was a real effort on Dignity's part not to go so far as to poke the hierarchy in the eye with claiming marriage," Liam said. Things were evolving, and politically, gay marriage seemed too fast at that point, he explained.

3. Interestingly, Pope Francis seems to support the legality of same-sex unions. On the one hand, he maintains the church's definition of marriage as strictly between a man and a woman. On the other, he endorsed civil unions for same-sex couples in the 2020 documentary *Francesco* by Evgeny Afineevsky, saying, "Homosexual people have the right to be in a family. They are children of God. You can't kick someone out of a family, nor make their life miserable for this. What we have is a civil union law; that way they are legally covered." The Pope also endorsed civil unions as an alternative to same-sex marriages while serving as archbishop of Buenos Aires. See Caitlin O'Kane, "Pope Francis Says Parents Should Support Gay Children Not Condemn Them," *CBS News*, January 26, 2022, https://www.cbsnews.com/news/pope-francis-says-parents-should-support-gay-children-not-condemn-them/. Liam rejects such legal and semantic distinctions as they imply a second-best status to same-sex marriages and do not recognize them as equally sacramental.

4. For example, see *Gaudium et Spes*: "The well-being of the individual person and of human and Christian society is intimately linked with the healthy condition of that community produced by marriage and family. Hence Christians and all men who hold this community in high esteem sincerely rejoice in the various ways by which men today find help in fostering this community of love and perfecting its life, and by which parents are assisted in their lofty calling. Those who rejoice in such aids look for additional benefits from them and labor to bring them about" (sec. 47).

5. Richard Gaillardetz is great on "the paschal character" of marriage and its sacred pattern of life-death-life by which married partners grow in holiness. See Richard R. Gaillardetz, *A Daring Promise: A Spirituality of Christian Marriage, Revised and Expanded Edition* (Liguori, MO: Liguori/Triumph, 2007), especially chapter 4.

6. Adoption is sometimes presented as an unequivocally good option for those seeking parenthood. But it's important to consider how practically difficult (and sometimes expensive) the process of adoption can be.

7. In *Considerations Regarding Proposals to Give Legal Recognition to Unions between Homosexual Persons* (2006), the Congregation for the Doctrine of Faith opposes same-sex

unions in part because they "are not able to contribute in a proper way to the procreation and survival of the human race. The possibility of using recently discovered methods of artificial reproduction, beyond involving a grave lack of respect for human dignity, does nothing to alter this inadequacy" (sec. 7). The central argument against the use of artificial reproductive technologies is that it separates procreation from the unitive meaning of the sex act (in other words, procreation is meant to occur during sexual intercourse between heterosexual married partners and conception should not happen outside of that context). The magisterium also expresses concern for the possibility of discarded embryos during the use of reproductive technologies, which reflects "a grave lack of respect for human dignity." Here the CDF draws on *Donum Vitae* (1987). Both documents can be accessed at www.vatican.va.

8. Here Tom refers to Gregory Boyle, S.J., Jesuit priest and founder and director of Homeboy Industries, the world's largest gang-intervention and rehabilitation program. Boyle has written a series of excellent books related to Christian compassion, kinship, and tenderness: *Tattoos on the Heart*, *Barking to the Choir*, and *The Whole Language*.

9. For an outstanding examination of Christian hospitality, see Christine D. Pohl, *Making Room: Recovering Hospitality as a Christian Tradition* (Grand Rapids, MI: William B. Eerdmans Publishing Company, 1999). Another helpful resource on hospitality and its roots in the Bible is Alain Thomasset, SJ, "The Virtue of Hospitality According to the Bible and the Challenge of Migration," in *The Bible and Catholic Theological Ethics*, ed. Yiu Sing Lúcás Chan, James F. Keenan, and Ronaldo Zacharias (Maryknoll, NY: Orbis Books, 2017), 28–33.

10. Luke Timothy Johnson, *The Revelatory Body: Theology as Inductive Art* (Grand Rapids, MI: William B. Eerdmans Publishing Company, 2015), 6.

11. Congregation for the Doctrine of Faith, Considerations Regarding Proposals to Give Legal Recognition to Unions between Homosexual Persons (sec. 4), quoted by Pope Francis in *Amoris Laetitia* (sec. 251). Both documents can be accessed at www.vatican.va.

12. See Pope Francis's *Amoris Laetitia*, especially sec. 71 and following, for a summary of magisterial teaching on the sacrament of matrimony.

13. For example, see Michael J. O'Loughlin, "'It Just Hurts': Catholics React to Vatican Ban on Blessings For Same-Sex Couples," *America Magazine*, March 15, 2021, https://www.americamagazine.org/faith/2021/03/15/vatican-blessing-same-sex-unions-reactions-pope-francis-240249 and Madeleine Davison, "Memo to the Vatican: Same-Sex Couples Find God's Love in Marriage Too," *National Catholic Reporter*, March 25, 2021, https://www.ncronline.org/news/memo-vatican-same-sex-couples-find-gods-love-marriage-too. The statement met resistance from some leaders within the Catholic church as well; for example, see Phillip Pullella, "Vatican Ruling on Same-Sex Couples Prompts Defiance, Pain, Confusion" *Reuters*, March 17, 2021, https://www.reuters.com/world/europe/vatican-ruling-same-sex-couples-prompts-defiance-pain-confusion-2021-03-17/.

On the Belgian and German Bishops' votes to bless same-sex, loving relationships, see: "Belgium: The Pope Accepts Blessing of Same-Sex Couples," *FSSPX News Information and Analysis on the Life of the Church*, March 25, 2023, https://fsspx.news/en/news-events/news/belgium-pope-accepts-blessing-same-sex-couples-81151#:~:text

=The%20Bishop%20of%20Antwerp%20reaffirmed,of%20the%20German%20Synodal%20Path; The Associated Press, "German Bishops Vote in Favor of Blessing Same-Sex Unions in the Catholic Church," *America Magazine*, March 10, 2023, https://www.americamagazine.org/politics-society/2023/03/10/german-church-synod-same-sex-blessings-244883; and Renardo Schlegelmilch, "Germany's Catholic Church Approved Blessings for Same-Sex Couples. Is This a Revolution?," *National Catholic Reporter*, March 15, 2023, https://www.ncronline.org/opinion/guest-voices/germanys-catholic-church-approved-blessings-same-sex-couples-revolution.

Perhaps the CDF's harsh condemnation of same-sex unions is softened by Pope Francis's acknowledgment in *Amoris Laetitia* that, in light of mitigating factors and the need to value prudential judgments in light of conscience, "it can no longer be said that all those in any 'irregular' situation are living in a state of mortal sin and are deprived of sanctifying grace" (sec. 301). He offers examples of certain couples who are living together outside of marriage or who are divorced and civilly remarried, indicating that intention and context matter. The pope prefers to emphasize mercy, conscience, and pastoral care in particular situations. He warns that the church's moral laws should not be used as "stones to throw at people's lives" (sec. 305). At the same time, he maintains traditional teaching on marriage as between a man and a woman, open to procreation, and notes that a person who "flaunts an objective sin as if it were part of the Christian ideal" stands in need of conversion.

14. Pope Francis, *Amoris Laetitia*, sec. 305.

15. The United States Conference of Catholic Bishops offer a straightforward definition of sacramental marriage in response to the questions "What is marriage?" and "What does our faith tell us about marriage?" in *Between Man and Woman: Questions and Answers About Marriage and Same-Sex Unions* (2003). You can access this Q&A style document at https://www.usccb.org/topics/promotion-defense-marriage/between-man-and-woman-questions-and-answers-about-marriage-and.

For a feminist critical analysis of this traditional sexual ethic and well-developed alternative, inductive approach to Christian sexual ethics, see Karen Peterson-Iyer, *Reenvisioning Sexual Ethics: A Feminist Christian Account* (Washington, DC: Georgetown University Press, 2022).

16. United States Conference of Catholic Bishops, "Ministry to Persons with a Homosexual Inclination: Guidelines for Pastoral Care," November 14, 2006, https://www.usccb.org/resources/ministry-to-persons-of-homosexual-iInclination_0.pdf, sec. 3. This understanding of marriage is explicated in innumerable church documents, to which a quick Google search will attest. A couple of good examples are Pope Francis's *Amoris Laetitia* and the USCCB's 2009 pastoral letter "Marriage: Love and Life in the Divine Plan."

17. For a very accessible explanation of complementarity and how the notion is presented in magisterial teaching, see Michael Lawler and Todd Salzman, "Pope Francis Brings Nuance to Notion of Complementarity," *National Catholic Reporter*, May 29, 2015, https://www.ncronline.org/news/theology/pope-francis-brings-nuance-notion-complementarity. For a historical perspective on the development of ideas about sex and gender in medicine, illustrating how ideas about what is "natural" change over time and have been used to subjugate and control women, see Elinor Cleghorn, *Unwell*

Women: Misdiagnosis and Myth in a Man-Made World (New York: Penguin Random House LLC, 2021). For a critical perspective on complementarity, grounded in science and experience, see Cristina Traina, "How Gendered Is Marriage?" in *Sex, Loves and Families: Catholic Perspectives*, ed. Jason King and Julie Hanlon Rubio (Collegeville, MN: Liturgical Press Academic, 2020).

18. USSCB, "Ministry to Persons," 3.

19. Ibid., 3–4.

20. See Ann Schneible, "Pope Francis: Children Have a Right to a Mother and Father," *Catholic News Agency*, November 17, 2014, https://www.catholicnewsagency.com/news/30948/pope-francis-children-have-right-to-a-mother-and-father; also see United States Conference of Catholic Bishops, "FAQs on the Meaning of Marriage & Sexual Difference," *USCCB Promotion and Defense of Marriage*, https://www.usccb.org/topics/promotion-defense-marriage/faqs-meaning-marriage-sexual-difference.

21. Theological debates exist over how to weigh these different resources in doing theological thinking, and sometimes experience is placed under the category of reason (leaving tradition, scripture, and reason), but these sources are generally agreed upon by Christian theologians. While paying attention to people's experiences sometimes makes the theological process messier, I agree with Luke Timothy Johnson: "If there is the danger of running amok in the messiness of bodily experience and the ambiguity of claims to the work of the Spirit in human lives, there is certainly much more danger in proceeding as though God were not at work in bodily experience and the Holy Spirit were not active in human lives here and now." Johnson, *The Revelatory Body*, 6.

22. For example, see the USCCB's "Ministry to Persons," which states the following: "Catholic tradition . . . holds that the basis of morality is found in the natural order established by the Creator, an order that is not destroyed but rather elevated by the transforming power of the grace that comes through Jesus Christ. Good actions are in accord with that order. By acting this way, persons fulfill their authentic humanity, and this constitutes their ultimate happiness. Immoral actions, actions that are not in accord with the natural order of things, are incapable of contributing to true human fulfillment and happiness. In fact, immoral actions are destructive of the human person because they degrade and undermine the dignity given us by God" (7).

23. For this reason, biblical scholar Luke Timothy Johnson criticizes Pope John Paul II's reliance on Genesis to draw particular anthropological, even ontological, conclusions (expressed in his theology of the body, which emphasizes male-female complementarity) in a way that fails to "respect the complexity of the scriptural witness" (*The Revelatory Body*, 36). Johnson writes: "John Paul II's practice in reading scripture falls into [a] familiar and unfortunate pattern, whereby he offers the texts of Scripture as support for theological positions without the texts themselves being interrogated in their historical and literary contexts. I do not suggest that a complete historical and literary analysis is required before any passage of Scripture can enter a theological discussion; but neither can the difficulty and complexity of scriptural passages be ignored. The pope is not alone in acting as though Scripture offers a clear set of answers; in fact, for those who read it carefully, it presents an array of tangled questions" (37).

24. Gushee's *Changing Our Mind* is helpful and accessible. He notes that those who claim a clear biblical ban on same-sex relationships rely on the following "formula": "Genesis 1–2 + Genesis 19 + Leviticus 18:22/20:13 + Judges 19 + Matthew 19:1–12/Mark 10:2–12 + Romans 1:26–27 + 1 Corinthians 6:9/1 Timothy 1:10 [+Ephesians 5:22–33 and all other biblical references to sex and marriage assuming or depicting male + female]." He breaks down each of these passages using historical-critical tools and offers a theological interpretation of them in light of contemporary science, church teaching on love and belonging and care for the most vulnerable, and the experience of LGBTQ persons. Also see the "Outreach Guide to the Bible and Homosexuality" at https://outreach.faith/bible/.

25. Luke Timothy Johnson, "Homosexuality & The Church," *Commonweal*, June 11, 2007, https://www.commonwealmagazine.org/homosexuality-church-0.

26. Johnson describes this "process of faithful obedience to God's direction in human stories" in the Acts of the Apostles (chapters 10–15) in this way: "Luke's narrative shows how God moved ahead of the human characters in accepting Gentiles as righteous, and how difficult it was for the church's leaders to learn what God was up to. It shows, however, that Peter and Paul and James were open to the truth God wanted them to learn. They paid attention to human narratives—testimonies—that spoke of God at work among Gentiles in ways that not even Jewish believers in the crucified messiah could appreciate. The apostles had to be shown how the same Holy Spirit who had come upon them also came to those very unlike them, people whom they regarded as unclean by nature and evil in their practices. When shown the evidence of transformed lives, they saw and accepted what God was doing." Johnson, "Homosexuality & The Church."

27. Gushee, *Changing Our Mind*, 109–10.

28. I agree with Gushee when he identifies the rooted-in-Genesis-male-female complementarity argument as "the single most important biblical-theological-ethical issue faced by any Christian wrestling with the LGBTQ issue." *Changing Our Mind*, 81.

29. Ibid., 91.

30. Ibid.

31. Ibid, 94–95.

32. Theologian Susannah Cornwall writes: "The fact that the model perpetuated in Western societies, of male-and-female binary anthropology, continues to occur through identification with a *religious* ideology, gives the model more power and slows the process of disintegration as a 'given,' since there are multiple motivations for maintaining it. The patterns of power and prestige inculcated in it disincentivize those it privileges from leaving it behind." Susannah Cornwall, *Sex and Uncertainty in the Body of Christ* (London: Routledge, 2014), 89.

33. Kelly Brown Douglas, "Contested Marriage/Loving Relationship," in *Sexuality and the Sacred, Second Edition: Sources for Theological Reflection*, ed. Kelly Brown Douglas and Marvin M. Ellison (Louisville, KY: John Knox Press, 2010), 382–83.

34. Ibid., 381.

35. Ibid., 383.

36. Ibid.

37. Ibid., 387.

38. Susannah Cornwall's recent work focuses on the trans community. For example, see "Transformative Creatures: Theology, Gender Diversity, and Human Identity," *Zygon Journal of Science and Religion* 57, no.3 (September 2022): 599–615.

39. Drawing on Patricia Beattie Jung's work, Cornwall argues that "the elevation of a few verses of Genesis as uniquely communicating ontological truths about human sex is problematic." Putting science and experience in conversation with scripture complicates a simplistic reading of Genesis to uphold male-female complementarity as universal. See Cornwall, "Laws 'Needefull in Later to be Abrogated': Intersex and the Sources of Christian Theology," in *Intersex, Theology, and the Bible: Troubling Bodies in Church, Text, and Society*, ed. Susannah Cornwall (New York: Palgrave MacMillan, 2015), 148. She is drawing on Patricia Beattie Jung, "Christianity and Human Sexual Polymorphism: Are They Compatible?" in *Ethics and Intersex*, ed. Sharon E. Sytsma (Dordrecht: Springer, 2006), 305.

See also Christine Gudorf, "The Erosion of Sexual Dimorphism," in *Sexuality and the Sacred, Second Edition*, 141–64. Gudorf describes the erosion of the paradigm of sexual dimorphism (understanding virtually every aspect of sexuality as biologically fixed and determined by the binary division into male and female) that dominated the early modern West, including the Christian tradition. She notes several factors that challenged the sexual dimorphism paradigm, e.g.,: the emerging distinction between sex and gender that grew out of feminism and anthropological studies in the late nineteenth and early twentieth centuries; sex research (such as the work of Alfred Kinsey) in the mid-twentieth century; and biological research in the later twentieth century that point to sexual and gender diversity (Gudorf, 147–51). She writes: "Clearly . . . in terms of both the data on human sexuality today and the choices that are made by human societies about sex, it is no longer correct to distinguish sex and gender by saying that sex refers to our biological givenness as male or female and gender refers to the traits and roles that a particular society and individuals construct for male and female persons. Today we should recognize that both sex and gender are socially constructed categories; both sex and gender must be interpreted" (151). Gudorf notes how challenging this paradigm shift from sexual dimorphism is for religious communities—their teachings about marriage and sexuality and the interpretation of sacred texts.

40. Cornwall, "Laws 'Needefull'" 154.

41. Ibid.

42. Ibid., 164.

43. Ibid.

44. Ibid.

45. Todd Salzman and Michael Lawler, "Human Dignity and Homosexuality in Catholic Teaching: An Anthropological Disconnect between Truth and Love?" *Interdisciplinary Journal for Religion and Transformation in Contemporary Society* 6, no.1 (July 2020), 126. Here they draw from USCCB *Always Our Children*, adding emphasis. They also suggest seeing CDF, *Persona humana*, no. 8.

46. It seems that some traditionalist Catholics want to downplay this by turning to the language of "same-sex attraction" rather than orientation, which implies less stability in the person than the language of orientation.

47. Salzman and Lawler, "Human Dignity and Homosexuality in Catholic Teaching," 126–127.

48. In their description of ethical sex, Salzman and Lawler refer to the important work of Margaret Farley, *Just Love* (2006). Farley takes a virtue approach to sexual ethics. In June 2012, the CDF issued a notification against Farley's *Just Love*, which can be accessed here: https://www.vatican.va/roman_curia/congregations/cfaith/documents/rc_con_cfaith_doc_20120330_nota-farley_en.html. For a response to that notification by a renowned Catholic sexual ethicist, see Lisa Cahill's "Vatican Dogma v. Margaret Farley's Just Love," *Guardian*, June 18, 2012,

https://www.theguardian.com/commentisfree/2012/jun/18/vatican-dogma-v-magaret-farley-just-love.

They also draw on James Keenan's "Virtue Ethics and Sexual Ethics," *Louvain Studies* 30, no.3, 180–97.

In 2010, the Committee on Doctrine, United States Conference of Catholic Bishops reviewed Salzman and Lawler's *The Sexual Person: Toward a Renewed Catholic Anthropology* and judged it to depart in methods and conclusions from official Catholic teaching. You can access their statement here: https://www.usccb.org/resources/Sexual_Person_2010-09-15_0.pdf.

49. Todd Salzman and Michael Lawler, *The Sexual Person: Toward a Renewed Catholic Anthropology* (Washington, DC: Georgetown University Press, 2008), 152. Emphasis mine.

50. Along with Johnson and Gushee above, Salzman and Lawler think it best to uphold all persons to the same ethical standards.

51. I sometimes hear a slippery slope argument regarding same-sex relationships—that is, if Christians move beyond a strict definition of marriage as between a man and a woman and allow same-sex marriages, where will it end? Will we soon allow marriages between adults and children, for example? In my view, this argument plays on homophobic fears and isn't reasonable. Including same-sex couples in the definition of sacramental marriage is actually a conservative move (this is what Liam points out related to their experience preparing same-sex couples for holy unions), holding adult Christians to the same ethical standards. It is not a move toward relativism.

52. Cornwall, *Sex and Uncertainty*, 83.

53. Feminist theologian Elizabeth Johnson rejects the binary way of thinking about men and women inherent in male-female complementarity, "which rigidly predetermines the qualities each should cultivate and the roles each can play. Apart from the naivete about its own social conditioning, its reliance on stereotypes, and the denial of the wholeness of human experience that it mandates, this position functions as a smokescreen for the subordination of women since by its definition women are always relegated to the private, passive realm." Elizabeth Johnson, *She Who Is, The Mystery of God in Feminist Theological Discourse* (New York: Crossroads, 1992), 154. In *The Sexual Person*, Salzman and Lawler argue that "[t]he practical reason supporting male-female complementarity is to defend the absolute prohibition of ordaining women to the priesthood" (86).

54. To be clear, I did not ask a direct question about complementarity during interviews, unless it was a follow-up when the couples used the language themselves.

55. At the time of our conversation, they were together seven years, married two.

56. Stephanie Coontz, "How to Make Your Marriage Gayer," *New York Times*, February 13, 2020, https://www.nytimes.com/2020/02/13/opinion/sunday/marriage-housework-gender-happiness.html.

57. See Melissa Hogenboom, "The Hidden Load: How 'Thinking of Everything' Holds Mums Back," BBC, May 18, 2021, https://www.bbc.com/worklife/article/20210518-the-hidden-load-how-thinking-of-everything-holds-mums-back.

58. Cristina Traina, "How Gendered Is Marriage?" in *Sex, Love, and Families: Catholic Perspectives*, ed. Jason King and Julie Hanlon Rubio (Collegeville, MN: Liturgical Press, 2020), 83. She notes a historical emphasis on a woman's "natural" wifely, homemaking, and caretaking roles. Traina focuses her analysis in particular on the writings of Pope John Paul II and Pope Francis.

59. Ibid., 83.

60. Ibid., 85.

61. Ibid.

62. Ibid., 90.

63. Couples who face natural infertility and couples who choose infertility for nonserious reasons are morally distinguished from couples who choose to remain childless for other reasons. Repeatedly, Pope Francis has called the decision not to have children "selfish." For example, see Sabina Castelfranco, "Pope Francis: Don't Be Afraid to Have Children," VOA, January 6, 2022, https://www.voanews.com/a/pope-francis-don-t-be-afraid-to-have-children/6385264.html and Stephanie Kirchgaessner, "Pope Francis: Not Having Children Is Selfish," *Guardian*, February 11, 2015, https://www.theguardian.com/world/2015/feb/11/pope-francis-the-choice-to-not-have-children-is-selfish.

64. USCCB, "Marriage: Love and Life in the Divine Plan," 14–15.

65. Second Vatican Council, *Gaudium et Spes*, sec. 48.

66. Catechism of the Catholic Church, #1654.

67. USCCB, "Marriage: Love and Life in the Divine Plan," 15.

68. To maintain that infertile heterosexual couples are somehow more able to maintain "a conjugal life full of meaning" because they have a biological "fit" of male and female genitalia (even if they cannot reproduce) seems overly focused on the sex-gender binary and the physical rather than the personal and relational, as discussed in this chapter.

69. See the USCCB's webpage on The Promotion and Defense of Marriage, which can be accessed at https://www.usccb.org/topics/promotion-defense-marriage. Michael Lawler and Todd Salzman convincingly have called the church to provide more convincing evidence for their claims. See "Quaestio Disputata: Catholic Sexual Ethics: Complementarity and The Truly Human," *Theological Studies* 67 (2006): 640–42. Whether the Church should oppose fostering and adopting by same-sex parents is hotly debated and time and space do not allow me to delve into this here. There are legal and theological issues at play, questions about marriage and family and questions about religious liberty. See Adam Liptak, "Supreme Court Backs Catholic Agency in Case on Gay Rights and Foster Care," *New York Times*, June 17, 2021, https://www.nytimes.com/2021/06/17/us/supreme-court-gay-rights-foster-care.html.

For a view critical of the US Bishops position, see Craig Ford, "Bishops' Theology Is the True Scandal in Philadelphia Foster Care Case," *National Catholic Reporter*, July 2, 2021, https://www.ncronline.org/news/opinion/us-bishops-theology-true-scandal-philadelphia-foster-care-case and Andru Zodrow, "USCCB Drops Opposition to Catholic Agencies Serving Single LGBTQ Foster Parents," *New Ways Ministry*, July 13, 2022, https://www.newwaysministry.org/2022/07/13/usccb-drops-opposition-to-catholic-agencies-serving-single-lgbtq-foster-parents/.

70. The wording is as follows: "As experience has shown, the absence of sexual complementarity in these unions creates obstacles in the normal development of children who would be placed in the care of such persons. They would be deprived of the experience of either fatherhood or motherhood. Allowing children to be adopted by persons living in such unions would actually mean doing violence to these children, in the sense that their condition of dependency would be used to place them in an environment that is not conducive to their full human development." Congregation for the Doctrine of Faith, *Considerations Regarding Proposals to Give Legal Recognition to Unions between Homosexual Persons*, sec. 7.

71. Marshal Neal Fettro and Wendy D. Manning, "Child Well-Being in Same-Gender-Parent Families: Courts, Media, and Social Science Research," in *Contemporary Parenting and Parenthood: From News Headlines to New Research*, ed. Michelle Y. Janning (Santa Barbara, CA: Praeger, 2019), 283–301.

72. Congregation for the Doctrine of Faith, *Considerations Regarding Proposals to Give Legal Recognition to Unions between Homosexual Persons*, sec. 4, quoted by Pope Francis in *Amoris Laetitia*, sec. 251.

CHAPTER 3

Family

Tension, Integration, and Belonging

JENN AND STEPH MET THROUGH A MUTUAL FRIEND POST COLLEGE AND quickly became friends. Jenn had never dated another woman, she "never really had any interest or anything." One night the two were at a beer garden with a group of friends. Someone in the band invited Steph to come up on stage to sing—"she's a really good singer!" Jenn exclaimed—and "sparks flew." "We were both kind of like, *holy hell*," Jenn said. Fourteen years later, we sat at their kitchen table for a conversation about their marriage, with their two young children playing with a babysitter in the basement.

Both women come from Catholic cultural and religious backgrounds and identify as Catholic. In the beginning of their relationship, Jenn explained: "You know, we were scared. Totally scared. It took us a long time to come out to our parents. I'm an only child. Irish, Polish Catholic. Yeah. So we had lots of talks. A lot of conversations. A lot of tears."

For years, Jenn and Steph hid their relationship from their parents and families. Boldly, they decided to come out to both sets of parents over the same weekend. Steph spoke to her parents first. "[They] were horrible," Jenn said. "Basically the first comment was, 'Are you sleeping with her?' Her mom stormed out of the house." "The second comment was: 'Oh, I'm sick and tired of people like you hiding behind Catholic parish doors,'" Steph said. "And I went, 'People like me? What are you talking about? Gay people? I'm pretty sure you're talking about molesters, pedophiles. Really? Are you that ignorant to not see the difference between them?' They're very ignorant people. They're very educated people. I love my parents. There is goodness in them. But I struggle with them because as educated as they are . . ." they refuse to critically examine traditional, Catholic norms related to sexuality and marriage. "[My being gay] didn't fit their [paradigm] . . . I'm an Italian Catholic. We have a very traditional Italian family," Steph said.

"Okay. So that didn't go well," Jenn said. "And then I told my parents the next day, and *that* didn't go well." She described her mother's response: "'Oh my gosh. How could you? You're the only gay [family member]!'" Her mother sought some kind of explanation. "My mom did ask eventually: 'Is it about sex?' 'No, that's not it,' [Jenn told her.] You know it was very hard. A lot of words were said. Hurtful, hurtful words. Our relationship really diminished for a very long time."

"Yeah, with both our parents," Steph added. "We went for stretches without talking for a very long time."

"And then, in 2010 [the following year], you proposed in July," Jenn said, looking at Steph. Turning to me, she said: "Steph was just like, forget it. We're not wasting our time on you guys [meaning, their parents] anymore."

"That's what I felt like we were doing. We were waiting for [our parents' approval before getting married]," Steph said.

"We were ready [for marriage]. So Steph got the courage and planned this beautiful event, and then she proposed. I said yes, and she had all of our closest friends waiting for us upstairs."

"Good thing she said yes!" Steph said. "Because that could have gone poorly!" We laughed.

"But Steph was very smart with her [planning of the proposal and party] because I didn't think about my parents at the time. [My parents and I] weren't talking. And it was celebratory." After the party ended, the couple went to bed. "And then, no joke, at two o'clock in the morning, I woke up in a huge panic attack," Jenn said. "Screaming. Crying. *How are we going to do this? How are we going to deal with our parents and our jobs? Our jobs! Our lives!*"

"How do we navigate this? Where's the [guide]book?," Steph added. In addition to the lack of support from their parents, the two were particularly worried about Steph's job because she worked in a Catholic parish. (We'll read more of that story in chapter 5.) An occasion that should have incited pure joy—their wedding engagement—was marred instead by fear, worry, and panic.

"She was and is my rock," Jenn said, looking at Steph. "Because when our relationship started, I was in a very dark place, and she basically pulled me back out."

"I think we've been through the hardest stuff first," Steph said. "You know, I think other couples graduate into harder things. We were thrown into the pool, like you better swim or sink, figure it out. I think we just decided it was worth swimming . . . I felt like we had it piled on us right up front. I mean, we had two years before we told anybody."

"Well, we were hiding. We were still living that dual life," said Jenn.

"'This is my roommate,' yeah.[1] And I think once we cracked open the Pandora's Box of telling people—our family, our parents, and my cousin—they were the worst people. I must say they were the absolute worst. I mean, my cousin sent an email when they found out that we were getting married telling us we were going to hell," Steph said.

"No, no, no. It wasn't the marriage, it was when we were pregnant," Jenn corrected.

"Well, first it was the civil union. When they found out we were together, he sent that. Then he found out you were having a baby. I could probably pull up the email. I still have it. He basically said, 'I heard that you and Jenn are having a baby. And I would like to offer my help in finding your child a good Catholic home to be brought up in. We would like to find you a home so that your baby can be adopted into a good Catholic home.' And I was like, *You Mother-Father, You! Where do you get off? This was planned. And you're going to . . . ?* And he's probably ten years younger than I am. Now, when you have those kinds of things [happen], you're just like, *Wow. What?* My biggest frustration is when people use their faith as a weapon. And that's what I felt that our parents were doing. That's what I felt my cousin was doing. Faith is never intended to be used as a weapon. Never. And if they understood it, they never would."

Chapter 3

"I do a lot of retreats," Steph said. "I talk a lot about how God is an unconditional Lover . . . You are loved by the Author of love, and really it all comes down to unconditional love. If we all made that the baseline with everyone and everything, whether it's in your house, whether it's in your community, whether it's in your parish or school, or wherever you work. Now understand I'm not saying I'm the best unconditional lover. I don't do it fantastically all the time. But if the goal is unconditional love, that's where God wants us to be. Which, if you really put that as a framework to everything you do—whether it be with your kids, your partner, your friends or family, or whatever—it's a good framework. I mean even with our parents, how many times they were so hurtful to us. I would say, 'They're good people making bad decisions.'"

"Oh my gosh, you've said that so much. I'm surprised you don't have that tattooed," Jenn said.

Jenn and Steph described what kind of home they've created for their young children. They focus on being "welcoming, always." Steph said, "Come as you are. You pretty much walk into what it is. Like our house is not picture perfect. It's a shitshow. You just get what you get . . . Growing up, [my family of origin was] so big on you know, the Christmas card image. You know, you had to look good. I don't care if you fought like hell, the second you walked out the door, you pretended. And I just don't want to do that with our kids. I don't do that with our family [because] it's not genuine . . . Yeah. We're just come as you are. You know, a lot of people come to our house and say, 'Your house is just warm. I feel it when I come in, I can just rest there.' And you know I think it's a space that is filled with love and prayer. It's a space of welcoming and love."

"I'm sure my parents have done the best they can. I'm trying really hard to understand their limitations and how they were raised. . . . I've tried to be conscious of that piece. But all the things I hated about growing up in my house, everything is completely different in our house," Steph said. In their home, Jenn and Steph agree to place no conditions on love. They strive to do away with pretension in favor of authenticity.

"Both of our families, growing up, were churchgoers," Jenn said. "Every Sunday, every Sunday, every Sunday. Well, great. But our argument, what we talk about, is like, yeah, you could be a churchgoer like that. That was my parents' thing. . . . They're going to church every Sunday, ['Praying the gay away!' Steph interjected.] but what happens when you walk out of the church doors?"

"Going out to love and serve the Lord actually [should] mean something," Steph added, "[If it doesn't influence the way you behave] you're not a practicing Catholic. You're an image Catholic."

"Maybe that's what I'm trying to say. What's the right word? Hollow Catholic? A sheltered Catholic? I'm really not sure," Jenn said.

"You can go be present there. But *are you listening*?" Steph said. "It's a generational issue," she suggested, claiming that their parents' generation equated being a good Catholic with going to mass and "doing what they were told. They were very obedient. And have the priest over every now and then for dinner. I mean, it was like, you're a good Catholic if you do all those things. No, you're not actually. I mean, you're a good person for some of those things, okay. But you're not a good Catholic. Go now and love and serve the Lord means *go and do good* and *make church a verb*. It doesn't mean [come back on Sunday with your donation for the collection] . . . That doesn't make you a good Catholic. That just makes you a good churchgoer," Steph said.

Over the years, Steph's sexual orientation and partnership with Jenn has strained her relationship with her parents; in her words, they've made it a "roadblock." At one point, Steph and her mom "were just boxing over it." Steph asked her mother, "'Can you just tell me what this is about? Let's get to the center of it. Just be honest and I can handle it. Just tell me what I did.' . . . Then finally she goes, 'I'm embarrassed of you.' And I went, 'Okay.'" Steph came to understand that her parents were very concerned about what other people would think, about how Steph and Jenn's relationship would reflect back on them. Her parents wanted to control the public message. They wanted to be in charge of who, in their social circles, knew that Steph and Jenn were a couple.

"My dad straight up told me, 'It's my family and you don't get to tell my family.' 'Well, it's my family, too.' 'Yeah, but it's my aunt.' 'No. It's my aunt too.' [He] was like, 'You can't tell my people. You don't get to choose to tell my people.' 'Well, they're not just your people, they're *our* people.'" This back and forth between father and daughter points to the layers of complexity in the process of coming out within families and communities. There are often negotiations, differences of opinions, and compromises related to *whether*, *how far*, and *to whom* a couple (and, in turn, their parents and loved ones) should come out of the closet. In Steph's case, this was emotionally fraught.

Tensions increased when Steph's younger sister also came out as lesbian. In response to the news, her father sent them both a text that read: "I'd rather have cancer than have two gay daughters." "He'd [had cancer and] beat cancer, and he basically said, 'Look, I'd rather have to go through cancer again than have two gay daughters,'" Steph said. She tried to reassure her sister and keep her from self-blame. Steph felt frustrated that the family struggle of the previous ten years related to her own coming out did not make her parents "handle it better." She thought, "How do we keep unconditionally loving them?"

At one point her father told Steph, "I made peace with my Maker," which she interprets as comfort in his belief and behavior in light of his faith—a settled conscience. "He feels that God is okay with him acting this way . . . because the church says so. And what a terrible spot for [my parents] to be in because the church that they have given their world to . . . this church is saying to them: *You're right. It's not okay*. Well, what the hell? That's my kid! If I was them, and I was listening so closely, if I had to choose between my kid and my church? See ya church! And they, because of the obedience they've grown up with, the church has instilled that [its teaching against gay relationships] is more important. The [church] say[s] that [obedience to the teaching is] more important than what you're doing in your own family. That's so messed up . . . He feels supported by his faith in acting the way he has. And same with my mom. [Looking at Jenn,] Same with your parents."

Steph invited her parents to the courthouse when she and Jenn had their civil union. "I invited them even though the last thing I wanted was to have them there. But I said, you know what? Twenty years down the road I want to look back and say I still, even though dot dot dot, I still invited you to be part of that. Even though I shouldn't have, I still invited you. They said no. They straight out said, 'No, we're not going to be there.

And if you ever choose to have anything in the future, we won't be there either because we don't support your lifestyle."

"Ugh, that weird lifestyle," Jenn said.

When Jenn gave birth to their first child, it was a turning point in her relationship with her parents. Jenn identifies her mother's visit to see the baby in the hospital as "the changing point." She said, "With the birth of the kids, with my parents it's gotten so much better. ['Drastically,' Steph said.] Now is it perfect? No. But my parents welcome Steph. You know my mom, she even referred to the other day, she said, 'Oh, I was talking to Dad telling him that *the girls* are going to want to know what we want for Christmas' or something. But just saying *us*, grouping *us*. Or, one of my mom's friends passed away and Steph went to the wake with me and my mom introduced [her] as my partner. I don't think it was wife. But it was a big deal. I mean, we caught each other's eyes."

Their children have an excellent relationship with Jenn's parents. They spend two days a week with them while Jenn and Steph work. "My father is a better grandfather than he was a dad. He changes diapers and things like that. He would never do that with me. It's like, he's got it. He loves them unconditionally, you can tell. . . . So as far as my parents as grandparents, it's phenomenal."

"Mine are distant. They'll send a card. We'll send a card. They may send a text here and there," Steph said. "Very rarely," Jenn replied. They will attend large gatherings with the kids on special occasions like birthdays, but they won't just stop by or have the kids stay over. "There's definitely a disconnect between them and the kids," Steph said, in contrast to her brother's children, with whom her parents have a very close relationship and regular contact. Steph continues to work to try to nurture a relationship between their children and her parents—she reaches out to see if they want to meet up with the kids, maybe "grab a breakfast"; she tries to keep the door open. But "I'm doing it for the kids, I'm not doing it for us anymore."

"I'm done," Jenn said.

Steph believes that "over the past year [her parents] have gotten a little better." For example, they invited her sister and her partner to their home for Thanksgiving and Christmas, which is "a big deal." She thinks they may have learned something from their experiences with Steph and Jenn, after all, "because it didn't take as long for them to turn a corner."

"Yeah," Jenn agreed, "It's just . . . I've always told Steph, it's one thing to treat us differently or treat us like shit or whatever. It's us. You know, we can make it work. We can handle it.[2] It's another thing when you're affecting our kids. And you can see that her parents accept and love their other grandkids unconditionally where they don't [with our kids]. They're different."

All in all, Steph said, "We have moved. There has been progress. But it's been slow and painful." Jenn agreed: "It's been very much like the Catholic church. It's slow and painful. They move like the Catholic church. They're slow, slow, slow."

I offer Steph and Jenn's story as an entree into thinking about broader family relationships in the lives of the same-sex couples in my study. These relationships are often, though not universally, complicated, and are influenced by religious teachings and cultural messages about same-sex relationships and marriage. Certain key events—for example, coming out, getting married, and having children—often resulted in family tension or, by contrast, expressions of affirmation and belonging. This chapter will focus on stories of family rejection, tension, integration, and belonging. I will pay particular attention to how religious beliefs influence family relationships.

When Steve told his parents that he was gay and in a relationship with Luke, his parents said, "Oh no. That was their reaction. *Oh no.*" Steve and Luke began dating while in college, and, following graduation, lived together in five different places before Steve told his parents that they were a couple. "By that time, we'd lived together in all those cities. They just chose not to think about us that way. We were just good friends." Years later, when the two decided to marry, "[Steve's parents] were very comfortable with Luke and [thought] that he was good for me and we had a good relationship . . . [T]hey were very accepting of our relationship, but the fact that now we wanted to get married, which they considered a sacrament, was something they just didn't approve of." His parents continued to struggle to recognize the relationship and to "reconcile that with their faith." They are "very strong Catholics" and so they wondered,

"*How does that work?*" Steve believes his uncle, a priest, ultimately helped Steve's parents "work through" their concerns "in their own way." In any case, Steve said, "They're certainly accepting of us now."

Katie's parents also had a difficult time reconciling their Catholic beliefs with the news that their daughter was in a relationship. Katie explained, "I said, 'Oh, I'm with this woman,' and they're very Catholic, in a pretty conservative, rural area. So there was a lot of crying. My mom wore sunglasses to work for the two days after because she had just been crying and crying and crying. My dad didn't really talk about it because we don't in general talk about stuff like that. So yeah, I think it's just really hard for them to say—they whispered about the fact that I was gay, so that was kind of hard. But actually the harder part came when I said, 'Oh, and now we're going to have a commitment ceremony,' and the realization [that] *we actually have to deal with this woman coming into Katie's life and we have to figure out what to do about that.* So there were some hard pieces, like after our commitment ceremony when I came home and there's immediately pictures of my sister and their spouses and there was no picture of Sarah and me in the house. It's a little like, well, you know, we didn't supply them with one, whereas my other sisters did, [so] there are some things we can probably be better at."

It hurt Katie to see that her parents did not have any wedding pictures of Sarah and her in their home, while her siblings were represented. She took partial responsibility for not providing one, but she nevertheless felt slighted. Other interviewees had similar stories of feeling overlooked or snubbed, or—on the other hand—recognized and accepted, by family gestures large and small.

For example, when Steph and Jenn were having a baby, Steph's mother offered to throw them a shower, but only wanted to include immediate family. On the other hand, she'd hosted a large, inclusive baby shower for Steph's [straight] sister-in-law—it "was like everybody come and celebrate this!" It felt to Steph like a violation of the strict sibling equal treatment she'd grown up with,[3] and it became a source of contention. Both times her brother's wife was pregnant, Steph said, "the excitement [from my parents] was just like: I'm going to shout it from the rooftops! My mom and dad just oozed over that." Yet when Jenn was pregnant, "it was kind of this moment of like: *Wow, you really aren't happy about this.*" They ended up not having the baby shower and it caused a familial rift. Unfortunately, as noted above, the sense that Steph's parents treat her brother's children with preference over her own continues.

Another illustrative example came from Sofia, whose mother "is just uncomfortable, and was always uncomfortable, with our relationship and with the whole homosexuality issue. I don't think it was a church thing, though. It was just her own personal discomfort. But one Christmas, Frances [her wife] had a stocking on the mantel, which was [my mom's] way of saying she accepted our relationship."

"Her rule was the soon-to-be-spouse does not get a stocking until they're married," Frances said.

"Yeah. That's the rule. And so my sister was always advocating for us and she says, 'They're married. Frances gets a stocking!' So [my mom] did her whole glue and glitter thing. And she put a stocking up. Never, never said a word. But that was her thing," Sofia said. "And then . . . when we had just moved [into our new house]," we [planned] an open house that my sister and cousin turned into a shower for us, a wedding shower [after the fact], and my mother bought us a Kitchen Aid mixer. And when she gave it to me, she started crying. She says, 'I should have given this to you a long time ago,' meaning, I should have given it to you when you got married. You know, I just appreciate how my mom has kind of grown and changed with it."

Val, together with her wife Margaret for over thirty years, also told a story about small gestures, related to her twin sister. "Several years ago, she sent me a Christmas card. [It read:] Blah blah blah, I love you. And I called her and I said, You know, Margaret and I have been together for however many years it had been at that point. I said, 'You could have included her in the card.' I said, 'I don't need a card from you if you're not going to acknowledge this. So I don't need to hear from you.' I said, 'I appreciate the card, but I really want you to know that's how I feel, that you need to be respectful of this.' I don't know how long it took before the phone rang again and she called and asked to speak to Margaret."

"She asked me to forgive her," Margaret said.

"She said, 'I'm sorry. I realize this is not how I should be acting,'" Val explained.

Christmas cards. Daily language ("Saying *us*. Grouping *us*. Introducing her as my partner."). Pictures on the wall or side table. Baby showers. Homemade stockings. Kitchen Aid mixers. All of these gestures are meaningful. They signal either rejection or acceptance to these couples.

When I asked Val and Margaret what has been most challenging in their marriage, Val said, "I think greater acceptance in our families. Like my mom and my siblings and cousins. That's certainly evolved over time and is fine. But it probably took five years to tell my mom. We'd been together about five years and I said, I have to tell my mom. I figured, I may lose my relationship with my mom, but it's better that she knows than not know. And I knew after five years that we were going to be together for sure." Therefore, Val initiated some conversations with her mom, who lived at a distance. "And that was really tough. [Eventually,] I said, 'Do you think that you could consider Margaret your daughter-in-law?' And she said, 'Well, I really don't know what our parish priest would say about this.' And I said, 'Well, I can understand that. But, you know, we're still going to church and the priest at our parish has not thrown us out. So, you know, maybe you could just start to think differently.' And my mom said, 'Well, I'll think of her as a sister in Christ.' I said, 'Okay, that's a start.'"

Val had a more difficult time with her twin sister, the one who called to apologize about the Christmas card. At one point in time, she had converted from Catholicism to become a born-again Baptist and was quite open about her disapproval of Val's relationship. "She could not accept us." Val said, "When I was talking to my sister when she was very vocal in her upset with me, she said, 'Well, I really believe you are going to hell and that pains me.' And I said to her, 'I'm fine with my relationship with God. And I think God is fine with me. So you don't need to carry that burden. Let God and me carry on, you know? . . . Let God be God. And let us deal with God.'"

Val's relationship with her sister has improved over the years. Perhaps ironically, the sister "found out that her [own] son is gay." Val explained, "Once we got into that conversation, it was kind of like I got my sister back. *Now you can understand.* I mean it really took a lot of soul searching for her, but she finally got to a place where [she asked herself], *God, what are you telling me? My child? I love my child. So I don't need any of that stuff, that's B.S.* [meaning, religious beliefs about homosexuality and damnation]. And the same with one of my cousins who was pretty conservative. I just found out that her son is gay. So it's kind of like, after enough time, things get to be okay. And I think the okay-ness is not that we're in a same-sex relationship. It's the okay-ness that we're just regular folks. When my brother and his wife at the time, she's now deceased, came to visit, my sister-in-law said [with great surprise in her voice], 'Oh, I have these same plates from Crate and Barrel!' And it was like, well you know, we like the same things."

"And we do sit down and use knives and forks!" added Margaret, wryly.

Often the initial reaction of parents and siblings does not reflect where they end up over time. Katie's parents (recall her mother crying for days) have "moved for sure." Katie had a conversation with her dad "at one point, [who asked,] 'Have you talked to a priest?[4] Do you worry about going to hell?' I was like, 'No, Dad. And if I do, I know I'll be in good company. I'm not worried.' But once they met Sarah, they automatically liked her. In fact, I think they like her better than me some days. But I think it was just that whole: *How does this work? Because this is not actually okay on some level.* Some discomfort with that. And societal expectations, and their friends, and trying to communicate with people." Katie suggested that her parents struggled to reconcile their love for Katie, and eventually Sarah, and their deeply held religious beliefs: "*We love Katie and this Sarah seems okay, but it's not okay by the church's teachings.*" Here we have another set of Catholic parents asking: *How does this work?*

Today, "they love Sarah, [but] I think it's still hard for them to say gay, like there's still hesitation around that. But yeah, I think they've moved quite a bit as far as—I don't know if it's theologically, or if it's just: this is Katie and this is Sarah and we like her as a person. I also have a cousin who is gay, actually two cousins who are gay, on different sides of the family. And my one aunt had done a lot of work with her church, so I think she was really helpful to have in the family because she was kind of like, 'You know, this is going to be okay.' And my parents turned to her quite a bit and used her as a resource." In fact, I heard repeatedly how helpful it was when parents knew others (friends, family, coworkers) who were out of the closet, or who were loving a child or sibling who was out of the closet. Such relationships were invaluable—providing a frame of reference for their own experience, helping them process new information, feelings, and concerns.

When Megan (married to Mary, discussed in chapters 1 and 2) came out to her parents, she said, "My mom cried really hard and kind of, 'God, why did you let this happen?' sort of stuff." As noted, Megan and Mary fell in love in college, and struggled for years to reconcile their religious and sexual identities. Both sets of their parents are Catholic. They, too, took time to negotiate their thoughts and feelings. Megan continued, "My dad was okay. He gave me a hug and told me about a lesbian couple at work who 'make good cookies.' He thought it was okay and gave me a hug, and my mom and I struggled and went for a walk that day and she cried a lot. And it was super hard. We took a long walk and she didn't want me to think that [my sexual identity as gay] was for sure. If this was what was going to happen in my life, she wanted it to be later, not when I was—I must have been twenty-seven at the time—and she just thought I hadn't given men enough of a chance, or that there would be more of a chance for me to figure it out . . . We basically had to drag them to our wedding ten years later. Well, not drag, but handhold them along."

"I was thinking about that," Mary added. "I think our families were the biggest reason why we didn't do something more public and communal sooner. Because I think we were waiting for them."

"We didn't want to do it without them," Megan agreed.

"Megan told her sister and then told her parents. But there's all these other aunts and uncles and grandmas and, you know, lots of protecting. We can't tell grandma because she might have a heart attack and then she might die," Mary said. ["Have a stroke or something," Megan interjected.] "So we need to protect grandma and we need to protect . . ."

"She's still alive, by the way, ten years later," Megan said, with a laugh.

Megan said that she and Mary found the day of their marriage blessing [the one they had to handhold their families toward] to be "a magical day of conversion and healing that helped us live better together, and in our families." The couple decided at the time to not call the liturgy a wedding for several reasons. One was that the word wedding "had a lot of baggage" attached to it, "just so many expectations. This is how you do it, and this is what you do, and we were really breaking out of the mold in so many ways," Mary said. "And, this was not the start for us and we wanted to acknowledge the whole path that we had already walked. We wanted to honor that part of ourselves and not just say, Oh, here we're beginning now." Lastly, the liturgy took place in a United Methodist church that was still working out whether to marry gay couples, and the couple did not want anyone "to be brought up on charges" for hosting their ceremony.

Their carefully worded invitation read: *We are so grateful for your presence in our lives and we'd be honored if you would join us together with our families to celebrate and bless our love and life together*. "I feel like those two words [celebrate and bless] were very important to us. We wanted the community to come and say, This is good, and you are good, and this is something to be proud of. This is something to have joy around. This is something to rejoice in. Also that blessing part for the spiritual dimension, for the sort of religious dimension in a faith context. We want this to happen in a church and we want it to be churchy. Like jeez, I mean super churchy. That's just who we are and what we wanted. And we felt like for a lot of our relationship, we weren't blessed by others," Mary said.

They designed a liturgy that was a "mash-up" of the Catholic rite and the Presbyterian rite, also drawing on the Methodist book of worship and the UCC's book of worship. Their presider was an ordained Presbyterian. Since the ceremony was nontraditional, they invited her to wear whatever she wanted, maybe a stole. "And she's like, 'Hell no. This is for your families. They need to see that this church is legit and that the ceremony is legitimate and that you are legit.' And so she came out in her whole white robe and whatever.... [at first] I didn't necessarily think that was that important," Megan said. "And at the end of the day, it was."

The couple also invited a female Catholic mentor to preach. Mary said, "I think [the presider and preacher] both, thank God, had some sense of the larger context, that it was seventy-five percent Catholic people, and especially for our family, it's like the enormity of that moment for them." Mary believes that the sensitive and familiar choices made by both of the women during the liturgy "brought [family members] nearer. It sort of healed some things."

Megan also noted, "Our ceremony was the first time that our parents were in a room with other people . . . who knew we were together. So it was this moment: they were sitting in this room and they knew that their daughters were known. And I think that that was more powerful to them maybe than they knew [at the time]. It was more powerful to them than *we* knew it was going to be, for sure."

"These people came from all over to be [t]here, and the way they treated us and were celebrating us . . . I think it was kind of like, *They're okay. People love them and this is all right*," Mary added.

"I think that's exactly right," Megan said. "At one particular moment in the ceremony, we did the laying on of hands. So we were in the center, and we had everybody just come up and do some prayers. So Mary and I were in the center, and the presider was there. And then our parents were closest and then everybody else had their hands on them. And it was a moment of joy. And it was just like the popcorn of prayer, of things that the people wanted to bless us with or pray for us or whatever—[people said] 'love' and 'laughter' and 'health' and 'happiness.' And I think in those types of moments, [our parents] were being surrounded and being held up and blessed and prayed for as much as we were."

"There have been a couple of moments in my life that I feel were so filled with the Spirit and moving, that something had to have been [searching for the right word] . . . definitely, not ordained, but . . ."

"It was thin," Mary concluded.

"It was thin. And many people mentioned that. Our parents, our families."[5]

"Yeah," Mary said. "I mean [some of our friends] who are basically atheists, they don't really come to church, were like, 'This was really incredible. I've never felt anything like this before. I wish I could come to a church like this and believe in this type of a God. And [looking at Megan] your coworkers who are not necessarily people of faith. But also people of faith [commented on the power of the ceremony]—you know, the eighty-year-old sisters. It was a sort of culminating moment for us, but also for our families and our communities. Like, the ritual worked." *The Spirit was present. Relationships healed. The ritual worked.*

"After the wedding, all of a sudden my mom was carrying photos around in her purse so that she could tell people, you know," Mary said. "And she wasn't telling anybody up to the wedding. Then all of a sudden the wedding was over and within like two weeks she went out to lunch with her three buds from middle school, and then she went out to lunch with people she knew from high school or something, and she was whipping out the photos and laying them out for everybody. So there was something about that weekend and about that time and ritual and communal space that all of the sudden it was like, *Yeah, I don't care anymore if other people don't like this. Like here's the pictures of my daughters and this is gonna be great.* But again, that took eight years."⁶

The wedding event sometimes helped or forced families to come out of the closet more fully—this certainly was the case for Mary's and Megan's families. In a number of the stories I heard, wedding announcements and planning brought family tensions to the fore. Questions about who would be invited and decisions about who would attend were sometimes fraught, bringing to the surface feelings and concerns that may have been hidden.

For example, Dan and Jaime are very "family oriented." Nurturing good relationships with both sides of their families is a shared priority. Dan explained, "When we were getting married, one of the things we decided was very important was that our immediate families were active and we actually planned a ceremony [so] that each of our siblings and our parents would all have a role in the ceremony and that we'd all be together. That was one of the reasons we decided to have the ceremony in Mexico [where Jaime's family is from], because at the time his dad couldn't come to the States. So we planned for months and months, a year of planning almost. And Jaime's sister told us about a month and a half before the wedding that they weren't going to come. She and her husband weren't going to come because her kids wouldn't understand. It would be too upsetting for her kids."

"They wanted to come, but . . ." Jaime said. "My niece, she was going to be a flower girl. My sister was never very comfortable with me being gay. So when we were planning the ceremony . . . my sister was going to [do a reading] or something. And she said, 'Well, I'll attend, but the kids are going to stay in the hotel, the bungalow.' We have bungalows . . . every family has their own little bungalow. '[The girls] are going to stay there with my husband. And when the ceremony is over, I will bring them out.' And I'm like, 'Whoa. That's super rude, what you're saying.' And she's like, 'Because we haven't talked to them about gay marriage yet.'"

"And [my niece] is super young," Jaime continued. "And I think perhaps this is a time when you should tell your children because children will not see much of a difference. I think that it's harder to tell them when they are older, like it was a secret. Because secrets entail that there's something wrong about it." [Recall from the introduction Dan's response when he was college-aged, first discovering that there are openly gay people in the church—*why is this hidden*? Secrets imply there is something wrong with it.] "So my dad [said to my sister], 'Well, if that's going to be the case, you better not go,'" Jaime said. He was surprised that his father intervened in this way because Jaime's sister is the only girl in the family, and the oldest, and he perceives her as the favored child. He explained, "My dad said: 'You either go, or you don't go. If you're going to go, you're going to be present. If you're going to [keep your children away], it's rude.' I didn't say much to my sister about it, I was like, 'Well, do whatever you want.' I expressed my frustration. But having the support of my dad, that was very, very nice."

"His dad is a rancher from Northern Mexico. The area they're in is a conservative part of Mexico. It's not progressive in any way. Jaime had just come out to his parents a couple of years earlier. For him to stand up for us and really tell his sister, 'No, family comes first.' ['It's true. That's what he said,' Jaime interjected.] Yeah, that was a wonderful thing to see. And to continue to see. His parents came to the funeral when my mom passed away. Now my dad is dating someone and they're going to get married, which is all kinds of feeling for me, but we're all going to be there, and [Jaime's] parents are going to come."

Chapter 3

After Jaime's father talked to his sister, she changed her mind. Her whole family attended the wedding, "and the kids had a blast." As it turns out, "there was not an issue for the kids," Dan said. He noted a change in generational perspectives and experiences. "I think it's funny because we've had conversations with my nieces who very much [are] being raised [differently] now. In school they talk about being gay and boys can marry boys and girls can marry girls. So it's funny, kind of like the generational difference." Dan was far from alone in highlighting changes in generational attitudes and practices related to queer persons in families, churches, and society. It was a recurring theme in conversations. Perhaps you've noticed it popping up in various places. It will come up again moving forward.

Like Dan and Jaime, Jane and Maggie are focused on family. They'd been together seventeen years, and married three, when we spoke. "A big piece of what drew us together is our shared love of our families, being in big families, and being Catholic. All that that means," said Maggie. Jane is the oldest of eight kids, and Maggie is the youngest of six. They have twenty-six nieces and nephews combined, and they talked at length about the joy they take in spending time with their extended families. Jane said that when they got married, family members traveled to be present—"all of them came, and all of their kids. So that was an amazing feat." Maggie noted, "They'd been told by all their pastors that this is wrong. [Nevertheless,] they came. One of my sisters-in-law, I just couldn't believe. This was completely out of her realm. But you wouldn't know it there. Like the piece about love. This sounds corny, but it did overcome. 'Well, you're Maggie and of course we're going to come! This is your wedding! I don't know what it's going to be like, but we're coming!' I mean, I was blown away by that."

There was one surprising exception to this widespread family support. Maggie said, "[A]ll along Jane's family has been on board with us. I never met her mom [who had passed away], but her dad . . . He gave us his blessing." "Yeah, I mean . . . my parents were two of the most inclusive people ever," Jane said. She explained that her parents had taken in three cousins when Jane was young, "because of mental health and alcoholism issues in their family life." She considers one of those cousins a sister.

Years later, her parents took in and raised another cousin. "And any one of us could bring anybody home, at any time—no matter the gender, race—anybody could come to my parents' home. And did." Jane explicitly emphasized the profound hospitality her parents modeled for her and her siblings as a way to frame what happened with her brother, Bobby, which took her by surprise. "So just a handful of days before our wedding, my brother called to say that he and his wife and their eleven-year-old son were coming to town for the wedding. But only Bobby would be attending. He was RSVPing for his meal. 'We'll need one dinner, not three.' And they would be at the gathering the night before. But only he was coming to the wedding and reception. So it was like, 'Bobby, why aren't [your wife and Johnny] coming to the wedding?'" Jane continued. "'Well, you know, we just don't think it would be appropriate for Johnny.'"

"Johnny has only known me in relationship to Maggie," Jane explained.

"It's not like I'm new on the scene," Maggie said.

"Yeah. He's been to our home," Jane said.

"He clearly knows we're a couple," Maggie added.

"He knows we're together. We've been to his baseball games. We've been to other [activities of his]. So, *we just don't think it would be appropriate*? Okay, Bobby. 'What don't you think is appropriate?' 'Well, you know, the whole gay thing,' [Bobby said.] 'Really?' 'Jane, we love you, we just don't think it'd be appropriate to bring Johnny to the wedding.' And I was like, 'Okay. I don't even know what to say right now.' I mean, that is just ironic. Odd. It was hurtful. But I didn't want it to get in the way because it's like three days before the wedding, and I'm totally jazzed about who *is* coming."

"Right. Right. Right." Maggie nodded.

"And I know I said to Bobby, 'Well, what are you going to say to Johnny someday when he comes home and wants to talk about a friend, or . . .' 'You mean like a boyfriend or something?' 'Yeah, maybe. I'm just saying.' 'Well, let's hope we don't have to do that,' [Bobby responded.]

Chapter 3

Alrighty," Jane said. ["Love you too!" Maggie interjected, sarcastically.] "Yeah, just the irony of that."

"We didn't see that coming," Maggie said.

"No. We didn't see it coming," Jane agreed.

"In contrast," Maggie said, "I had my oldest brother and his wife, [who] live a pretty conservative life. I have been out to my sisters for fifteen years, but I'd never been out to him, and I have another brother I was never out to, he passed away . . . and I never took the opportunity before he died. But I never told my [oldest] brother, Mike. Then I told my sisters that we were getting married and they leaked it to him, as only sisters can do, I guess. And so he calls. We're actually on vacation with a sister of mine, and Mike calls, and I said to my sister, 'Mike is calling me.' 'Well, you better take the call.' And I'm thinking, *Well, you're the leaker*. So I go in the other room and: 'Hi, Mike.' 'Hi, Maggie . . . I heard you and Jane are going to get married.' And I'm like, *Oh shit. Okay*. 'Yes. Yes we are, Mike.' And he just leaped right into it. I mean, I barely said anything on the call. 'I just want you to know we're coming.'"

"He prefaced it by saying . . . ," Jane prompted her to provide more context to me.

"'Maggie, you know I've had my prejudices. But they just wouldn't stick. The truth is, they wouldn't hold up.' So he was kind of admitting why I wouldn't have come out to him, because I didn't have a lot of indication he'd be open to it. But by the time I was out, he was ready to go. He was like, 'You know what? We're not going to continue that stuff that Mom and Dad . . .' particularly my dad in his eyes, '. . . We're not going to continue to do that stuff Dad would do. We're just not going to do that.' Because my dad and his sister [Nora] were racist and bigots. Oh, awful. He's like, 'I'm not pulling an Aunt Nora on you. I wouldn't do that.' I'm like, 'Thank God! She's dead and gone. We don't need to bring Aunt Nora back. No. We don't need to repeat her in another generation. No. Let's let that go.' He was acknowledging that we're trying to do something different here now that Mom and Dad are gone."

"So they were here. They came. And they've been fine ever since," Maggie said. "Actually the hardest thing for me was, I went from not being out to being out to everybody pretty quickly because we were getting married. All my nieces and nephews I wasn't out to, although we'd been together for fifteen years. I spent all of my Christmases by myself with my family. I think Jane didn't come home until the Christmas after we were engaged, because I didn't feel like I could," Maggie said. "So, that Christmas I go home and now I'm out to everybody and we're getting married, all in like one day. And they're all like, 'Yeah, it's all cool, Maggie. It's great. What's the big deal? We're coming!' So I'm like, *twenty years of being tucked away and scared to death*? And you're like, *No big deal*? I'm like, I'm so happy. I'm affirmed. Got it. But [you have to understand that I've had] twenty years of feeling completely excluded and hated in this family for who I really was. So let me, I need a little time for what to do with *that*. I can't just jump into . . . so it was a jumbled mess. It took several years for that to recalibrate amongst my siblings and I. More for *me* to recalibrate. I don't know how much recalibrating they did. I needed time to process those resentments that I built up for so long. Then really just trust that they love me," Maggie said. "But things change over time. The world changed, and so did they. If we had come out in 2004 as we were living together . . . it would not have flown in my family, [with my] siblings. My sisters [then] were like, 'Yeah, keep that hush hush. Don't tell Mom and Dad.'"

"Well that's what I was going to say," Jane replied. "For me to be nonexistent and not a part of Maggie's life when she was home to now announcing we're getting married, and it's no big deal? Yes, it is. It's a very big deal that we are telling you we're getting married because for fifteen years we didn't tell you anything about [us]. You didn't know [me]."

"They were trying to say it's no big deal. Like, they're totally on board. Dismissing how we were made to feel prior to that. . . . I think the overlay of why it wasn't okay, the seed of that really was the Catholic church identity piece. On top of having no one around them that was gay or that was out to them," Maggie said.

Sometimes siblings were surprisingly open, as they were in Maggie's case. For example, Liam told a story about coming out to his siblings as he geared up to come out to his parents. He said, "I think I told two brothers and a sister at that point and they were like, 'Yeah, so? You don't think I knew this?' I'm like, 'No. No. This is the biggest secret of my life!' They're like, 'Shut up.' They just didn't care."

Liam's husband Marty talked about their large families on both sides and how "becoming part of the parent-club" brought them closer to certain siblings and relatives: "My mom's one of nine, so there's tons of aunts and uncles and there's the full range of intolerance to acceptance and celebration. And for those that had the most difficult time, once we became parents, they got us now. *Oh, you worry about what you're going to do with the kids for the summer! You worry about camps!* They got our lives, and connected more deeply with us. [T]here's tons of cousins on each side . . . both sides of the family just scooped [our kids] up."

On the other hand, as in Jane's story above, sometimes siblings refuse to be open with their children about the gay identity or relationship of an uncle or aunt (claiming that it would be "upsetting" or "inappropriate"), or in extreme cases, cut off relationship on account of it. Recall the story of Michael and Brian, the couple acting as "surrogate fathers" for Brian's deceased brother's two sons (discussed in chapter 2). Brian added an additional layer to the story when he told me that he has another brother, Jacob, from whom he is estranged. Brian and Jacob did not speak to each other for twenty years because Jacob "didn't like" that Brian is gay. "They barred me from seeing their kids," Brian said. The two began speaking again when their other brother was dying. "We did start talking from that point," Brian explained. "But you know there's so much that's gone on in twenty years . . . I have another whole bunch of kids, but I haven't seen them or talked to them in twenty years. They're older . . . they're adults now. Maybe we'll have a different relationship now that they're adults. [We'll] see how that goes. That's all beginning to change, hopefully in a good way."

Relatedly, Tom said, "In my own family there have been difficulties, not being sure about [my marriage to Mark.] And what I finally said to my niece, [whose] daughter just finished first grade, was: 'I don't want Sally to grow up not knowing gay people who go to church and gay people who give money to missionaries and gay people who love their nieces and give them Christmas presents. I don't want her to grow up not knowing gay people because that's how I grew up. And that wasn't good. I want her to know she has two uncles who are married to each other, who send her books and who pray for her and who love her. I want her to grow up knowing that. Now you can tell her whatever you want about the morality of that situation, I can't control that. [But] I want her to know that those two gay uncles love her and pray for her and care for her."

The stories in this chapter illustrate that families sometimes find it difficult to accept their gay loved ones and their relationships, and that lack of acceptance is often rooted in religious teachings that condemn same-sex relationships, as well as cultural messages and experiences. Sometimes parents and family members who initially express disappointment, even rejection, eventually "move" toward greater acceptance, openness, and affirmation. Other times, couples find acceptance and affirmation from their families from the get-go, and are grateful for it. William and Mateo are one such couple. "Our families are awesome. Yes. Yes. They are incredible . . . especially for gay people because often you don't have supportive families." The couple described an engagement party that Mateo's family hosted (to which William's parents came) that typifies their sense of familial belonging. Mateo's family lives in a town close to the Mexican border, and his family planned the party around a cultural festival that takes place in that border town. About sixty or seventy guests arrived to celebrate the couple, many driving two or three hours from Mexico.

"This was an important moment for us because we had this party planned, and everything was catered and all that stuff, but the turnout just blew us away . . . not just cousins but aunts and uncles and the parents of aunts and uncles, like all the generations showed up in a really big way. And we had just kind of tried it, because nobody had tried the same-sex thing in that context. It's not a particularly a conservative bunch, but not particularly progressive either. But we were like, This is just what we're doing. My mom was always very supportive[7] and she was like . . . this is who you're marrying. This is family. This is how it's going to go. And my mom fills the role of matriarch in that space. So her sort of saying that, holding that, opening that space for us, people showed up in a huge way. Driving three hours there and three hours back. And it was just really powerful, and not just for us," Mateo said.

"There was a really beautiful moment when we were looking through the guestbook and a young cousin of ours, who at that point was in her early twenties maybe, who is lesbian, had written us this note. [She wrote about] how much fun she had had and how this made her feel like she could get married, like she could marry a woman. And that was really touching because we weren't trying to be advocates for anything, we were just trying to be ourselves and be among our family. I think it was really meaningful for people. In fact, a colleague of my mother's is a gay man who spent his life as an advocate . . . for children . . . but has been closeted for his whole life, with the exception of being out to a few friends, including my mom. Seeing this go down and the Mexican-ness of it and the celebratory tone of it and the way the family showed up, well, it just had him in tears. He was also a little drunk! We were like, *You need to calm it down!* [laughing] But he was very moved and continues to talk about it all the time."

This story of warm, affirming, family celebration—so meaningful not only for Mateo and William, but for family and friends of multiple generations—is a powerful bookend to the story of Jenn and Steph that began the chapter. Recall that on the night of her engagement to Steph, Jenn woke in a panic, screaming and crying, fretting over how their parents and community would react to the news. A stark contrast, indeed.

What becomes clear in these stories is that families have choices to make, large and small, that foster feelings of rejection or belonging, shame or unconditional love. People have various roles to play in moving families toward deeper experiences of love and belonging.[8] Sometimes it's a parent who sets the tone, opens the space, for other family members to follow or to step into, such as Mateo's mother, and Jaime's father. Sometimes it's a sibling who "advocates" for greater acceptance in the family, such as Sofia's sister, who helped Frances gain her rightful stocking on the mantle. Sometimes it's a priest, or an aunt, or a knowledgeable family friend who helps a confused, Catholic parent answer the question: *How does this work? How do I love my beautiful child and also maintain my Catholic identity and values?* Sometimes it's a sibling who simply says, "I know.

Shut up. Who cares?" And sometimes it's an invitation from gay couples themselves, via a well-planned marriage liturgy, an honest conversation (and another and another and another), or an ordinary, married relationship well-lived.

Notes

1. I heard from a number of couples about the challenge of introducing their partner to strangers or relatives, not knowing whether that person will be receptive to same-sex relationships. One tactic, which Steph refers to here, is to introduce the partner as "my roommate."

2. "We've both gone through counseling. Not because of us, but because of what we've experienced with our parents. I mean, I was on what we call 'the red couch' for ten years because I was very depressed because of what was going on with my parents," Jenn said.

3. "My parents were really big about being equal on everything. When we had Christmas, everyone had the same amount of stuff. Or it was like, 'We spent the same amount on each of you, just so you know if you see more on this pile.' Everything was very equal. And they made it very clear. If one got it, the other one got it, if one didn't get it, the other one didn't get it either," Steph explained.

4. In fact, Katie had reached out and spoken to a priest, who was very helpful. More on that in chapter 4.

5. The concept of a thin space is ancient and rooted in the Celtic tradition. Julianne Stantz explains that "[t]he Celtic imagination considers sacred places to be 'thin,' or places where the veil between the worlds of heaven and earth seems especially permeable, and the worlds discernably close to each other . . . Entering thin spaces is an opportunity that we don't normally have—to slow down, to pause, to look with fresh eyes, to recover a sense of wonder about the world." Julianne Stantz, *Braving the Thin Spaces: Celtic Wisdom to Create a Space for Grace* (Chicago: Loyola Press, 2021).

6. Emma and Christina experienced their wedding in a similar way, as healing for them and their families. Emma said, "The wedding helped with her family and the wedding helped with my family. And when those relationships are aligned to who we are, then that brings so much joy."

7. For context, Mateo was raised Roman Catholic in a Mexican-American context. His father's family, while culturally Catholic, "did not really identify with their Catholicism." Mateo said, "My mother was very intentional about forming us because she has her own arc. She has her own story of Catholicism. She still identifies as Catholic. She's a very progressive woman" and a Zen teacher.

8. For an excellent website with information and resources on how to increase family acceptance and support for LGBTQ youth—and why this is crucial for well-being—see www.lgbtqfamilyacceptance.org, a collaboration between the Family Acceptance Project at San Francisco State University and the Innovations Institute at the University of Connecticut. Find out more about the Family Acceptance Project at https://familyproject.sfsu

.edu, and the Innovations Institute at UCONN at https://innovations.socialwork.uconn.edu/about-us/.

For a specifically Catholic perspective, Fortunate Families, a Catholic ministry for LGBTQ persons, families, and friends, is helpful. See https://fortunatefamilies.com/.

Chapter 4

Church

Tension, Integration, and Belonging

"Being someone who realized they were gay from a very young age . . . never thinking that I would be able to get married, I used to think of marriage as just a legal arrangement, a piece of paper; it was a legality. I've since learned how much it means. One [benefit is] social status—recognition that your relationship is serious . . . You know, I'm not a fifty-five-year-old person with a boyfriend. I have a husband. It's marriage. But the fact that someone will commit themselves to you for life. It is amazing. It's very affirming. It just feels wonderful knowing that someone will do that with you," Luke said. He and Steve wed after twenty-nine years together.

Luke noted that their decision to marry "was actually [a] pretty practical one." He highlighted the complicated history of gay marriage in the United States, and their own efforts over the years to gain the legal benefits of marriage. At one point, the couple registered as domestic partners "because I felt like we needed to stand up and be accounted for," though it "had no benefit whatsoever." But, Luke explained, "Every time we moved we've had to hire an attorney and do wills and health care power of attorney and all the legal stuff to make sure that if one of us were in the hospital that we could visit each other in the ICU and make decisions for each other because otherwise we could be locked out." When DOMA was overturned by the Supreme Court, Steve and Luke decided to marry, primarily for "pragmatic" reasons.

Chapter 4

"Being raised Protestant," Luke said, "I never really thought of marriage as a sacrament. I often just thought of it more in the layperson's perspective: it's a contract and its purpose is passing on property, that sort of thing. But . . . the day when we got married, standing up there and having someone say that they want to be bound to you for life, was just overwhelmingly powerful. Just amazing. I've always felt that Steve was a gift from God. I felt like our relationship was a gift from God. Now I can see how the act of being married itself [is spiritually meaningful], because you're standing up and declaring your love and commitment before God and everyone. So I have a new perspective on it than I had for most of my life."

The couple relishes the "companionship and compatibility" of their marriage. Steve explained that they share "a lot of the same values" and "just love being together." He said, "we still have the flame of love alive and well and lit between us, which I really appreciate." Luke sweetly expressed gratitude for how "demonstrative" the two are in expressing their mutual love and affection: "My favorite parts are going to sleep at night with him next to me and waking up with him next to me. It's just really nice." Their stable married relationship grounds them and, in turn, allows them to do good work in the world. Steve said, "I think through our committed relationship we're able to commit to other things in society that [are] important to us. Having our relationship and our home life stable, in place, enables us to be more productive, [to be] difference-makers with those outside our relationship and also with commitments that we . . . enter to improve our community, our church, our work, whatever." In other words, it enables them to be outward-facing, contributing to the common good.

They've enjoyed many years of stability and joy ("nirvana" as Luke described it) in their relationship and marriage, but their start was rockier. Steve struggled to accept his sexual identity and reconcile his relationship to his family and their shared Catholicism. "I was born Catholic, raised Catholic, and [am] still a practicing Catholic, and really never had a break from the church," Steve explained. He indicated that "the biggest challenge was in the early years" of his relationship with Luke: "I was very career focused and really was not accepting of being gay. It took years for me to get through that . . . there was a lot of processing and difficulty I had to go through, and patience [from] Luke. [The] processing and acceptance I needed to do about who I was, it took some time."

Steve believes that his family's Catholic identity was a major cause of the challenge of accepting who he was as a gay man. "It also was generational. But I think with my parents and my older brother who look at the world as like, 'Well, what does the Catholic church say?' I think that was a big part of it. And then also being very close with my family and not willing to alienate them, [wanting to] retain their acceptance and approval, and on the other hand, having all these feelings and want[ing] a relationship. And that was the conflict with me—in the middle and trying to figure it out. I needed to do something. So for years I was trying to bridge both [loci] of importance in my life—my family and Luke—and they were in conflict. So that was in the early years, and in time we worked through that."

Steve explained how he worked through that "limbo land," where he sat uncomfortably in the middle: "You're trying to play both, I don't want to say sides, but both sources of importance in your life and appeal to them both, and there's an irreconcilable conflict between them, at least at that time. It's very stressful being in that situation, and eventually something has to change. What happened was Luke [finally said], 'You've got to make a decision. We cannot be just perceived as friends. That's not going to work.'" In an attempt to get unstuck, Steve went to speak with a priest, "because associated with my parents was the Catholic church. That's where they were coming from. And so here was a representative of the Catholic church. And I said [to him], 'I feel like moving towards accepting who I am as being gay is a moving away from the church.' He says, 'Well, you're here now. That tells me a lot.' That was pretty powerful." In Steve's mind, the priest's words "basically meant I could still be with Luke and not pull away from my family." Steve wrote a coming-out letter to his parents. They read the letter, but did not call him for weeks. "I finally had to call them. And it was a confrontation. But we worked through that and overcame that, and they had to acknowledge Luke as more than a roommate."[1]

Despite its official teachings on same-sex relationships, Steve consistently felt committed to the Catholic church. He said, "One of the positive values of my parents is commitment and allegiance to institutions and value-sets that you were raised with, that you consider good . . . There [are] institutions we have in society that we don't always agree with or [with which] we have problems . . . This is more of the cognitive or analytical view of faith. There's more of the spiritual side, but the cognitive view is just because you don't agree with everything within an institution, is your commitment so weak that you're going to shun that institution for either something else more to your liking or, for nothing at all? I've never thought that way. I felt, you know, if there's a Catholic parish that I don't particularly like, [then I'll find another]. When we moved [to a new city, there were] probably six or seven churches I went to until I found one I liked, and got Luke to go there too.

"On the spiritual side, I've always believed that [spirituality] is part of us as human beings," Steve continued. "There's a whole component that you have to explore, honor, [and] recognize—your spiritual life. And if you don't, then it's just dormant. You know, it's almost one of the senses. [If] you choose not to use or recognize it, it can calcify. So I've always . . . consider[ed] myself a spiritual being . . . and I always get value and fulfillment by practicing that. And one of the things is attending church, attending mass."

Steve described his appreciation for the mass, which nourishes his spirituality: "[T]here's a certain flow and pattern to the mass that I like, [and] maybe because I was raised that way, that I've always liked . . . There's plenty of priests that speak of the importance of God's relationship with each of us. The importance of His love in us and how fulfilling that is. And then also our obligations, [our] commitment to society and the importance of us—individually [and] collectively as a church—acting on those obligations. So I find that of value. That's usually when the church is at its best, when it's appealing to those better angels of our being, pulling them out and getting us to act on those qualities that we all have, [reminding us] that we can make a difference in the world."

In sum, Steve continues to actively participate in the Catholic church because he believes in loyalty to institutions, none of which is perfect.

He's also motivated to worship in community because of his (basic anthropological) conviction that human beings are embodied spirits, and our spirits need nourishment to grow. For Steve, the Catholic mass tends his spirit. He is willing to search for a Catholic parish in which he and Luke feel comfortable, where they regularly can be reminded of God's love for them as well as their obligations to contribute to the common good.

Luke and Steve are currently practicing in an inclusive Catholic parish, and both identify as Catholic; Luke converted from Protestantism as an adult. He explains: "I was raised Baptist. I went through a period of many years where I was very earnest and serious about it. And then as I got older—junior high, early high school—I became aware of the people in the church, not necessarily from the pulpit, but elders of the church, deacons of the church, Sunday school teachers, and the things they would say. There was a lot of prejudice and bigotry, especially racial things. And a lot of anti-Catholicism and frankly slight ignorance. That was before I realized I was gay. It really turned me off. . . So I walked away. I slammed the door and walked away. And then I figured out I was gay. You know the message was very clearly: *You are not welcome*. So I had a lot of anger and animosity for decades. And I was the person who would argue anyone down if you ever talked about God or organized religion. In retrospect, I realize that I allowed people to tell me that I was not welcome at the table when I was welcome at the table all along. So I did that to myself by allowing people to make me feel that way. I attended mass with Steve on and off throughout our relationship many times, [but] most of the time he just went on his own."

Luke credits a particular priest, "who gave wonderful homilies," with "reaching" him. Fr. Bill has since passed away, but, Luke said, he can "put a little notch in his belt" for "bringing me back to the faith." "So I joined the Catholic church. I'd been baptized elsewhere, so I went to RCIA." ["You need to say how you got there," Steve interjected. "What else was going on in your life that year?"] "Oh, I also stopped drinking. Is that what you mean?" Luke asked Steve, who nodded. "Yeah. That's part of it too because having a higher power is part of AA. But where I was going with this was: [Steve's] parents came to my first communion on the Easter Vigil, so they drove from [another state], which was very, very meaningful. It definitely said a lot about the legitimacy of our relationship at that time, and this was before marriage."

"Yeah. Yeah. We'd been together twenty-seven years," Steven added.

"Which actually really surprised me. I didn't expect that at all. [Looking at Steve,] I think you were surprised too."

"I was surprised," Steve agreed. "I think in their mind, you becoming Catholic somehow made our relationship more legitimate. You know in a weird way."

"Both of his sisters married non-Catholics who converted," Luke explained. "His brother married a Catholic, so three of the four married non-Catholics, who all converted. So I guess [Steve's parents] were like, 'Oh, we got the last one!' They got a microwave or something out of that!" Luke said, laughing.

"I guess they thought, If we can't make him straight, at least he's going to marry a Catholic!" Steve replied.

At one point in our conversation, Luke admitted, "I am not particularly wedded to Catholicism. There are many things I do like about it. I love the comfort of the ritual and dignity of the mass. I like the [order of the mass], you have the liturgy [of the Word] and then you have the eucharist, the Last Supper recreated, so I think that's wonderful. And I enjoy that. I like the universality . . . of the church, the multiculturalism of it. I like the history of so many people who are now saints—and if they're not saints, they're scholars and well received—mysticism, meditation, things that in the Protestant faith really aren't discussed or may even be frowned upon.[2] Learning from the past. In fact, many times . . . these people were . . . criticized or persecuted by the church. But now they are canonized and have become saints."

"So there are things that I definitely admire about the Catholic Church, and I'm happy to be a part of it. But truthfully, if I found a church community elsewhere that met my needs and it was not Catholic, I could happily attend it. I'm not restricted by the dogma of any organized religion or denomination. I have a little book *The Catechism of the Catholic Church* . . . I've read some of it, but I'm not particularly too concerned about what's in it. I'm going from what's in here [pointing to his heart].

Steve is a cradle Catholic [and attended Catholic schools most of his life], so I think Steve is a cultural Catholic as well as a religious Catholic, and that's a big part. Because I don't have that cultural Catholicism—I have it from a religious perspective—I'm not quite as wedded to it."

Luke continued: "Something that does strike me as a little frustrating is when you tell people who are Protestant or who are not religious that you are Catholic, nine times out of ten the first thing you're going to hear is 'How can you be part of that church where they abused children and then hid it and moved the priests all around, all because they were worried about protecting their property?' And there's no argument about that. I can't, I'm not going to defend that at all. So you would think that a group of people . . . mostly older men who are part of the hierarchy of the church, would have learned from that and would be a little more open and accepting [and more cautious about] . . . anything having to do with them trying to dictate sexual mores. That's my little diatribe there. So, I am basically [Catholic] because of Fr. Bill and a wonderful parish. I would like to find something similar here."

Luke explained that "the diocese here has started an outreach to the LGBT community," rooted in the parish they currently attend. "So they're trying," Luke said, "and I feel it's important to step up and be accounted for. If we're asked and we're invited, we should show up. So that's what [we're] doing." Steve and Luke appreciate the local bishop's support of the gay community through their parish. The bishop has "visited the LGBT social at our parish twice. He came and he's given mass and then walked around the [parish hall] where we're all having tacos and cookies and greeted us."

"There [are] three times I can think of over the years that I've cried, really cried of joy at mass," Steve said. "One was when my sister got married . . . I guess I was just so happy for her. She was the first one of the siblings to get married. The second time was when Luke was walking in the procession with Fr. Bill leading the procession, and he was with a group of six or so catechumens at Easter Vigil, and I was there by my parents. And then the third time was at the [diocesan-wide] mass that the bishop said here for the LGBT community two years ago. The church was full, with the mayor, and the whole mass was so moving because it

Chapter 4

was basically the church officially saying that 'You're God's children too, even with you being gay, you are fully accepted and we welcome you.' That was huge! Being raised Catholic, being a part of that was very emotional."

"And that's why we feel it's important to participate in [our parish], since they're doing the LGBT ministry there, and they're trying to reach out. So even though I wasn't raised Catholic, I understand what it means to someone like Steve and religion in general," Luke asserted. He noted that when Steve and Luke were younger, not many Christian churches were gay-friendly. "And now many Protestant churches are gay-friendly. So when I mentioned that I'm not strictly wedded to [Catholicism], if Steve wasn't culturally Catholic, I would very likely explore a gay-friendly Protestant church. Because, for instance, I went to this retreat at the diocese," a training for people who want to be ministers in their parishes. "They had a PowerPoint up, and they were talking about being a eucharistic minister and . . . one of the PowerPoint things was: *If you're married, your marriage should be in accordance with the church.* That doesn't apply to me. So I'm like, *Well, do I remove myself? Do I recuse myself?* But [our parish] also had this thing about, 'You know we need you.' They did announcements, and I'm sitting in church, and they said, 'We need more volunteers. We're understaffed. We need eucharistic ministers, liturgical ministers. If you're interested, please see me at the end of mass.' And suddenly, I'm like, *All right, God. Well, here's my call. Your ask! I'll show up.* Then [at the retreat] I'm like, *Well, God called me, but the PowerPoint says I'm not welcome.* So then I just figured, *Screw it. I'll just keep doing what I'm doing*. But you know, those are the little things you have to think through. *You just told me I'm not welcome. So.*"

Steve notes that, while some people in the church might be pushing the gay community away, there are also those who are pulling the community in. He believes that those who are pushing queer people away are "either ignorant or misguided" and will, over time, "see that their stance is really not in the best interest [of the church or] consistent with the teachings of Jesus Christ."

"I would say that the Vatican is not the church. The diocese is not the church. The building is not the church. The people, the *gente*, are the church. *Where there are two or more gathered in my name, I'm there*—so that's the church. And so you don't change things by walking away, you change things by staying," Luke replied. "I graduated high school in 1982, and at that point in time you could still be fired for being gay. You could easily be severely beaten or possibly killed walking into or out of a gay bar. It was not criminal at that point, but ten or fifteen years before, it was criminal. You could be arrested. They raided gay bars—you know, Stonewall was '69. I look back now that I'm older and realize what the generation just before me did by standing up . . . Steve and I just missed by the skin of our teeth the AIDS epidemic. It was all around us, but when we came of age and came out, we knew about safe sex because they were literally just figuring that out. So people just a couple years older than us did *not* know, and many of them died. And so, when I look at the people who got their skulls cracked open with billy clubs, lost their jobs because they got arrested walking into a gay bar and the police raided it, all the ostracism they went through, people who passed away from AIDS, and everything they suffered through, which gets me now where I can be legal and married and the way things have changed. . . . It's the same perspective on the church. We can show up. We can be there. If people don't like it, they can leave, or they can give us the stink eye. But we can show up, participate, be worthy of respect (as we are), and do our part to change things over time."

"Change doesn't happen quickly. It happens over time," Steve asserted. "I've often said that the LGBT Pride parade is more of a festival and [doesn't] carry [the same] importance as it has in years past. This year it was the fiftieth-year anniversary of Stonewall . . . A week ago yesterday, I was with a group of twenty-five Catholics that walked in the parade together for the first time. We carried a banner that said: *We are all God's children*. And there was a Franciscan and a nun in a habit [who] walked as well, and we wore shirts that said *Roman Catholic* on one side and on the back it said, *It's our church too*. And that was a huge statement. It's courage, but it's also sending a message, and that is the essence of social change like pride, and why it exists." Courage + Community + Sending a message of basic human dignity and inclusion = "the essence of social change."

Chapter 4

"And while he was doing that," Luke said, "I was sitting in a basement conference room at the diocese looking at a PowerPoint slide that said not to be a eucharistic minister. I would have been [at the parade], but I had agreed to that commitment earlier and didn't realize what day it was when I signed up for it. So there's a kind of dichotomy there."

There's a dichotomy there.

I offer Steve and Luke's story as an entree to thinking about how the people in the study have navigated (and continue to navigate) their church communities and wider faith traditions, as LGBTQ individuals and couples. Of course, experiences vary. As in families (discussed in chapter 3), in faith communities, the interviewees sometimes felt rejected, hidden, or on the margins. Other times, they felt welcomed, embraced, and integral. Strangely, though perhaps unsurprisingly, many felt *both* welcome and unwelcome, whether periodically, situationally, or simultaneously (as illustrated by Steve and Luke's "dichotomous," push-and-pull experiences). Testimony from these couples shows that experiences of church—positive and negative—profoundly are shaped by: official church teaching and practice; spiritual mentors; church leaders; cultures within parishes; families; and small communities within the larger church or in parishes. To be sure, experiences are multilayered and complicated.

Keep in mind that, in order to participate in the study, couples had to have some "meaningful connection to the Catholic tradition," understood broadly. It was not necessary for *both* spouses to be Catholic or to have grown up in the Catholic tradition, as long as at least one of them had a (self-identified) meaningful connection to Catholicism. Most people in the study identified as Catholic. Some folks were Catholic at some point in life, but no longer identify strictly or easily as such. Many, such as Steve and Luke, are Catholic *and* practicing in a parish. Others are Catholic and seeking to find a parish that is welcoming and affirming. A number of folks are practicing in non-Catholic churches, and a subset of those officially belong to those Christian denominations (for example, Episcopalian, ELCA). Still others find themselves outside organized church communities, whether temporarily or permanently, and are finding other ways to sustain themselves spiritually and maintain spiritual community.

Moreover, couples are not always in agreement about whether or how to participate in church communities.

I hope that reflecting on the experiences of these couples in their faith communities can help us think more deeply about what it means to "be church" when the body of Christ is diverse.

"I grew up in a deeply evangelical family," Kevin told me. "My mom played the piano at the Baptist church. My dad is a Deacon. My grandfather, who had this kind of oversized place in my life, was an educator and a pastor in the Baptist church." Kevin's life revolved around church. "When I was a little kid, I'd walk out of church and the pastor would be like, 'There's preacher boy!' I would stand on the pulpit and give the benediction at the end of the Sunday night service. This religious identity was huge to me. And then this identity as gay was the most scary, horrific, disgusting, awful thing it could be."

As a very young man, Kevin remembers burning a rag as a symbolic gesture, while " . . . asking God to burn away my sexuality and my gayness. In the backyard, I remember it so vividly, just begging God to take this away. In college, I went to an evangelical university. I have memories of hiding under the desk just sobbing and asking not to be gay, begging not to be gay. I went to seminary . . . [where] they were boldly evangelical. [I] literally had a pretty significant breakdown midway through seminary. I walked into a church sanctuary [where] I was an associate pastor. I looked at the stained glass image of Jesus, . . . cursed, and was like, 'You can't take this one thing away from me? I give you everything and you can't take this one thing away from me?'"

Kevin began therapy "and was lucky enough to be with a good therapist" who was a professor at the seminary. The therapist "started helping me to see that I was okay," Kevin said. He continued on a conflicted journey to reconcile his sexual and religious identities. "I dated, particularly a girl named June, and thought that would help me be straight. We broke up and got back together again. When I told her I was gay, she was still ready to get married. So, [that's] how deeply entrenched all this was." Kevin moved on to work in another couple of evangelical, educational settings, as a teacher and minister. When the latter institution took "a harder and harder line on LGBTQ kids, that just finally broke me,"

Chapter 4

Kevin explained. He decided to come out. He'd been reading, reflecting, and striving for integration. He'd joined the Episcopal church. "When I publicly came out, I lost my ordination from the church I had been ordained at," Kevin said. He lost his job and his home.

As next steps, Kevin discerned a monastic vocation (ultimately deciding against it) and moved to a major city, where he met and still resides with his husband, Timothy. He found a welcoming and affirming Episcopal church to attend. "When I came to the city, just recently I had come out," he said. "I was freaking out, like I didn't know what was going on. I was wounded. I was hurt. I was acting out. It was a horrible time for me. But my ass was in church every Sunday morning, most every morning, because there was this disconnect of: The church has rejected me so hard—like my community, all that stuff—and so *I'm hurting over here*. But I still [came] into the place where I felt accepted, I felt the Divine, I felt loved . . . even though I was going through all this other pain." Kevin got to know the rector at the church, an out gay man who became a spiritual mentor. The church began to feel more and more like home, and Kevin felt emotionally and spiritually ready to begin dating.

Kevin and Timothy met online. They started emailing, then texting regularly. "So at one point I was petrified of coming out to Timothy [by telling him] that I went to church," Kevin said. "So many people have come to [the city] who have been beaten up by the church or by homes and been kicked out, all those things. I knew plenty of [people] that would look at people who go to church now and be like: *What idiots. They don't know what the hell they're doing* . . . But I was like, *Shit, I've got to come out*. So it was Saturday night and I texted him: I've got to go to bed. I have to get up early tomorrow morning because I go to this liberal, progressive Episcopal church [and he named the church]." Timothy quickly texted back, indicating that he knew the church and was friends with the rector, who, as it turns out, had also become a spiritual mentor to him. After leaving the Catholic church, Timothy had discovered "a real home" in that very church community. Kevin was both "baffled" and relieved—his fears of "coming out" as religious were unfounded, and his commitment to be both gay and actively religious were not only affirmed, but shared.

About a year and a half later, the two wed in that Episcopal church, together creating "a great liturgy" that highlighted their "two backgrounds coming together." Kevin and Timothy designed the liturgy hoping to connect to "everyone in the congregation," though those gathered came from diverse perspectives and religious traditions. The two melded liturgical resources from various Christian traditions, creating "something new" that reflected their understanding of marriage as fundamentally about the mutuality and equality of spouses rather than some "heteronormative deal." Accompanying traditional scripture readings and a eucharistic blessing were some traditional evangelical hymns, the litany of the saints, and the witness of two "best persons" who happened to be women. It was a wonderful celebration and gathering of family and community.

Unfortunately, because Timothy works in a Catholic institution, some conservative Catholic groups found out about the wedding, took issue with the marriage, and began a campaign to get him fired. His workplace "got apparently three thousand plus letters asking for my being fired. And you know the Cardinal Newman Society and the Church Militant people . . . they know how to mobilize their troops." (Four years later, Timothy "routinely, like once a month" received "a hate letter" at work.) The conservative Catholic groups utilized social media to spread stories and rally people, and the church where Kevin worked also began getting phone calls. "This is where I got really offended because some of the comments accused him of being a child molester," Timothy said.

"A child molester, because I worked with youth. So that pissed me off," Kevin replied.

Kevin reflected on his role as a youth minister—mentoring explicitly focused on helping young people know that, whoever they are, "they are loved beyond measure," no matter their gender or sexual orientation. "We want them to know they are loved. That they are deeply and unconditionally loved. And known. And seen." Kevin understands his marriage to Timothy as "sacramental in a way of showing: whoever you are, you get to be you." It was difficult for him to understand the vitriol coming from the conservative groups in response to their marriage. "We have emails and letters coming in, because we love? We're both in fields that are so focused on making the world better. You still have the audacity to come after us? The wedding blessing [states]: *What God has brought together, let no one [tear apart]*. . . . [Their behavior is] just horrid. It's evil to me."

The couple was extremely grateful for how people rallied around them. Kevin's coworkers were fiercely protective and supportive. Timothy's institution was as well, issuing a public statement in support of Timothy's constitutional right to marry.

Looking at Timothy, Kevin said, " . . . [E]xcept being angry for you and with you, the thing that was most painful to me was when they would in these articles and statements and letters and stuff, they'd put marriage in quotation marks. And I would be like, *No! No! A priest stood up. It was the day after Obergefell, in our church. Our parents were sitting right there. Hands were placed on us and prayed over us. And you have the audacity to put marriage in quotation marks? The agony and the pain and the struggle that it took for both of us in our histories to get to that altar. And you have the audacity and this flippancy to put it in quotation marks?* It still offends my spirit. Because *how dare you*. How dare you put quotation marks around that."

Gianna and Kathy have been together since 1991. They married religiously in 1997 and legally about twenty years later. Together, they've raised two boys, who were late teenagers when we spoke. Gianna and Kathy both identify as "cradle Catholics" and chose to raise their boys in the Catholic faith. Gianna comes from "a very Catholic, Italian family" and went to Catholic schools. Kathy's father was not Catholic, but her mother and grandmother are, and Catholicism "was always a big part" of her life. She said, "We were a big part of the parish when I was younger. We would meet my grandmother at church and then she'd come over every Sunday and hang out with us on Sunday afternoons." This weaving of church and family echoes Kevin's experience as a child—for many, church and family cannot be easily separated in shaping one's sense of self.

When Gianna and Kathy met, Gianna was "coming out of another relationship which had been fairly long-standing"—eleven years. "It had gone south kind of suddenly," Gianna said. "I think that I brought into that relationship the idea that you get together and you stay together. You stay together and you weather life's storms and celebrate the meadows and you go on, and that's not what happened. So I think when I met [Kathy], that whole theory of life was being uprooted. Then I met a lot of other people and just was getting to that point of: *Well, I'm having a whole lot of fun and making up for lost time, [but] this isn't right. It's just not the way life was meant to live.* And you know, [Kathy] was struggling a lot with her sense of identity and the Catholic church, and her sense of God and how God was, accepting [her] sexuality. Thankfully for some reason that was never really a theme in my life." Gianna believes that the two met for a reason. She was able to help Kathy come to terms with her sexuality and religious identity and, in turn, Kathy "brought a sense of rightness and religion back into [her] life."

"I always believed I'm God-created and He doesn't create mistakes. So whatever this is about [meaning, her sexual orientation], it's created for a reason and you just move forward with it," Gianna said. She had no difficulty accepting her sexuality or reconciling her gayness with her Catholicism. Kathy said, "With Gianna, she's always been able to embrace it. It's been a part of her and she's accepted it from a very early age, [looking at Gianna] as early as you can remember."

On the other hand, Kathy "always struggled with [her] Catholicism and being gay." She came out in college. In her twenties, she found herself "at a surface level of . . . spirituality" and "started diving down [deeper] into" her faith. She read "a lot of Catholic books" that "drove me into a deeper wanting to get closer to God and become more religious, to really strive for it. But as I was getting there, everything I was reading was *Oh yeah, and you're going to hell* kind of thing. For me, that was very real and is very real still. It was very real that I could be really driving myself away from God and going to hell. That was really tough."

"I had some major struggles, and I remember a couple of times thinking: You know, if somebody just hit me on the road . . . I would never consider suicide, just because, but if somebody just hit me and just let me go at this point, then it would be a relief to me," Kathy recalled. The effort to reconcile her sexual identity and her religious identity felt unbearable. Death looked like relief.

"That's where Gianna picked up and she's like, 'You need help. You really need some help. This is real[ly] serious.' And I started seeing a spiritual counselor and a psychologist. The spiritual counselor was a gay ex-priest, which was to me very enlightening—that he could be where he was and so spiritual, but acknowledge his homosexuality. Through Dignity, I was meeting with a group . . . which was never something I'd be comfortable with, but I would go downtown, and it was once a week or once every other week, and we'd meet in the basement somewhere and it was just discussions about where people were. And the people helped there. And one of the priests that was part of Dignity, I met with him a couple of times one on one, and that was like *Oh, wow*. It was amazing."

"I know it was really tough for Gianna because I was at the point where I had to make this decision, and . . . I [thought], *If I continue on a path of our relationship, then I'm deciding to go against God or away from God, or accept the consequences.* That was real. That was a tough couple of years, actually. [Looking at Gianna,] I still think it's amazing that you hung in there with me all the way." The language that Kathy uses here is similar to the language that Steve used at the beginning of the chapter. Both worried that moving closer to acceptance of their sexual orientation and toward a loving relationship meant moving *away* from God and church. For them, the highest of stakes. Both spent years in the agonizing middle of two poles of meaning and sustenance that seemed impossible to integrate, while their partners patiently waited and supported. For Steve, a priest's reassurance—"You're here now. That tells me a lot."—helped him to overcome an either/or framework. Kathy also found a way forward with the help of "amazing" and revelatory conversations with an ex-priest, who modeled a way to be both gay and faithful. She also benefited from open conversations with other Catholics who were gay, simply talking about "where they were."

Dignity was instrumental for both Kathy and Gianna in learning how to practice their Catholicism and be gay and in relationship. The group became an important and cherished source of support and community. Gianna explained that when they were younger, "being gay and being religious were two very different things." People were often "hurt" in churches and "felt like they had to get away." Gianna was one of them—before finding Dignity, she found Catholic churches "tough to go into." Yet Dignity allowed them to "meld" being gay and being religious.

They found a safe and affirming worship community and an environment in which to deepen their knowledge of the Catholic tradition and their spiritual lives. They learned about the "primacy of conscience"—that "we can think for our[selves], even though we're Catholic." The two "met a lot of friends [through Dignity] . . . the people we ended up meeting were just incredible. And that's where we ended up talking through marriage . . . [W]e had a couples' group there. That kind of kicked it all off, because I had never thought about marriage, that it would be possible," Kathy said. Possibility became reality: the two did marry, and they subsequently started a family.

When Kathy and Gianna adopted their two children, a priest they met at Dignity baptized them. The couple took the boys to mass every Sunday at their parish church, where the family continues to practice. "[E]verybody is used to seeing us together. We have people that we always sat by and they all watched our kids grow up—you know, kind of neat," Kathy said. While Gianna and Kathy were not "super blatant" about the fact that they're married, they "never hid it." They function on a kind of "don't ask, don't tell" policy at the parish. In their children's religious education program, Kathy said, "We always fill out the forms that we're both parents." She told me that when one of their sons was preparing for confirmation, it "somehow came out" explicitly with his religious-ed teacher that the two are married. "I said, 'Yeah, she's my partner.' And she just said, 'Well, God bless you guys,' or something like that. It was very affirming."

Over the years, they've felt welcome in their parish, though they did mention one negative experience that stood in contrast. A "very, very fervent deacon," at the parish spoke out when marriage equality was being debated in their state. Gianna said, he " . . . began to speak about [same-sex marriage] as an abomination, blah blah blah. [However,] all of the sudden it just stopped, and that whole message went away. . . . I suspect he really was self-anointed at that point . . . I really think that he kind of spoke out of line, and I don't know that it really represented what the parish itself believes. He's still a part of us." This dynamic, in which church leadership did not seem to match the ethos of the wider community, is one that other couples discussed as well. A couple examples will be highlighted below. It can be tricky when priests are moved in and out of parishes, yet the people who remain must deal with ongoing effects of changing leadership.

In light of the church's official stance against gay relationships, Kathy and Gianna thought about "looking elsewhere" for worship, but repeatedly decided against it. Kathy explained: "For me, there's a familiarity [in the mass]. It's deep-rooted, like family. And it goes back. It brings back, for me, family as well. My mom, my grandmother, meeting her at church. . . . There's a familiarity to it."

"Communion is very important" to both of them. "I see the Catholic church as a vehicle," Gianna said. "And it's also something [that] has been created mostly by men. It's a vehicle for God's message, but it's not God in and of itself. It was created by Jesus. But it's been formed and carried on by men, and as humans we all have our faults and our failings . . . I've grown up, and in some sense have an agreement with the Catholic church that there are some things I'm just not going to accept for myself that I understand is part of them and their doctrine. But you know I enjoy and believe and see the beauty in the ancient ritual in [the mass] and see the connection back to Jesus. We relive the last supper at every communion, and that's beautiful. And that's Jesus. What the priest says standing at the pulpit is not necessarily always God-given."

Marty and Liam were also very active in Dignity, through which they celebrated their holy union. Ten years later, they wed legally, though "they never thought [they'd] see gay marriage in [their] lifetime." As previously discussed, they adopted two children (Marcus and Kayla) out of the foster care system and committed to raising them Catholic. The kids "went through The Rite of Christian Initiation for Children. It was at St. Mary's that all that happened. Introducing our kids to a life of faith to give them a tradition was something important," Marty said. "But right around that time was when Ratizger became pope. And when he said gay parents do violence to their children, [it] was incredibly hurtful. I've often said if I've ever done anything holy in my life it was raising these two kids and giving them a home. And because we didn't image male and female that somehow we were causing damage to them, when the reality was that leaving them in a foster care system with no parents is where trauma and damage is done. So the idea [that] what was most holy to us could actually be called sinful and damaging, there was a sense of: *You don't understand the reality of our lives, of our lived experience, where grace is."*

In spite of the negative assessment of same-sex parenting, which Marty identified as out-of-touch and hurtful, Liam and Marty *loved* St. Mary's. "It's a giant city church" comprised of four language-communities, Liam explained. There was an unofficial "kid's section" of the church, where many of the families sat, which was "wild. Because there are a lot of babies. We procreate a lot. But the interesting thing was: There were gay and lesbian families there, and there were mixed-race families there. There were single moms, families by adoption, families by my-sister-can't-take-care-of-this-kid-anymore. I mean, every stripe of human being you could ever imagine was there. And it was like we all take care of each other's kids."

"You couldn't tell [by] looking whose kids belonged to whom. It was that kind of place," Dan added.

"Because often, when they turn a certain age, like ten, they're like, 'I want nothing to do with you. I will be in church, but I'm sitting with Jayden,' right? A great experience," Liam said.

Liam and Marty served as ministers in the parish. In fact, they were personally invited by one of the parish priests, Fr. Peter—"an inclusive and wonderful guy." Fr. Peter told them they have gifts to bring to the community, telling them: "You'll be a lector" and "You look like a eucharistic minister," Liam said.

Fr. Peter "had only one sermon ever: 'God is love,'" Marty interjected.

"Yeah. He never changed topics," Liam said. "[We thought,] *You've gotta spice it up here, you know, power of evil? Something. Give us something,*" Liam responded.

"Nope! Nope. 'God is love. Until you get that down, I'm not giving you anything else!'" Marty said. Liam and Marty responded affirmatively to the invitation from this parish leader, whose one sermon in word and deed was love. They got "really involved" at the parish as ministers. The family flourished in a thriving and diverse church community, of which they were an integral part.

Chapter 4

Then Fr. Peter left the community and "a new guy came in"—Fr. Don. The first Sunday that Fr. Don preached, Liam and Marty greeted him after mass. They introduced themselves and mentioned that their children "need the sacraments. We said we'd like to come talk to you about initiation for our children," Liam said. "So, weirdly, we never hear from him. But, you know, he's new, busy. Whatever. Fast forward three months. It's the third Sunday of Advent, pink, Gaudete Sunday. I'm a eucharistic minister and so I go do the whole thing, pray beforehand, and Don was fine I guess. And then I get a call at home, like it's seven, and it's Fr. Don. He goes, 'I need to talk to you.' I'm like, 'Okay. What?' He goes, 'Well, you're not going to be able to serve anymore as eucharistic minister.' I'm like, 'What?' I thought he was joking. He said, 'Yeah, you're living in a relationship without the benefit of marriage.' So I say, 'I have an idea. Marry us.' 'Of course you know I can't do that,' [he responded.] 'Well, I'd like to understand your reasoning.' His whole reasoning was blabber. You know, Marty and I had done marriage preparation for Dignity. We prepared ten couples for it. I had the theology down pretty well about primacy of conscience and that the sacrament is between two adults, that the community witnesses through the person of the priest, blah, blah, blah. We've wrestled with the church teaching and we know what it is. And as we stand before God, this is where we stand."

"So he says, 'Listen, I know you're really smart, but this is just what it is, okay? So you're not going to be able to serve.' I said, 'Did you make this decision? Or did someone else make this decision?' He said, 'It's my decision.' So I got off the phone." Liam and Marty wrote to Fr. Don's superior,[3] asking whether Fr. Don speaks for him, and inviting him "to come to dinner at our house and meet our family and have a conversation. He writes back [about] four days later. I get a letter back saying, 'I really appreciate the letter. This is a local parish issue. I want you to know that I am thinking very clearly about this, but I have to let the parish leadership handle that.'" The next day, Liam got a call from the priest [Fr. Rick] who was the "overall [canonical] pastor" at St. Mary's, asking to talk. He came to Liam and Marty's home for dinner. The kids were "adorable" and "on his lap within twenty minutes of eating." Ultimately, Fr. Rick "says, 'Look, we got to work some stuff out and I need some time. I'm going to ask you to just take a leave of absence as a eucharistic minister for a little while." So Liam and Marty took a break from ministry, while their children entered into the process of initiation at the parish.

I'd like to highlight a couple of things about this story. One is the paradox of the couple being asked by one priest (who knew about their marriage status) to more fully participate in the parish by engaging in ministries, and subsequently being told by another priest *in the same parish* that they could not minister because they were together "without the benefit of marriage." *I thought he was joking.* The second is the way that Liam chose to handle Fr. Don's decision. First, he asked Fr. Don to more fully explain his reasoning and—in turn—offered his own, informed theological perspective to explain his dissenting view. He followed up by inviting those with decision-making power into conversation around the dinner table, in their home—in the hope of better understanding one another and finding a reconciling solution. Having this encounter in Liam and Marty's home opened a door for the priest to see *the reality of their lives, their lived experience where grace is* in order to gain a richer understanding of the implications and impact of official church teaching and the on-the-ground application of it. The church could use more of this kind of honest dialogue and encounter between the laity and ordained about church teachings, understanding that would require *openness* on both sides and incredible *courage* and *charity* from those with less (or no) decision-making power, who are also most impacted by said teachings. Pope Francis's move toward synodality seems to be pushing us in the right direction, toward these types of encounters.

In the case of St. Mary's, Fr. Don left within months, but "in the meantime, there's a lot of unraveling of a lot of stuff," asserted Liam. He and Marty were not the only gay parishioners to be affected, and it "created this rift in the community," Marty said. At the liturgy during which catechumens were initiated into the church (of which their children were a part), there were about "thirty catechumens. It's like they're coming in droves. [St. Mary's is the] kind of place that draws people. And so the adults come up first and they do their thing, and then they bring the kids up," Liam described. He explained that, for children participating in the liturgy, parents stand with them instead of godparents. Therefore he and

Chapter 4

Marty stood up with Marcus and Kayla. Liam teared up as he continued the story: "I'm going to cry. When they acknowledge the parents are there, not the godparents, Fr. Rick says, 'And how 'bout those dads?' The place erupts in applause, like jubilant applause—clearly the spirit of the place. Yeah. The people were with us, and we had a spiritual leader who was able to see that the people were with us."

"But the irony of 'No, you're not allowed to be here and do public ministry . . . [Liam] would have been a eucharistic minister that day, but he was not allowed," Marty added. "Yet our kids could be celebrated. Our relationship could be recognized." (*The irony*. This so clearly resonates with Luke's experience above: *There's a dichotomy there*.)

"Yes, our parenthood of those children was acknowledged. It's like the microcosm of the whole thing. That's the struggle right there," Liam replied.

As a result of their being dis-invited from ministry and the wider rift that occurred in what had been a radically inclusive community, St. Mary's "stopped feeling like home" for Liam, Marty, and their kids. "We needed help raising two kids. We needed a community of people that were going to help be our village. And [being removed from ministry because of marital status] was a clear: *Whether you're part of the village is a question*, so it never really felt the same to me. You know, we're two white men raising two black kids, there's enough going on just in that description to feel like, *Okay, I'm going to seek support*. Well, in a place where we had formerly found a great deal of support . . . [to be] just kind of dismissed . . . Yeah, [that sense of being supported] really stopped. But it's also after that whole period when Ratzinger said gay parents do violence to their children. And so I think that's when the real break with St. Mary's was. [Looking at Marty,] You really said to me, 'I can't do this anymore.'"

"Right," Marty confirmed. "I felt the hypocrisy. I was being a hypocrite. When a church says it believes that about me. You know, *I'm not welcome here*. I'm clearly told *I don't belong here, nor is my family recognized or valued as other families are*. So since family was so important, Liam got on the board of the children's school. We plugged ourselves in with the soccer moms. If the church wasn't going to meet that kind of need . . .

And we're still a new family, so that's challenging under any circumstances. So we tapped into where resources were for us . . . we plugged into Rainbow Families which was a community of gay and lesbian families in [the area]." They sought the support and community their family needed elsewhere.

When I spoke with Marty and Liam, they were not actively practicing in a parish community. Whether they would re-engage was an ongoing question. "It is a tension in our relationship," Marty said. "Liam loves community. He's drawn to the eucharist. Having a worshiping community is something that's really important to him. We have good friends, one woman who is an Episcopal priest. We'll often go to the Episcopal church. The Easter Vigil is his all-time favorite, and we've been pretty committed to getting to the Triduum and being part of that. If we're with family for Christmas and Easter, we'll still participate. He misses that regular community and would love to find a Catholic community. I've become interested in mindfulness. I'm in a two-year program to become a certified mindfulness instructor, so meditation and prayer to me have been meshing together. So I'm Catholic in the Richard Rohr sense of the word. I recently read Paul Knitter's *Without Buddha, I Could Not Be a Christian*. And that really captures where I am. So I'm not as drawn to the institutional church. But I can tell you the Catholic church informs my sense of grace and sacraments and incarnation. All the major themes in my life are rooted in the tradition I grew up with. So in one sense I feel more Catholic than I've ever been in my life. Liam's explicitly Catholic. I'm implicitly Catholic. Figuring all that out gets tricky sometimes."

"Yeah," Liam agreed.

Bernadette and Anne, who met as Catholic Workers and adopted two children out of the foster care system, also find relating to Catholicism tricky. They've never really been connected to a parish, but they live on "the same block as a soup kitchen run by [a men's religious order]." "For twenty-eight years . . ." Anne said, " . . . that's been our church. And it's been really nice because it doesn't have the politics of a parish . . . it's basically just liturgy and then they go and run their soup kitchen all day. We walk down the block and [run our community organization]." Anne has been described as a "radical Catholic," which may be "as good as anything" to describe her, she stated. But, "I want to disassociate myself from the Catholic hierarchy. I one hundred percent believe in Jesus and the Gospels and the mass and much of the tradition and the cloud of witnesses and the whole package, minus the hierarchical structure and all the unjust laws it imposes. I have explored and looked into other faiths over the past several decades and haven't ever really been drawn to any of them. Part of that is an ethnic thing. I feel ethnically Catholic. . . . As long as we can go to mass at the soup kitchen, I feel fine. Although I would admit that [with] each of these new scandals [that] seem to be coming almost daily, I want to publicly detach myself from this church. Though I'm not sure how one does that."

"It's really difficult for me because I feel the same," Bernadette replied. "Very Catholic. It's very much a part of me and I can't express enough how much my life and my values are shaped by the Catholic Worker. I think if I left everything, I would still have my life rooted in the works of mercy. Catholic social teachings are just core to who I am, what I believe, what I love about the church. And I have a deepening appreciation for the early church and the history of the mystics and contemplative prayer. So I never want to be too far from all that. At the same time, the only way for me now to stay is to actively work for change, and that becomes challenging."

Bernadette explained, "We did not realize how insulated we were for so many years with most of the fabulous priests who would come to 'our house'"—the priests were "progressive" and would "say mass and go down and work in a soup kitchen. They're living out gospel values. So that was our world." In this environment, the couple "didn't connect to any church hierarchy." "But we've heard!" Anne said. "Our volunteers would come in with stories of the progressive church and all the wonderful things that happened, then the pastor gets changed and they repaint the building and fire all the committees and undo everything that the church community built up for twenty years. I feel like we've been secondhand witnesses to many of our friends' pain." Pain like what Liam and Marty—alongside others—experienced at St. Mary's.

With less "insulated" eyes, Anne and Bernadette have recently spent time working for church reform. For example, they work in solidarity with survivors of clergy abuse and are in favor of ordaining women; they'd like to see changes in church structure. In true activist-style, they organize and travel to bishops' meetings, doing political work that aligns with their commitment to mercy and justice. Yet Anne said she's "not sure how much energy [she's] going to continue to have to do this church reform work." She has little confidence that change is possible: "I feel like it's a hopeless battle. We have a better chance of stopping nuclear war. A lot of our friends are working on stopping nuclear war full time. I think they have a better chance of succeeding than us."

"Oh, I hope you're wrong!" Bernadette replied. "At one point a priest friend of ours said, 'Oh my God. You can't go out there and fight Goliath.' I don't know. I keep thinking maybe we're at a tipping point where some change will happen, and that would be beautiful."

In the meantime, Anne and Bernadette's sense of Catholicism is not bound up with the church's hierarchy. Their "very Catholic" spirits are nourished by their social justice work (rooted in the gospels), daily prayer practices (for Bernadette, centering prayer in particular), regular mass attendance, "surrendering" as parents, and reading and reflecting on scripture or other spiritual readings to determine "how they relate to [their] lives." They keep *being* church, living out their Catholicism with others, and trying to hold out hope that church teachings and structures may change for the better.

Again and again, stories I heard illustrated that practices within— and the overarching "spirit" of—particular parishes profoundly affected experiences of church and whether folks felt truly welcome. You may remember Brian and Michael, who've taken on special responsibility for their nephews after they lost their dad. Brian describes himself "as a Catholic," who has "never really been a fallen away Catholic. I mean in college I maybe didn't go to mass every Sunday. But there was a chapel on campus and the opportunity was there, and I even went to mass while I was there." However, "I thought of it more as an obligation," until he and his husband Michael moved, six years earlier, to the city where they now live. "I would always say to myself, if I just get one thing out of this [mass], it was a successful trip. So when I opened myself up to that, long before I even came out, I was getting things out of going to church . . .

But it wasn't until I arrived here and went to [the open and affirming Catholic parish] down the street" that Brian really felt welcomed. "The priest was wearing a rainbow stole and he was doing the mass for Pride and he talked for the whole twenty minutes about the marginalization of gays in the church and how we should all be together and one, and welcome these people as your brothers and sisters. The whole place stood up and clapped. Being from the Midwest, we never heard anything positive coming from the pulpit about gays and lesbians."

Brian "found his way" to another gay-friendly Catholic church in the city, which has a supportive priest and a ministry for LGBT parishioners. "Then I realized, *Oh my gosh. You can be welcomed in the church. All they have to do is turn the welcome sign on,* you know?" He continued, "I feel like I've had a renewal and awakening in the church because of this church here. I know you're not supposed to fall in love with the preacher and the [particular] church and all that, it's about the universal thing, but the universal church doesn't really welcome me." He referenced an incident that had just occurred, when "[The local bishop] was advising, 'Don't go to any Pride events. It'll harm your children.' Okay. That kind of mentality needs to change. So that's why I'm here, to help change it. Give my witness. Give my point of view. You know, I'm a person. I'm a human being. I'm baptized in the church and therefore am a member of the body of Christ. And so I'm staying. You can't kick me out. You can't. You shouldn't be saying all that stuff if you're going to be a loving, open church. Especially in light of the sexual abuse crisis, where they've been harming all the children and we've been sitting on the sidelines, [feeling] outside the church, saying: *Can you let us in?* That part hurts. The hierarchy doesn't even want to see your face. But I'm going to bring my face around and show up and talk out loud, but not be rude. Say my piece because my relationship is with God. I've talked every day to Jesus and the Lord God and Mary . . . I say my prayers in the middle of the day . . . that will never stop. No matter what they say about me, that won't stop. My relationship with God has never been stronger. I feel confident about myself and who I am, and I feel like the church needs to reach out to us. We certainly are reaching up to them, asking them to give us a chance, give us a platform to say: 'Hello guys, we're here.'" This echoes what Maggie wants from the church, as noted in the introduction. *We're here.* Take that as a starting point for dialogue. "I feel bad that ultimately the hierarchy is sort of dug in."[4]

"You're more engaged than you have ever been, too. When we first met, you went [to mass] . . . out of duty, not out of a desire to really be part of a community," Michael said.

"Now I feel part of the community. Yeah," Brian replied. "And I'm shocked at the young kids. These guys are twenty-something year olds and they're some of the liveliest members of the church, most active. Some of us older guys, if you're older than fifty, you've been listening to the catechism of 'intrinsically evil.' 'Disordered' and all that . . . You wouldn't be on this planet without a disorder. The world is disordered. You know, but to point fingers at [LGBTQ persons] and . . . scapegoat [them], that's problematic. The Catholic church is huge. It could change this whole tide against gays all around the world if they could wrap their arms around this. Do some studies. Do something. Read a book. Commission studies. Where's all that?"

Brian repeated that it is the first time in his life that he "actually feel[s] a part of the Catholic church . . . You know, you're always on the edge because they were always talking so poorly about you. But this place [meaning his current parish], they say at the mass: All are welcome. Well you know all *are* welcome because you feel welcomed and you feel a part of the community. You feel a sense of contentment. Then you can think about your faith or think about yourself and how you relate to the rest of the church. The renewal . . . comes from being welcomed by the community and being part of the community, feeling like you have a voice in the community, feeling like you're heard, that you're not pushed aside, marginalized, scapegoated, treated as less than, less than human. You get that when you go out into the general world. They tell you all kinds of things about you[rself], keep you from housing, social security benefits for your spouse . . . it's an uphill battle every day. Why should I have to do that even inside the church itself, where I'm supposed to feel loved?" Brian continued.

Michael, a non-Catholic who often worships with Brian, said: "I think being an outsider also inside . . . I've noticed that there is a sense of pride amongst members here that I haven't seen in general, just about being Catholic. [For instance, Brian] talking about where he worships and how he is part of that community. That's something that is really interesting to find, specifically with this parish. A lot of the social programming allows for that as well. It is community both inside of these walls and outside of the walls . . . We have friends. Before we would rush in and rush out of a mass, in another place. . . . Here you have friends in these walls. People gather. After church, people stay for half an hour and just gab in the back of the church. That's friendship. That's people coming together and say[ing], *How was your week? What's going on?* We have a friend who is sick, and they're like, *how can they help?* . . . That's what you hope a community is like, right? They look after each other and they socialize together and they celebrate things happening in their lives." Brian adds that "it's about fellowship, community, helping others out, giving back to the community." *Church as a community of friends*, united in friendship with one another and God, through the power of the Holy Spirit.

Michael's parents were periodically practicing Methodists. He attended a Quaker school, a faith he described as "super liberal and flexible and there's no hierarchy. It's very like, be yourself." Growing up, many of his friends were Jewish. He had "a black mitzvah." He was surrounded by "a very diverse group," but he didn't know many Catholics. Today, he considers himself more "Quaker-like" than Methodist: "I really love those values and I still consider those my values."

When he met Brian, Michael had only "perceptions" of what Catholicism was, based on "what was being said about the Catholic church—that they were not for people like me, and it was not going to be a welcoming environment. A lot of what I had were the headlines that were out there in the news. When we were dating—we've talked about this many times—I struggled with [Brian] being Catholic. It was a point of contention. I just didn't understand the duality of how Brian could be a practicing Catholic and still be gay and merge these two things together in his life. It was really a point of conflict, because at that point I kind of saw it as a weakness, that he couldn't find the gumption to break away from something that was not supporting him. I wouldn't say we fought about it, but we had many intense discussions about it."

After dating five or six years, Michael came to understand more fully Brian's connection to the Catholic church. "He was raised this way, and he was able to make his own peace . . . he was able to find his own relationship with God in his own way. It wasn't like . . . I was going to be able to break him of that. Fast forward to today—not even today, maybe five years into it—I started to understand *that was just who he was* and he's very principled and very structured. And I was like, I actually like [that] . . . he is very principled and very structured . . . He knows who he is. He's very disciplined about the things that make him a complete person. He has values and a point of view, but also he's dependable that way. He's very centered."

In years past, Michael would sometimes attend mass with Brian, especially when they lived near Brian's family.[5] "I would go because it was a family thing. He'd often go with his mom and nieces and nephews . . . you don't want to be the person who is not going to mass with the whole family, right? That's just how you become part of the family. It drew you into the whole family . . . [they're] very Catholic so it's part of how you bond with everyone. I don't have to believe everything in order to [participate] . . . At the same time, I started to get more out of it." Michael now regularly attends mass with Brian in his open and inclusive parish. He's moved from being "fearful" of Catholicism to being "open and appreciative. I sing the praises of this organization and I [better understand that] it is different in every parish, in every community, and you can't judge it all together. I have the same hopes and dreams as Brian does for the church to change. For me, it hurts seeing him deal with it, understanding and acknowledging it's not going to change in our lifetime, like overnight. But I really do respect all the work that's being done and I encourage it. It's a part of my life now, the Catholic church. It's something I embrace. I find myself on the other end now, talking to my friends growing up. They're trying to understand where I stand with it, and where Brian is, and I'm having to play this role of defender, explaining what it means to be in this duality of not being fully embraced by the church but yet finding a place in the church where you are accepted."[6]

Chapter 4

Let's return to Dan's story, which was highlighted in the introduction of the book. After struggling in high school and college to integrate his sexual and religious identities, to the point of being suicidal, he took a break from the Catholic church. He left in anger, wondering why the presence of LGBTQ persons was hidden. As already noted, he returned to the church years later. The story of what brought him back is compelling.

Dan was living in a big city, across the country from his parents. They kept encouraging him to go to mass at a parish nearby, where a retired priest from Dan's home parish (growing up) had been transferred. When his dad would come to visit Dan, he'd meet up with the priest. "But it really wasn't until my mom had been sick for years and years—she fought cancer for a very long time. I went back home for about a month. A little over a month. We were caring for her at home until she passed. Jaime came out for the funeral. It was really nice. All the family came together. After I came back to [the city]—it wasn't right away, it wasn't until the summer that I started coming. [I] was kind of feeling a bit lost, still grieving. I'm like, I might as well give it a shot. So I came [here, to the parish]."

At mass, someone from the LGBT ministry group [Dan now serves on the ministry team] got up and made an announcement. It's "what they do at the end of every 5:15 mass, about being welcoming. That was huge for me!" On the ministry team, Dan noted, "We talk about being very thoughtful and basically doing our mission statement . . . in the announcements, saying all are welcome and it doesn't matter. . . . not just LGBTQ, but you are welcome no matter what point you are in your journey of faith. That was just as powerful to me, too, because it wasn't like [you have to have] this black and white understanding of your faith or the Sunday school version. It's like [we're] all kind of struggling with what being Catholic means to us and it's a safe place to have those kinds of conversations."

Dan emphasized how important that announcement was for him: he was welcome as a gay man and as a spiritual seeker who could question and examine religious teachings. He noted how mundane announcements seemed as a child ("just get through" them and "go have donuts"!) but this seemingly small gesture of welcome was "huge" for him. The clear message is repeated every week: gay parishioners do not have to hide here. (This reminds me of what Brian said: *All they have to do is turn the welcome sign on.*) Dan remained "standoffish," but he came back to mass again. "It took me probably coming to mass a couple of times before I went up and introduced [myself]. Actually, I went to faith sharing, and that was the first [LGBT ministry] event that I did. That was the beginning of starting to find community again. So that brought me back. I became more and more involved here . . . it really was [finding] community after so long [that] I started to feel some of those same feelings of belonging that I hadn't felt since high school and college."

In this gay-friendly parish, Dan could return to the comforting ritual of the mass in his time of grieving. "It made me feel closer to my parents, just to experience that. But as I met people and started getting involved with [the LGBTQ parish ministry], that was my first real opportunity as an adult to start looking at my faith and what I believe and why." Dan said, "I grew up with a very strong, unquestioned faith." It's a struggle for him to "reconnect" after "dismissing all that." He continues to discern: "What does it mean to be Catholic? What does it mean *for me*? [In light of] the Pennsylvania crisis that came out about a year ago . . . I'd say the last year has been particularly rough and really a lot of anger and questioning of things. The important thing is . . . where I stand in my faith now, I still feel a sense of community . . . I'm surrounded by people where we're all kind of struggling to grapple with: What is our faith? What holds us together? How do we exist as a community within this larger hierarchical institutional church?" Dan indicated that the LGBTQ ministry in the parish "really helped facilitate" this reconnection with the Catholic church. "I would not have just walked into a Catholic church off the street and been active. It's been that personal connection that brought me back." *He belongs.*

Jaime goes to mass with Dan occasionally, but is "much further away" from a full reintegration into the Catholic church. At the same time, the couple plans to foster and adopt children and are in agreement that they "want to educate them about being Catholic." Raising their children Catholic is important to them both because of their own upbringings in the faith tradition, which engrained a "basic value system" that continues to guide them. Catholicism provided a core sense of morality—"why we have to forgive people, why we have to help others." They want to pass that on. Yet they foresee a struggle. Dan longs for their marriage to be recognized as valid and sacramental in the Catholic church: "Especially if you are thinking of children. Our marriage is not less than the marriage of these other straight couples." Dan asserted that when the magisterium does not recognize their relationship as equal and sacramental it "puts us at a disadvantage. And I don't know how our kids are going to process that, and how we can raise them without having any bad feelings toward the Catholic church when they see that the marriage of their parents is not being recognized. We probably have to bring them [to church], but at the same time warn them that we are here, but really we are not necessarily super welcome. That's the kind of dissonance that will be difficult to work around if we want to bring them to a Catholic church."

"I see what we have, and [it's] like my parents' marriage," Dan continued. "Our relationship is just as strong. It might look different, but I know I want to spend the rest of my life with Jaime. And that's a source of frustration and anger with the church when they see our relationship as less than . . . if we could have our marriage recognized by the church as sacramental, that's something we would want." Jaime agreed. He understands their marriage as sacramental and like his parents' marriage, who are "very stereotypical Catholics from Latin America." Jaime said he tries "to follow the same type of values and practices" he's seen modeled for him by his parents. "I don't see [our marriage] in a different way. I don't know how to do it in a different way."

Jaime said it's challenging to identify as a "hundred percent Catholic," because "every time you say ['I'm Catholic'], at least from my way of thinking, you are comfortable at some degree about not being recognized from the church. That makes it more difficult if you're thinking of having kids eventually. I can stand some sort of rejection. But I think it's unfair for me to put that burden on my children if we have children. That makes no sense." This sentiment harkens back to Jenn (in chapter 3) discussing the family rejection that she and Steph and their children feel. It is one thing to experience mistreatment or a lack of recognition or full integration as adults, she explained. It's another to subject one's children to that.

A sense of protection kicks in. Perhaps compromises one was willing to make for oneself seem less tenable when children are involved. As discussed above, this struggle was part of the reason Liam and Marty are no longer practicing in a Catholic parish—they attributed their departure from St. Mary's to a lack of full recognition of their marriage and family by church leaders and how that would affect their children.

Being fully recognized and known—truly seen, welcomed, and celebrated—is plainly the opposite of being hidden. It allows for and nourishes freedom and authenticity. Toward the end of my conversation with Kathy and Gianna, Kathy said, "To this day, I still don't feel like I would be able to hold [Kathy's] hand in mass. You see the older couples. You see all the couples go through their various stages in church, right? [Recall her commenting on how 'neat' it is that they've sat in the same section of church every Sunday and the community has watched their kids grow up.] You have the younger couples, and then you have the ones that are having their babies, and then their kids are teenagers and you know, kinda in that survival mode. You see the older ones . . . [Looking at Gianna], every now and then you do reach out to touch me, and I'm like [she flinches and pulls back] kind of one of those things. I would like to be able . . . My guess is as we get older, when we're ladies it's okay if you link your arms together or something like that, because you're now helping each other . . . I think it would be a great day if you could just be yourself in church, and be yourself wherever you are. Not just be yourself, but show your love and affection."[7] *Be yourself, express your affection, and not have to hide.*

Duality. Irony. Dichotomy. Dissonance. Inside and outside, welcome and unwelcome, at the same time. These are some of the ways couples described their experiences in churches. Couples struggle to find their place within institutional Christian churches (with their respective, official teachings about marriage and family) and in local church communities. They long for familiar and beloved ritual, spiritual nourishment, belonging, community, and full integration. They want to be explicitly recognized, authentically known, and unconditionally loved. They seek to maintain tight connections between *family* and *religious* identity and rituals. They want their gifts to be appreciated and utilized in parishes and parish-sponsored outreach efforts. They desire their relationships, children, and families to be honored as *equal* and *graced*.

Sometimes, queer couples find church communities that satisfy these longings. They breathe. They heal. And they thrive. The Body of Christ would do well to listen to these couples—and others like them—about the kinds of messages, attitudes, and practices that create and maintain hospitable communities. And on the flip side, what harms the spirit and drives these siblings in Christ away.

Notes

1. As noted in chapter 3, Steve's parents initially said, "Oh no" when Steve came out to them; they moved past their initial dismay with the help of Steve's uncle, a priest.

2. To be fair, attitudes and experiences within Protestantism on these matters vary significantly based on denomination and local community.

3. The parish is administered by a religious order.

4. Here Brian acknowledges the efforts of Fr. Jim Martin and Fr. Bryan Massingale. He's "thankful that they're there" and opening up conversations about queer people in the Catholic church.

5. They've since moved farther away from Brian's family.

6. Michael and Brian's interview was so rich. I've woven much of their interview into the text. They describe themselves as "the interracial, intergenerational, gay couple." One could add interreligious. What became clear through our conversation is how much unity they've found in diversity, how much joy and connection in the exploration of differences. At the conclusion of their interview: Brian said, "I love you" to Michael, and Michael responded, "I love you too." With tears in his eyes, Brian said, "I still love him, from the day I met him. You'll always be the love of my life." "Thank you," Michael responded, adding "Is this an interview or a therapy session?" Indeed, the two shared from the heart. I am beyond grateful for their willingness—and the willingness of all of the couples in the study—to open themselves up, giving me a glimpse of their love.

7. Kathy acknowledges that this hesitancy to be openly affectionate is partly generational. She and Gianna were in their late fifties when we spoke. Kathy said, "We came from a time where you just couldn't. It wasn't a comfortable thing . . . Something would happen. Not like Stonewall, [but something] would happen. I never feared I would be arrested, but . . ." She notes that "the younger generation" "feel very free to do that [meaning, show affection in public], and I think it's wonderful."

CHAPTER 5

Catholic Institutions

Tension, Integration, and Belonging

TONY IS A FORMER PRIEST WHO'S "BEEN INVOLVED IN CHURCH MINISTRY [his] whole life." He comes from a large, Catholic family, and from the age of seven or eight, he thought he was called to the priesthood. As an adult, he entered seminary and was "in the religious life for six years."

He had what he describes as "an aha moment" while in Rome studying: "I went to one of my favorite churches. I sat down in front of the statue and I said, 'Okay, God. I need an answer. Is this what I'm supposed to be doing? Through all of this, I knew I was gay and did not hide it. If anyone ever asked, I was always very truthful. And as clear as day, God basically said to me, *Get up and leave.* And I did. I left. And never looked back. I tell people all the time that religious life was huge. I grew a lot. It was huge for me. So I don't look back on it with regret at all. It was a good time for me. But I also knew it was time to leave. And it gave me the opportunity to meet him." Tony turned to look at his husband Pete, to whom he'd been married eleven years. You might remember Tony and Pete from chapter 1; I discussed their fidelity to one another, expressed in joint care of Tony's elderly mother.

Since leaving the priesthood, Tony's been a jack of all trades in Catholic settings, working as a youth minister, pastoral associate, parish administrator, and professor. But it was his most recent experience in parish work that radically changed his life. "Three years ago, the bishop called me and asked me to go with a priest to St. Rose of Lima to overhaul the place," Tony said.

"It was in the heart of a gay neighborhood," Pete added.

"It's in a gay neighborhood," Tony confirmed—a detail crucial to what follows.

The once vibrant parish—standing room only at masses—had been "ruined" when the former bishop placed an extremely conservative pastor there, Tony explained. Participation in the parish "went down to nothing." Tony's bishop hoped to revive the place by sending him to work with a new pastor there.

Within weeks of Tony's arrival at the parish, tragic circumstances meant the pastor he'd been asked to work with needed to be replaced. Thankfully, another pastor was assigned to the parish, who "worked great" with Tony. The two began to resuscitate parish life. The pastor encouraged them to actively reach out to folks in the local community, making connections through the LGBT Center. They did that outreach work together. "It was really good," Tony said.

Tony's description of their efforts to leave the church walls and go forth into the community reminds me of Pope Francis's description of the church "as a mother with an open heart" in *Evangelii Gaudium*. The Pope praises a church that goes out to others "to reach the fringes"; a church with open doors; a church "where there is a place for everyone" and where the prodigal son can return home.[1]

It was really good.

Some older parishioners, "angry" with changes at the parish, would "go after" the pastor. In response, Tony said, "[h]e'd basically say go find a new place if you're not happy. And he could. He was the priest." Tony felt protected by him as they ministered to the LGBTQ community, but eventually the pastor got called elsewhere and left. At that point, the bishop named Tony as parish administrator. According to Tony, that "was when the hate started."

"They could come after me. I wasn't a priest. And so the old guard [at the parish] started telling lies . . . [such as] I locked them out [of the church building] because I 'hate Mary' and they had to pray the rosary out in the parking lot. They even took pictures of themselves locked out.

[Also, they claimed] I was putting abortion material throughout the parish. Not true," Tony said, emphatically. Apparently, someone found a pamphlet with information about birth control and abortion that was sent by the county in an envelope with someone's marriage license; Tony said they "took a picture of it, sent it to Church Militant and Life Site News," and claimed that Tony had spread such material "all over the parish." Local people who read the information on social media began reacting.

At the time, St. Rose of Lima parish leaders were planning an "*Always Our Children* mass," intended to be a "big welcome" for members of the LGBTQ community.[2] Unfortunately, what should have been joyful was tainted by violence. Tony explained: "The police department had to get involved. There were snipers on the roof" because people were threatening to kill him. "It was horrible."

In spite of the threats, the "mass went off beautifully. It was packed." Tony recalled one attendee in particular, who approached Tony after mass. The seventy-six-year-old man told Tony, "'I have not been at mass since I was eighteen years old when I told a priest I was gay, and he told me I was not welcome.' The man was crying. He said, 'I finally feel like I can come home again.'"

"I have many of those stories," Tony added. Prodigal son-like stories of return. Stories of belonging. Stories that Tony holds close to his heart.

Once the *Always Our Children* mass was over, the negative commotion "really died down," Tony said. He assumed all would be fine. But the calm was short-lived. Harassment "ramped up again" following the release of the Pennsylvania report[3] about widespread sexual abuse by priests. Tony said, people "decided to come after me because, of course, [they falsely assumed] I'm a gay man, so I'm a pedophile. I started to get many emails that I was a pedophile and I needed to resign immediately."[4] Some were from parishioners who would sign their name to correspondence, so Tony knew who they were. Others used false names. Detractors were coming from inside and outside the parish.

"I fought back," Tony said, believing they'd "gone too far." Tony hired a lawyer.

CHAPTER 5

People were "calling the parish—I mean, off the hook—screaming, sending mail, sending me email. A lot of it would be anonymous. I didn't even know you could send emails that you can't track, but you can." People threatened to "throw Molotov cocktails into the church. One guy wrote on a . . . site that he was going to stand across the street on the roof and snipe me off when I walked in." The police department got involved again and brought in the FBI "because it was so bad." Apparently in some warped attempt to protect the purity of the Catholic faith, people used lies, threats, and violence as their tactics. They terrorized Tony. "They lit the doors of the church on fire one Sunday morning," he said. "They broke into the offices and wrote NO FAGS on the wall."

It's important to note here that this sort of treatment of any person is explicitly condemned in Catholic teaching and calls for active resistance. In *Fratelli Tutti*, Pope Francis writes:

> [T]here are those who appear to feel encouraged or at least permitted by their faith to support varieties of narrow nationalism, xenophobia and contempt, and even mistreatment of those who are different. Faith, and the humanism it inspires, must maintain a critical sense in the face of these tendencies, and prompt an immediate response wherever they rear their head. For this reason, it is important that catechesis and preaching speak more directly and clearly about the social meaning of existence, the fraternal dimension of spirituality, our conviction of the inalienable dignity of each person, and our reasons for loving and accepting all our brothers and sisters.[5]

"Through all of this, I want to say that the bishop was supporting me," Tony stated. As folks in the diocese were vehemently and publicly complaining to the bishop about Tony, he was Tony's loyal and staunch defender. "He even called me and said, 'I'm going to hire armed security for you while you are at work.'" The bishop—who called Tony to this ministry—was doing his best to protect him, publicly and privately.

In light of the scary details of this story, I turned to Pete and asked what it was like for him to see his husband endure this at work. "Well, at some point it was like *enough already*," Pete replied. "One day they put a photograph of me [on social media] and referred to Tony as a 'homosexualist,' whatever that means. [T]hey called me his sodomitical partner. I guess they were trying to find scandalous pictures of us, but all they found was a picture of me, him, and his mom in the kitchen one day, and another one of us fully clothed on the beach." When harassers put up a post that included a link leading to Tony and Pete's home address, Pete had had enough. He told Tony, "'Do something else. It's not about winning all the time. Because even if you win, you're losing because you are miserable and people are following you around.' I was like, 'Why? Enough of this Catholic shit. Be done with it.'"

Pope Francis acknowledges the danger of social media—including Catholic media—to destroy peoples' reputations and tear them down (the Pope has been victim to this himself). In *Gaudete et Exsultate*, he writes:

> Christians too can be caught up in networks of verbal violence through the internet and the various forms of digital communication. Even in Catholic media, limits can be overstepped, defamation and slander can become commonplace, and all ethical standards and respect for the good name of others can be abandoned. The result is a dangerous dichotomy, since things can be said there that would be unacceptable in public discourse, and people look to compensate for their own discontent by lashing out at others. It is striking that at times, in claiming to uphold the other commandments, they completely ignore the eighth, which forbids bearing false witness or lying, and ruthlessly vilify others. Here we see how the unguarded tongue, set on fire by hell, sets all things ablaze (cf. *Jas* 3:6).[6]

Tony and Pete's description of what they experienced is a painful illustration of the effects of such "verbal violence" and vilification. Indeed, the church building itself, along with Tony and Pete's life, had been set ablaze.

"I'm very good at filtering out all the noise and stuff," Pete added. "But when people are saying they might kill you . . . even though most of that stuff is just [coming from] a loud mouth, the way the world is now, you don't really know."

"So that was the final straw," Tony said. "They put our home address up [through a hyperlink] . . . That was the day I finally called the bishop and said, 'I can't do this anymore.'" Tony gave the bishop one month's notice.

"I was always supportive of what Tony had going on until people started to say we should die or whatever," Pete said. "To me it's not worth dying for. I don't want to be a martyr for these people. Like, it's not happening."

It's clear that when Pete encouraged Tony to "be done" with the "Catholic shit," he was referring to the moral-policing and harassment Tony faced from certain parishioners and ultraconservative Catholic organizations related to his gay identity, marital status, and ministry to the LGBTQ community. Pete was referring to Tony's work in a Catholic parish that had been made untenable, even dangerous, presumably by other Catholics. Pete was not suggesting a rejection of the whole of the Catholic tradition. In spite of everything, during our conversation Pete stated: "I was born a Catholic, and I'll die a Catholic."

Pete believes Catholicism is "true" and "real." He has a deep appreciation for the tradition. He takes comfort, he said, in knowing *what we are* and *what we believe*. He likes knowing he could attend mass anywhere in the world and "know exactly what was happening during mass." He "think[s] that [liturgical consistency] is something that sets Catholics apart and ties us together as a people . . . you don't have to be any color or come from any part of the world to be Catholic." Pete identifies with the saints and values the moral grounding the church provided him as a child. "[G]rowing up as a Catholic and going to CCD and going to church and having my mom always take us there was an important foundation in my life." Pete added, "I don't ever remember as a child in church being told anything about being gay, ever. You know, I don't know if it was the church I went to, or maybe it wasn't an issue back then, but nobody ever made me feel bad about who I was as a child when I went to church."

"But now they do," Tony responded. Gesturing toward Pete, he said, "His sister-in-law had to call me very recently because [Pete's] nephew is in CCD and has a good friend whose parents are lesbians. And they were told, 'No. Your kids can't be here [in religious education].' . . . And that's the same church [Pete] went to growing up."[7]

In the interview, Pete described his complicated relationship to the church. "It's really kind of weird because even though I'm not a churchgoer, I still identify very heavily as being Catholic." He feels "sad when [his] relatives are not choosing to have their children be Catholic." Tony described Pete as more of a cultural Catholic. Pete's Catholic identity is wed to his family and cultural identity. Pete is willing to go to mass, and doesn't "fight it," but Tony is the one in their relationship who has initiated regular mass attendance, rather than limited, special-occasion mass attendance, such as on Easter, Christmas, or for celebration of family sacraments. In the beginning of their relationship, Tony and Pete "went every Sunday. It wasn't even a question." But their weekly mass attendance has waned, Tony said, "and I think a lot of it has to do with the hate that was brought toward me. I mean, [Pete] has even said to me, I don't know if I believe in God anymore. Because it is so disgusting."

The disgusting treatment Tony endured while working at St. Rose of Lima has challenged Pete's faith in God and negatively impacted the couple's already-complicated relationship with the Catholic church. At one point in the interview, Tony faced Pete and asked, "But what do you *really* feel about the church?"

In response, Pete expressed criticism of the institutional church. He condemned clergy sexual abuse and the "spin" and "clever wording" that serves to cover up abuse. He doesn't "particularly care for any organization that has zero female input," which he thinks is true of the Catholic church. He is disgusted when the molestation of children is made into "a gay problem" which is "a big old bowl of shit, and they're trying to tell me it's a bowl of cherries." He condemned what he sees as an inordinate focus on the "sin" of gay relationships rather than "really listening to what Jesus said."

Pete suggests the church would be better off concentrating on Jesus's message and example: "Be kind. Don't judge people. Let the stranger in. You know, those kinds of things. *Here's this prostitute you're going to stone to death . . . Any of you never sinned before? Oh, no? Only the person who hasn't [sinned can] start throwing rocks.* You know?" Pete continued: "I just don't like that people seem so willing to not acknowledge their own problems, or where they're wrong, or where they're not exactly one hundred percent

Chapter 5

living the gospel, but when you try to call them out on their own shit then they have an excuse." He expressed frustration with what he sees as the misplaced priorities of church leaders. Ultimately, and importantly, Pete expressed a desire for them to emphasize and live out Jesus's ministry, focused on inclusion, forgiveness, and welcoming.

Let's return to St. Rose of Lima. A month after Tony gave his notice to the bishop, the church was overflowing with people for what Tony calls his "closing liturgy." A wide array of friends and supporters filled the church—Catholic, Protestant, Hindu, and Jewish. Some folks traveled hours to be there. It was standing room only. "It was absolutely incredible," Tony recalled. A beautiful, expansive, and bittersweet experience of church to end Tony's time at the parish.

"And so I left. I left horrified that I was having to leave. But I left more sad that so many of these people had found a home again, [but] most likely they were not going to have a home, which is what really pisses me off." When Tony thinks about the folks who found true belonging at St. Rose of Lima and yet were re-alienated due to Tony's upsetting departure, it continues to weigh on him.

"Just to end that story . . . Pete tells me this is what I need to focus on. And I try to . . . It's hard for me, but I try. I have received emails, social media contacts, letters in the mail from literally all over the world. And ninety-nine percent of it has been positive. I've received things from bishops. About a month and a half ago, I received a letter from the secretary of state of the Vatican, telling me that the pope was standing with me in solidarity."

Due to such support, Tony believes that the ultraconservative Catholics who harassed him and pushed him out of the parish ultimately lost in the long run. For Tony, the generous and genuine experiences of support and community win out. Nevertheless, many LGBTQ persons, like Tony, continue to face challenges as workers in Catholic institutions.

Notably, Pete reflected on the stark contrast between the Catholic settings Tony has worked in and his own work environment, which is not religiously affiliated. Pete explained that in his workplace, there is no need to "tiptoe around" and worry about "using the H word—the husband word" for fear of negative repercussions. At work, "I can be as gay as I want, I get all the benefits for him that I want, and he gets my pension.... [N]obody can ever tell me to not be gay, or be less gay, or tone it down. And I like that." Pete "likes the idea" that his organization recruits gay people, seeking out people from the LGBTQ community to enhance the workforce, as opposed to Catholic institutions where the message is: "it's okay to be gay but just don't practice."

I offer Tony and Pete's story as an entree to thinking about experiences that married, queer persons have as workers in Catholic institutions. Many stories of LGBTQ persons being fired from Catholic institutions have been widely publicized in the media in recent years, particularly as same-sex marriage has been legalized in the United States. I certainly did not anticipate focusing on this topic when I began interviewing couples about their marriages and faith commitments. However, reflection on fraught experiences within Catholic parishes and schools surfaced organically in conversations. I concluded while reviewing transcripts that these stories ought to be included in the book. Just as interviewees variously and sometimes simultaneously experienced rejection, exclusion, integration, and belonging in families and church communities (as discussed in chapters 3 and 4), they likewise had varied experiences in Catholic institutions in which they work. Some distressing experiences related to working in Catholic settings have been noted in the stories you've read thus far, but will be the focus of this chapter.

I heard powerful testimony about the daily vulnerability, and sometimes terror (as illustrated in Tony's story above) felt by gay and lesbian persons in their work environments, and related negative effects on their spirits and their married and family relationships. In contrast, I heard about the freedom that accompanies full support and authenticity in the workplace, and the positive effects that has on persons, marriages, and families. These experiences should give us pause and prompt us to consider what is at stake for LGBTQ persons in Catholic institutions, and for the whole people of God, especially when the message *it's okay to be gay, but just don't practice* practically functions to keep too many LGBTQ persons from being free and authentic at work, and too often feeds the moral policing of some Catholics by others, with social media as a common and dangerous tool.

CHAPTER 5

Working in Catholic Institutions
Steph and Jenn

Following her college graduation, Steph got a creative job in the city. When she was laid off, she "went kicking and screaming into the Catholic church" as a youth minister. Folks who knew her told her she'd be great at it, but Steph resisted. "I was like, no. I don't want to. I'm not the poster child for the Catholic church. I'm the last person that I feel should be doing that. Then slowly but surely I [got] what's been coined before as a God wink. I use God nod because in my world it's like a two by four to the head. Like, 'Are you gonna hear me now? Can you hear me now?' I just felt I was being called that way." So she took the plunge to answer the call. At the time of our interview, she'd been doing parish work for about eighteen years.

Steph recalled experiences in her time as a minister that she named *God-incidences* instead of *coincidences*. She said, "I've just kind of been placed for reasons and then I'm gone. I feel like I'm just getting plopped there, picked up, moved over, and plopped to wherever I'm needed." In our conversation, I was struck by Steph's vivid language of prayerful calling. She has a palpable sense of God placing her in particular settings in order to build young people up and strengthen their faith. She repeatedly used the language of vocation to describe her work in Catholic youth ministry. Each morning and evening, Steph asks God: "'Where do you need me today?'" And, however reluctantly, she goes where she is called. Steph acknowledged, however, that "working for God" in the church is "a stressful calling to have" as a queer person, particularly as a married queer person raising two children.

Steph's wife Jenn named the "constant fear" Steph manages related to her job. She told me how nervous Steph is to go to work every day, wondering: "*Is this going to be my last day?*"

Steph told an illustrative story about the daily vulnerability she feels at work. "So my second year there, I went in and the pastor said, 'Hey, do you have a minute?' I said, 'Yes.' He said, 'I want to talk to you in the office. I got a letter from a parishioner.' And I was like, *Okay. This is the moment. Steph, pull yourself together. Don't cry. Pull it together. This is going to be fine. Whatever happens next is gonna be fine.* And I talked to myself all the way down that hallway. I sat down and he said, 'I got a letter from a parishioner and I'm just going to read it and we'll talk about it afterward.' And I was like, *This is it. This is it.*

It turned out that the letter was about a fundraising event for teenagers. A parent disapproved of how goofy the teens were acting. "So he's reading the letter and he's like, 'Apparently she wants her money back, but didn't leave her number, so . . .'" He was joking about it, but in my heart I was prepared for: *I don't have a job tomorrow night.*" Steph was mentally doing damage control—worrying about how the news of her dismissal would come out, and how her family and the teens she works with would be affected. "You know, I worked so hard to give teens faith, that me being fired, I'm afraid, would break a lot of that for them, which pisses me off. [I] don't want to be the reason that they want to walk away, you know?" Steph's immediate concern for how her departure would affect the people she ministers to reminds me of Tony's parallel concern about how his leaving St. Rose of Lima might affect the parishioners who had found a home there. These sorts of fissures in church communities that result from the departure of a trusted LGBTQ minister, teacher, or administrator are real, devastating, and deserving of fuller attention.

Thankfully, it was not the day for Steph to be fired from her job at the parish. But the story powerfully shows the culture of fear that has been created in the Catholic church for LGBTQ workers who are married. Steph described the "constant conversation" she has with God as she attempts to reconcile her firm belief that God is "challenging [her] to stay in this arena" with the intense difficulty of doing so. "We box over that," Steph said.

She believes in working for change from the inside of the church. "If I'm outside complaining and fighting a problem, it's not going to do any good. It's like someone throwing rocks and they'll just ignore you. But if you're on the inside and you're genuine . . . I feel like you change hearts easier that way . . . because it's about changing people's minds and hearts more than anything. And I feel like that's much more successful from the inside out than the top down. But that's the struggle, because you have to do that cautiously and strategically . . . you have to think about who you tell and how you trust," she said. Adding, "There is so much trust and faith in God in that piece." She tells herself, "*When it's my time to go, I guess it's my time to go.*"

You have to think about who you tell and how you trust. In light of the well-publicized firing of LGBTQ persons in Catholic institutions, Steph and Jenn are *cautious* and *strategic* about their words and actions. While some folks at the parish know that Steph is lesbian with a wife and children, her policy is to not discuss this with any of the teens. If someone asks, she won't lie. But unless a person is eighteen, she doesn't reveal this part of her identity or family life. When civil unions were legalized in their state, she and Jenn purposefully conducted their civil union in another county because they "didn't want anything published" in the county where Steph works, lest someone do an Internet search, out them, and get Steph fired. Steph and Jenn baptized their children "*incognito*" rather than openly at the parish; luckily they knew a priest who would do so quietly. The couple told me that they long to attend mass together on Sundays as a family but do not for fear that someone in the congregation would see them, object, and report them (say, to the pastor, or to the bishop, or to an ultraconservative Catholic group), resulting in Steph losing her job. They want their children to be formed in the Catholic tradition and celebrate the sacraments, but as their kids approach school-age and the possibility of religious education, the prospect is "terrifying" for Jenn and Steph because the children are being raised in a same-sex household. "Steph always says that she wants to do it from the inside and affect [the Catholic church] and make a change that way," Jenn said. "But there's still a lot of discrimination out there and . . . with our kids . . . it's one thing if it's just us, but it's another thing when our kids are going to be involved in it."

Granted, whether or not Steph *worked* in a Catholic parish, Jenn and Steph would face some of these issues—such as worrying about whether their children will be discriminated against in church settings and what they will be taught about themselves and their non-normative family in religious education. Nevertheless, the fear of job loss is an intense layer on top of these other concerns. Catholics ought to take very seriously the fact that some parents who want to raise their children in the tradition feel the need to baptize their children in private rather than openly in the community, when baptism is fundamentally *about* entrance into the full body of Christ as equals and siblings loved by God.⁸ Further, I suggest we should be concerned that a married couple who longs to attend mass with their children are too afraid to do so because one of the spouses works for the church. It is counterintuitive and unjust.

Steph and Jenn talked with me for over two hours in their home, reflecting on a wide array of topics: their deep love for each other; the faith that sustains them; their complicated relationship to the Catholic church; negotiating family rejection (discussed in chapter 3); parenting two children, raising them toward virtue; and more. We shared laughs as they told their stories, even about difficult things. But tears were also shed. It was when Steph talked about her experiences at work that she cried.

"Now I feel like God's saying, 'Don't give up on me yet.' And when you feel that in your heart . . . that chokes me up [she starts to cry] . . . because there are a million times when I go to bed angry. You know this church breaks me. . . . It breaks me and exhausts me. I love the church. I hate the church. I am hurt by the church. I'm wounded by the church, and yet I love it so much that I want it to be better. I want it to be better for these kids [she ministers to] who want to say, 'Screw this, I'm out.' I want to give them a reason to stay, because there is something good and something worthy in it . . . [but] it's so broken. It's so broken."

Steph asks God for strength to keep doing the work. She tells God, "'You better show up with some energy. You better show up with some guts. You better show up with some peace and some love and you better do it fast.' . . . [L]ast year I was really close to being like, *I'm out*, and something always drags me back in. It's usually some kid that sends me something that says, 'You're the reason why I'm sticking around. You're the reason why. You show me faith I didn't know I had.' So it's the teens that feed me so much and keep me hopeful. But if it was up to me, which I clearly feel like it's not, I'd go to work at a job where I don't give a shit what anyone thinks," a job free from the difficulty and risk she faces in parish work.

If it was up to me, which I clearly feel like it's not . . . Here we encounter more powerful language of vocation. Undoubtedly, Steph has a choice

CHAPTER 5

about whether or not to continue her work in Catholic youth ministry where she: faces daily vulnerability; needs to be constantly cautious and strategic; and is unsure who to fully trust besides God. Yet she also feels *compelled* to follow where she believes God is leading her, even when she feels *broken* and *exhausted*. "I think that's a struggle in my world . . ." Steph said, " . . . because [we're] not just playing with a job here, but with a calling. We're playing with my faith."

Frances and Sofia
Frances is another woman in my study who felt called to use her gifts by working in a Catholic institution. Unfortunately, unlike Steph, she *was* fired. "I lost my job because of our marriage," she said.

Frances had worked at a Catholic school—run by an order of progressive Women Religious—for eight years. "It was a dream job" in religious education, she said. She loved working with kids, faculty, parents, and board members. "I mean, it was an amazing job. It was kind of like being the pastor of a parish but without doing the sacraments." She reveled in this amazing dream job until she made a recommendation about the curriculum that upset a parent, which set off a chain reaction ending in her termination. "I would still stand by that decision—that recommendation, [actually], it wasn't my decision—but [the parent] was upset about that, and then found out that we were married and just went on a mission to get me fired," Frances stated.

She and Sofia married in 2007 when "marriage was just becoming legal, and so the church was just at the time wrestling with LGBT identity. Marriage wasn't even an issue at that point. And so people weren't getting fired because there wasn't a reason to fire according to the church's stance. So it really wasn't in our thinking," Sophia said.

"Yeah," agreed Frances.

"And we knew the [Women Religious] really well. So when Frances interviewed for the job, she had a discussion with the sister who hired her. She said, 'You know, we're married. Is that going to be a problem?'" The sister went back to the Leadership Council and indicated that she wanted to hire Frances, asking if that would be okay. "They said yes," Sofia explained. "And then her caveat was: your relationship will be accepted among the faculty and most parents because it's a pretty progressive school. But there is an element of conservatism, and so you might not want to be open with the parents. So that's how we lived our lives for eight years—kind of half in the closet, half out."

Sofia indicated that many of the parents, but probably not all, knew about their marriage. She and Frances don't know how the student's frustrated mother found out that the two were legally married. "*That* became the issue. The issue wasn't that we were living together; [the fact] that we were married was the issue," Sofia said. The mother subsequently "sent a letter to the principal, the board, the sisters, and then somebody contacted the bishop," Francis said, describing the bishop as "extremely homophobic."

"The sisters chose not to stand by Frances," Sofia said.

Frances described the experience as "extremely painful." She said, "It throws all your conceptions of church, of a religious order, up in the air. *Who are we? Aren't we people who say that everyone is made in the image of God? That we all have dignity? That we have a right to work? [That] we have a right to petition, to have a conversation about an issue instead of just a decision being made and then being silenced?* With the sisters, their whole approach to decision making had always been feminist—circular, it's a process. And that was not our experience [in this case], and it is really disappointing and hurtful." Indeed, Frances felt as though important convictions in Catholic teaching—about inherent dignity, the right to work, and subsidiarity—had been neglected in her termination and the lack of process that accompanied it.[9]

As disappointed as they were in decisions made by the Women Religious in charge of the school, Frances and Sofia ultimately believe school leadership was forced to fire Frances by the hierarchy, and that the sisters had also been wronged. Relational tensions unfortunately increased when Frances and Sofia decided to talk to the press against the expressed wishes of the Women Religious. Sofia explained that the incident quickly became "high profile, extremely high profile, more than we were really comfortable with. But it was high profile because the parents were wealthy in that community." ["And well-connected," Frances added.] "And well-connected . . ." Sofia agreed, " . . . and so the media was on it right from the start."

Frances and Sofia questioned why the Women Religious did not want them telling their story to the media: "Why?" Frances wondered. "You've really been hurt by this church in the same way we have. You have been forced to do something you didn't want to do—I believe that—by men who don't understand the implications of that [for Frances, for the Women Religious, for the school community] . . . so why are you so upset? We're trying to say this is a problem in our church and it's an abuse. It's an abuse of power and it's an abuse against a marginalized community. But [the sisters are] afraid. I think they're afraid of that power that the bishops have."

While they felt unfairly treated, even abused, by some members of the church, Frances and Sofia simultaneously found "amazing" support by others in the various communities to which they belonged. For example, Sofia described a "huge alliance of people in the school community who were trying to fight" Frances's termination, and were working to get her job back. While Sofia and Frances had little hope that the decision to fire Frances would be overturned, they nevertheless appreciated that others were speaking out about what they identified as *an abuse of power against a marginalized community.*

Further, the couple's parish community provided support in ways that both surprised and nourished them. At the time of the incident, Frances and Sofia were taking "a sort of break from church," particularly from the parish that they'd been actively involved in for years. They'd left the parish two years prior out of frustration related to dwindling lay participation. "Our church was very lay led, lay involved, and slowly lay leadership became more and more eroded. We got a new pastor, and that was sort of the nail in the coffin for us . . . We were just feeling really frustrated," Sofia said. Ironically, it was that same "new pastor" who reached out to support them when Frances was fired. He "welcomed [them] back to the church because he wanted the community to pray with us, and it just changed everything . . . he even offered us money," Sofia said. "I mean, this church has paint that's chipping and falling down into the pews, and the man wanted to know if we were okay financially."

While the couple declined the offer for financial support, they accepted the offer to come back to the church to pray with the parish community. The pastor organized and celebrated a special mass during which "there was an outpouring of support" and a blessing for Frances and Sofia. "The homily was all about justice, speaking out," Frances said. She described the deep meaning of being blessed by members of the parish, people that they knew and admired. These folks "are really big into social justice, and here they are blessing [us]. For me it was just like, *Wow, this is so moving*. The sense of being called and being sent forth to be this prophetic voice was just so powerful," she said.

"And there was real risk involved for the pastor," Sofia noted, especially in light of the media attention. So many people were following the story. "He was taking a huge risk not to be penalized or punished by the bishop. He did it despite that. And he stayed involved. He joined an LGBT support group that we were invited to participate in because he wanted to show support. He really became active in that community and still lends support in some ways. He was trying to live up to what he preached every week. And I commend him for that." The initial hospitality extended by their pastor, and the concrete and ongoing solidarity in that church community, *changed everything*. Frances and Sofia felt blessed, literally and figuratively, and they rejoined the parish, despite ongoing concerns about a lack of lay leadership. "We always say: It's about relationships," said Sophia.

Christina and Emma
Married partners and parents Christina and Emma have both worked in Catholic institutions. At the time of our interview, Emma worked in a Catholic school that she experienced as very hospitable. "I've been really fortunate in some respects. I'm in a school where the faculty and staff are so understanding and respectful. It's not like that in other places. It feels like a cross-cultural experience to enter into a magisterial document [which morally condemns same-sex relationships/marriage], if that makes sense." She said being out with faculty and staff at work "has been really, really valuable"—"it's just a nonissue."

Chapter 5

On the other hand, Christina felt less free to be out in the Catholic school where she'd been teaching. It was summertime when we spoke, and she'd recently quit the job, determined to avoid working in another Catholic institution. She told me about how, in her time there, "everything [was] so hyper-managed." For example, she and Emma had to carefully consider whether or not to wear their wedding rings to work. And she had to restrict what (if anything) she said about her spouse and daughter at work. Like Steph above, she needed to be *cautious* and *strategic* in her work environment, thinking about *who to tell* and *trust*.

Christina felt constantly vulnerable. She said: "I was teaching Christian Sexuality, and I'm just thinking, *Oh my God, are they going to find out that I'm married to a woman?* . . . At any moment I could lose my job. *So, why again am I here doing this?* But it's like, *If you're going to fire me because I have a kid now, go right ahead . . . we are living our life as faithfully as we can be, and it is so clear to me that your resistance doesn't have anything to do with me.* Whereas before [at an earlier time of life], there was a lot of self-doubt and internalized homophobia, internalized everything—like *oh man, I'm not a guy, I'm not worth it in the Catholic church,* you know—but now it's clear. *Oh, wait a minute!* I am finding my own dignity in this."

Emma talked about how they needed to "measure the risks" of being out to people and open with their affection in public. "The other day there was this family, we were out and about walking. I was like, *Welp, I can't be out in front of that family.* You know, you have to measure the risks, where it's like, *there's no risk in not holding your hand right now, but I'm not compromising my relationship or my love for you because there are so many other spaces where I can hold your hand. So I can choose this space where that's not necessarily a priority. We don't have to.* I'm not in love with the fact that we can't just be who we are everywhere. But at the same time, I weigh that against losing my job."

This is the kind of mental gymnastics and negotiating many LGBTQ persons who work in Catholic institutions must do to maintain their jobs. Note that it is not just when Emma and Christina are physically in their work environments that such measuring of risks is required, but while conducting day-to-day activities that straight couples likely take for granted, such as taking their young daughter for a neighborhood walk.

Emma said that she and Christina are in a process of "becoming integral," of learning how to live with integrity and authenticity in all of the communities and spaces in their lives. Emma reflected on the challenging early days of their relationship, when she was trying to negotiate her faith with her queer identity but felt she couldn't talk with other people about it. She explained, "It was this really quiet, silent journey, like trying to figure it out on my own and operating in [my] life [while] keeping an important piece out of it constantly in conversation and pronouns and the other stuff . . . it doesn't allow that part to grow, or to thrive, or to have breath." As time went on, she said, "We were able to share more of who we are with other people and grow as a couple in a context that isn't just ourselves. And so it became much more free. Much more healthy. You can't underestimate the power of just having freedom to mention your partner's name and what that does psychologically and emotionally and relationally. [It] definitely made an impact. So as I came more out, our relationship improved and we were able to have more spaces to be who we were together."

"I think that process won't end until we're completely who we are one hundred percent of the time, which having a child is absolutely calling us to, which is why that question of how can we get jobs that are not paid for by the Catholic church is a higher priority," Emma said. For Emma and Christina, growing in authenticity, becoming who they believe they are called to be, means forgoing work in Catholic institutions.

Jane and Maggie
When we spoke, Jane and Maggie had been married three years and together for seventeen. Both had extensive experience working in different Catholic institutions. When they were living together and considering marriage, Maggie was a Catholic school administrator. She said, "I knew I loved Jane, and I knew we were in love. There was no question. I was sure that I'd be spending the rest of my life with you [looking at Jane]." But when it came "to the marriage piece," Maggie hesitated; she worried both about how her family would respond and about her work situation. She explained, "I didn't think I could get married and [keep her job in the Catholic school]. It was also the time morality contracts were

starting to brew. So I was like, *Well, I'll be fired*. I'd be fired because we were living together, much less getting married. I mean all those layers were just added to [factors under consideration.]" She and Jane went through a long discernment process, eventually deciding to marry. The 2015 Supreme Court ruling "accelerated" their decision.

At the time of our interview, Jane had recently retired from a progressive Catholic college in which her queer identity and marriage to Maggie was accepted without question. She was grateful to have worked in an extremely supportive and diverse work environment. However, things were trickier for Maggie in the Catholic setting where she worked. She sometimes worried that openness about her marriage, for example, would upset important donors who could decide to withhold their financial support. These sorts of situations are quite common for workers at Catholic institutions, keeping people (in Sofia's words above) *half in the closet, half out*. Maggie told me about a "super-conservative" Catholic woman who sits on their advisory board, and "long story short: I had to tell her about Jane and I . . . So I thought, *This probably isn't going to go well*. But it was one of those moments where I had to trust because I had to tell her. And she was like: 'Oh how nice you have somebody. I was worried you didn't have anybody.'

"'No, I do. Yeah.'

"'Oh, that's nice. That's nice.' . . . I mean, *it just didn't matter*. I feel like with the church, it's the leadership [that are most concerned]. The people don't care. I mean, there's a few, but by and large, the people don't care," Maggie said. She and Jane believe that most lay Catholics are "already there" in terms of acceptance of LGBTQ relationships and same-sex marriage. In fact, studies bear this out. Gallup polling shows that since 2011, a majority of Catholics have consistently approved of same-sex marriage, "with an average 59% approving from 2011–2015, rising to an average of 69% since 2016."[10] In fact, US Catholics' support "has consistently exceeded the national average by five or more percentage points since the 2000s."[11] Most Catholic lay people, especially in Maggie and Jane's urban environment, support same-sex marriage. Maggie said, people who *do* accept magisterial teaching on the matter (including board members and donors in her workplace) "might be uncomfortable. That's okay. But they don't hate you and say you shouldn't go to communion." For Maggie and Jane, it's ordained leaders in the church who are the main problem.

The couple longs for both a change in magisterial teaching and more openness and honesty from church leaders. They were adamant that the teaching—*it's okay to be gay, but don't practice*—is harmful to LGBTQ persons and the church and needs to change. Bluntly put, Maggie said: "The teaching is a joke. It's a total joke. Who's doing that? Whoever is really living that teaching, I feel bad for them."

"I truly believe that God's will for all of us is to live joyful, happy lives in freedom," Jane added. "*In freedom,*" she repeated, implying that magisterial teaching undermines the freedom of queer persons to be themselves fully and enter into loving relationships that help them flourish.[12]

"In freedom, right!" Maggie emphatically agreed.

"And in service to others. God's will for us is to be happy and joyous and free, and if all the persons in the hierarchy of the church could come out, the world, the church, would be a different place," Jane said.

"True. Yeah. Yeah," Maggie said.

"Help us," Jane pleaded. "Just be like, 'You're all okay. You're okay. We're okay.' That self-hatred you are living in is crippling you and the vision of Jesus for the church, or the Holy Spirit for the church. It's like: you're living a lie. So stop it. Accept God's love and mercy. It's there for you too. . . . Come on, join the party. Come to the table. We're not separate. It's not you guys are up here and we're down here. We're at the same table. So come around."

"It would help if more men who were in the hierarchy who know they're gay would out themselves. Yeah. But they're so scared of losing their [jobs]," Maggie said. She mentioned a good friend of theirs, who is a priest and pastor—he chooses not to come out because he fears losing his position. "He's not in a relationship with anyone. He's living a celibate life. He lived a gay life prior, was with someone prior to becoming a priest, so he knows who he is. And he's made his choice [to live as a celibate priest] and it's wonderful. That's all good. I just want him to be able to be free about that because it would help everybody loosen up the edges. But yeah. He'll lose his job and his retirement. I mean his livelihood. So he's sixty-something years old and he's like, 'Maggie, if I did this, *I'm out*. And where am I going to end up at sixty? I don't have anything to take care of myself.' So that's practical."

"He's really clear about praying to be true to who and whose we are. He says that all the time," Jane added.

"He is. But he can't do it himself. He goes as far as he can without losing his job," Maggie stated. "I mean, he's the kind of guy you need to step out."

"Yeah, well . . ." Jane said, " . . . he does so in ways that he can. I'm just saying that it's time to [be free from] the bondage and the fear . . . the people living in it have to come to it in their own time." Jane's convinced that if "the privilege and clericalism" could "be undone . . . so many things would change."

In a February 2019 *New York Times* article about gay men in the Catholic priesthood, Elizabeth Dias wrote, "Fewer than about 10 priests in the United States have dared to come out publicly. But gay men probably make up at least 30 to 40 percent of the American Catholic clergy, according to dozens of estimates from gay priests themselves and researchers. Some priests say the number is closer to 75 percent."[13] Bryan Massingale, an openly gay priest and Catholic social ethicist, thoughtfully reflected on his own decision to publicly come out as gay in a conversation for Outreach's Outspoken Webinar Series.[14] Massingale acknowledged the difficult position gay priests are in, particularly in light of the magisterium's official position on homosexuality and ordination. A November 2005 policy statement from the Congregation for Catholic Education indicated that homosexual men are to be excluded from ordination, asserting that it is impossible for them to achieve the "affective maturity and spiritual fatherhood" required for priestly ministry.[15] Massingale suggested that if more gay priests *did* come out, they would do so as "a service to the church," helping the church "recognize what has always been true"—that there are gay men serving the church "with fidelity, and with honesty, and with dedication as deacons, as priests, and as bishops." Massingale added, "If we could only be honest about that, I think that would also help us to deal more honestly with issues of sexuality, of same-sex sexuality, of transsexuality." Massingale believes that out-gay-priests serve as models to help the church see that it is possible "to be gay and Christian and mature and a spiritual leader."

Biblical scholar Vincent Pizzuto, referring to the 2005 policy statement, pointedly writes: "We must ask on what basis the Church can claim that *without exception* all homosexual men are unfit to serve as priests when *in fact* homosexual priests and bishops have been serving the Church with great dedication, effectiveness and fidelity throughout history," as Massingale rightly highlights above.[16] He argues, "Even today, a preponderance of the priests who are being directed to enforce this unabashedly homophobic policy statement are themselves homosexual—a fact that is absurd and duplicitous." Pizzuto believes that any authentic solidarity with LGBTQ persons in the church must begin with "an honest disclosure of this truth."[17]

Jane and Maggie see possibilities for positive change should more gay ordained men publicly come out, while at the same time sympathizing with practical considerations related to jobs and livelihoods which may keep them from doing so. Were the magisterium to revoke what Pizzuto identifies as the "unabashedly homophobic policy" related to ordination, undoubtedly it would open up space for more honesty and integrity—personal, interpersonal, and institutional. Surely it would have positive ripple effects for LGBTQ laypersons in the church. In Jane's words, *so many things would change.*

CHOOSING SCANDAL (THE GOOD KIND)

We see from the testimony in this chapter that the problem at hand is multilayered and complicated. In some Catholic settings, LGBTQ persons are fully out and integrated; their marital status is accepted on par with their straight colleagues, and they feel secure at work. In other cases, LGBTQ workers feel vulnerable and insecure as a result of lay Catholics who function as self-appointed moral police, playing Catholic "gotcha" at the expense of persons. These lay Catholics often wield social media as a weapon in ongoing cultural and religious wars.[18] As a result, some queer married persons go to work each day wondering if it will be their last—fearing job loss from a single email to a superior, or a social media post or campaign about their marital status. In these cases, the response from those with decision-making power—whether they be school administrators or pastors or diocesan leaders—is, of course, crucial. In Tony's case, we saw the local bishop fully support him, concretely defending and protecting him, when Tony was harassed and threatened. In Frances's case, school administrators chose to fire her, though Frances and Sofia believe they did so out of fear and coercion.

While we can't know exactly how much pressure school administrators faced in Frances' case, it is clear that bishops in general *do* hold power over Catholic school administrators, including the power (in some cases) to terminate *them* if they do not cooperate, and/or to remove the ability of the school to maintain its Catholic identity. Presumably, it matters whether the school is diocesan (directly under a bishop) or run by a religious order (in which case there may be more of a buffer, or more independence in decision making), but determining how much freedom administrators truly have in light of pressure from a local bishop is difficult. Administrators can be wedged between a rock and a hard place, weighing important goods that have high-stakes personal and social consequences, depending on how a bishop chooses to wield his power.

Rev. Bryan Massingale suggests that many queer persons working in Catholic schools and parishes are trapped in what he calls "the open closet." While Catholic institutions may offer "private toleration" for gays and lesbians, when same-sex relationships are made public, "these Catholics risk stigma, condemnation, and losing their jobs."[19] Massingale argues this is a flawed-paradox because justice (the cardinal virtue by which we give people what they deserve and include them in a common good) is inherently public. He points out that justice is "the social face of love."[20] Following this logic, the community lacks justice when queer married persons are required to endure "the open closet" or negotiate a life *half in the closet, half out* in order to keep their jobs.

The Catechism of the Catholic church states that persons "who have deep-seated homosexual tendencies . . . must be treated with respect, compassion, and sensitivity. Every sign of unjust discrimination in their regard should be avoided."[21] Those who fire queer married persons from Catholic institutions argue that the action is essentially *just* discrimination because employees are expected to uphold Catholic teachings, whether or not they have signed an explicit morality contract. Such firings are sometimes justified as necessary in order to avoid "scandal" or moral confusion for others in the community. As Catholic ethicist Christopher Vogt explains, "Church and school officials are seeking to avoid scandal in a theological sense" by "seeking to suppress behavior that would serve as a stumbling block for the faithful or lead some people away from the faith altogether."[22]

Yet many have pointed out that it is most often LGBTQ persons who are singled out as defying church teaching and fired.[23] While a few lay ministers and teachers have been dismissed "for violating church teaching on other issues (e.g., in-vitro fertilization or pregnancy out of wedlock) the majority of dismissals have been related to sexual orientation and same-sex relationships."[24] One may grant that leaders of Catholic institutions are within their authority to fire people when they disregard church teaching, but also submit that the practical application of that authority is often unjust. It is worth quoting Fr. James Martin, S.J. here at length:

> [I]f adherence to church teaching is going to be a litmus test for employment in Catholic institutions, then dioceses and parishes need to be consistent. Do we fire a straight man or woman who gets divorced and then remarries without an annulment? Divorce and remarriage of that sort is against church teaching. In fact, divorce is something Jesus himself forbade. Do we fire women who bear children out of wedlock? How about a person who is living with someone without being married? Those actions are against church teaching too.
>
> And what about church employees who are not Catholic? If we're firing employees who do not agree with, or adhere to, church teaching, do we fire every Protestant who works in a Catholic institution, because they do not believe in papal authority? That's an important church teaching. Do we fire Unitarians who do not believe in the Trinity? Do we fire all these people for all these things? No. Why not? Because we are selective about which church teachings matter.

> Moreover, requiring church employees to adhere to church teachings means, at a more fundamental level, adhering to the Gospel. To be consistent, we should fire people for not helping the poor, for not being forgiving and for not being loving. That may sound odd, but why should it? Jesus's teachings are the most essential "church teachings."[25]

Clearly, Martin is not advocating that firings be made more regular and expanded to include anyone who disobeys church teaching (who would be left?), but to make a point about how unfairly these expectations for employees get applied, with LGBTQ persons as primary targets. He argues that "[t]he selectivity of focus on L.G.B.T. matters when it comes to firings is, to my mind, to use the words of the Catholic Catechism, a 'sign of unjust discrimination,' something we are to avoid (No 2358)."[26] The editors of *America Magazine* concur with this judgment in a 2016 editorial, stating, "The high public profile of these firings, combined with the apparent lack of due process and the absence of any comparable policing of marital status for heterosexual employees, constitute 'signs of unjust discrimination' and the church in the United States should do more to avoid them."[27]

While discussing her own termination from a Catholic school, Frances referenced this language from church documents, saying, "I just find it atrocious to put justice and discrimination in the same line." She noted that doing so allows the firing of LGBTQ persons to be framed as just. She asked, "How can we ethically approve of that and stand by it?" Bryan Massingale points out that while Catholic documents affirm the human dignity of LGBTQ persons, calling for them to be treated with sensitivity, respect, and compassion, "this dignity is highly qualified and conditional." He writes: "All 'unjust discrimination' against homosexual persons is proscribed and condemned. Yet this phrasing allows for 'just' or legitimate forms of discrimination. Indeed, it is taught that discrimination and inequalities in the areas of housing, teaching, coaching, adoption/foster care and military service are not only justifiable but indeed at times mandatory. This ostensibly is required to protect the unique status of heterosexual marital and familial love."[28] In their editorial, the *America* magazine editors acknowledge that "sometimes an employee of a

Catholic institution can cause scandal by his or her public words or deeds. But it is also true that treating employees unfairly, by holding them to different standards or dismissing them abruptly or without consultation, can itself cause scandal."[29]

I think it's worthwhile to reflect briefly on the notion of scandal here. Doing so brings us squarely into a consideration of who we are called to be as a church and what values and practices we should prioritize in light of the gospels. Christopher Vogt insightfully reflects on scandal as it pertains to the firing of LGBTQ ministers and teachers in a chapter in *The Bible and Catholic Theological Ethics*; his perspective on the topic is informed by the work of two other Catholic ethicists—Angela Senander and Lisa Fullum. He argues that, however unwittingly, scandal can occur when strict adherence to church law is applied in an attempt to avoid scandal—resulting in what Lisa Fullum calls "opposite scandal." The *America* editors identify such scandal as occurring when LGBTQ persons are held to different standards and terminated without due process. Frances' treatment as she describes it seems to illustrate just such scandal. Recall her confusion about how her firing squares with other church teachings about how all persons have dignity and the right to work, about how we honor subsidiarity in decision making. The testimony above shows that removal of LGBTQ ministers and teachers *divides Catholic communities* and *serves as a stumbling block to the faith*. For example, recall: the parishioners at St. Rose of Lima who were alienated from church (again) with Tony's departure; Pete's admission that he's not sure he believes in God anymore because of the "disgusting" way that Tony was treated; the teens who told Steph that her presence is the sole tether to the Catholic faith—if she goes, they go; and Jenn and Steph's reluctance to worship together and decision to baptize their child in private.

Vogt invites us to think differently about scandal, shifting from a disproportionate focus on scandal as caused by any dissent from church teaching (and thus a legitimate reason to fire queer married persons from Catholic institutions). He proposes a broader theological understanding of scandal, rooted in scripture and focused on Jesus's own teaching and life as scandal. He writes:

Chapter 5

To say that Jesus Christ caused scandal is to say more than that he put forward a challenging call or message; it is to say that Jesus and his disciples engaged in behavior that many people regarded as morally offensive and wrong. Scandalous behavior runs contrary to social conventions and often against the law and accepted norms of morality as well. Jesus became an offense or scandal by challenging individuals' most cherished beliefs and violating their assumptions about the way the world should be.[30]

Consider, for example, how offended some people in the gospels were by Jesus' inclusive table fellowship. He ate with tax collectors, prostitutes, and those considered "unclean," calling those very people to discipleship. Likewise, he willingly harvested food and healed on the sabbath—all against the letter of the law. Upsetting. Unacceptable. Pharisees, who knew the law well, regularly objected to Jesus's behavior and called him out on it, finding it scandalous and in clear violation of accepted norms of morality. Yet Vogt points out that Jesus' scandalous behavior was actually "revealing God's kingdom" of mercy and inclusion. His scandalous behavior was inviting folks to see the law anew.[31]

Elizabeth Johnson points out that "Jesus is both faithful and free regarding the great Jewish tradition of Torah."[32] He knew the scriptures well, and honored them. But he occasionally "broke the Torah" and when he did it "gave scandal."[33] Crucially, Johnson notes: "In every single case when the law was set aside, it was because the well-being of someone was at stake. In the face of the sick, the suffering, and the hungry, the sabbath observances were given second priority."[34] What took first priority was the law of love—the love commandment that asks us to love God and neighbor. "In other words," Johnson writes, "love is at the heart of the reign of God; not an easy love but a self-giving love on the model of God. Such love grounds the law, puts it in correct perspective, and fulfills it. Loving in this way, Jesus himself creates a liberating life-style and shows a wonderful freedom to do good."[35] *Faithful and free. Free to do good.*

Through his characteristic behavior and his preaching—especially his parables—Jesus upset accepted norms and expectations, flipping social conventions upside down. He invited followers to think and behave in new and surprising—sometimes upsetting—ways in order to build up God's inclusive kingdom marked by love of neighbor, especially the vulnerable and outcast. He showed a pathway to discipleship through scandal. Jesus showed by example how we can—no, should—reevaluate and even break rules when they divide folks into insiders and outsiders, worthy and unworthy, when human dignity and inclusion in community are at stake. In his day, those who clung too tightly to the law and (unjust) status quo missed out on the opportunity for conversion. The same is true today.

"The Pharisees were scandalized by the message of Christ. Their sense of certainty regarding the Law and what constituted holy living made it impossible for them to respond to God's invitation in Christ. One can see similarities between the mistakes of the Pharisees of Jesus' time and some responses to contemporary controversies about gay marriage," Vogt argues.[36] He suggests that myopic focus on church laws keeps some Catholics from recognizing that we are in a moment of discernment. A broader theological understanding of scandal, informed by the New Testament "should lead us to ask whether the phenomenon of gay men and women promising loving, lifelong commitment to each other should be an occasion for Christians to be scandalized in the very different sense of seeing long-held certainties unexpectedly overturned by the living God."[37] I believe we are being called to discern the answer to this question.

"When you go back to the root of what being a Christian is, it's following the gospel, and Jesus was not exclusive. Even when he tried to be, he was challenged and then he opened his heart and learned," Frances said.[38] "So I think if the church can go back to its roots of the simplicity of the teaching [that] all people are made in the image and likeness of God, then we don't have to go any further than that. I think we get into trouble when we have teachings [that question this core anthropological belief, asking:] So what are *they*? And why were *they* created? And out of what were *they* created? . . . I think opening the door to same-sex marriage is a way to unravel this twisted teaching that has all of us wrung like a rag trying to make ourselves spin it so that people don't see how messed up it is. You know, to see all these people fired and all these communities

CHAPTER 5

suffering. And all these principals and pastors, trying to support a teaching that is very difficult to support. And the people in the pews as well as probably more church leaders have family members who are LGBT too. And that relationship changes you and opens you to understanding this group of people, and you can't just keep standing in that space when you know and love somebody. I just don't think most people can, you know?"

I hope the stories in this book, the experiences of LGBTQ persons that we know and love, will help guide our collective discernment on the issue of same-sex marriage. The Living God seems to be moving us from one space to another, and deeper into the kingdom of God.

NOTES

1. Pope Francis, *Evangelii Gaudium*, November 24, 2013, https://www.vatican.va/content/francesco/en/apost_exhortations/documents/papa-francesco_esortazione-ap_20131124_evangelii-gaudium.html, sec. 46–47.

2. This is a nod to "Always Our Children," a 1997 pastoral message from the US Bishops Committee on Marriage and Family on care for homosexual persons that can be found at https://www.usccb.org/resources/always-our-children.

3. You can find the grand jury report at https://www.attorneygeneral.gov/report/. As described on the site, it "serves as the holding ground for the results of a two-year grand jury investigation into widespread sexual abuse of children within six dioceses of the Catholic Church in Pennsylvania and the systemic cover up by senior church officials in Pennsylvania and at The Vatican."

4. On misguided connections between homosexuality and pedophilia, see James Martin, "Pedophilia and Homosexuality," *America Magazine*, April 13, 2010, https://www.americamagazine.org/content/all-things/pedophilia-and-homosexuality and Thomas G. Plante, "No, Homosexuality Is Not a Risk Factor for the Sexual Abuse of Children," *America Magazine*, October 22, 2018, https://www.americamagazine.org/faith/2018/10/22/no-homosexuality-not-risk-factor-sexual-abuse-children.

5. Pope Francis, *Fratelli Tutti*, October 3, 2020, https://www.vatican.va/content/francesco/en/encyclicals/documents/papa-francesco_20201003_enciclica-fratelli-tutti.html, sec. 86.

6. Pope Francis, *Gaudete et exultate*, March 19, 2018, https://www.vatican.va/content/francesco/en/apost_exhortations/documents/papa-francesco_esortazione-ap_20180319_gaudete-et-exsultate.html, sec. 115.

7. Catholic schools and parishes face decisions about whether to include and how to treat children of same-sex parents. In 2019, St. Ann Catholic school in Kansas City made national news for denying a child admission to kindergarten because the child has same-sex parents. The archdiocese advised against admission and released a media statement explaining their position, which can be found at https://www.documentcloud.org/documents/5761141-Archdiocesan-Media-Statement-Regarding-Same-Sex.html.

The decision was met by widespread protest in the community. "Catholic School in Kansas Faces a Revolt for Rejecting a Same-Sex Couple's Child," Christine Hauser, *New York Times*, March 8, 2019, https://www.nytimes.com/2019/03/08/us/kansas-catholic-school-same-sex-parents.html.

Here is a more recent statement from Colorado, "Denver Archdiocese's LGBTQ Guidance to Catholic Schools," found at: https://www.documentcloud.org/documents/23218852-guidance-for-issues-concerning-the-human-person-and-sexual-identity. It states that when same-sex couples approach a Catholic school seeking enrollment for their child(ren), "The child or children in their household likely see the same-sex couples as a family like any other and two mommies or two daddies as a normal parental relationship. Enrolling a child under these circumstances is likely to lead to intractable conflicts. *A Catholic school cannot treat a same-sex couple as a family equivalent to the natural family without compromising its mission and Catholic identity and causing confusion about the nature of marriage for all students enrolled*." Causing confusion = scandal.

8. See John Baldovin, S.J., "Pastors Should Baptize the Children of LGBTQ+ Couples Says Liturgical Theologian," *Outreach: An LGBTQ Catholic Resource*, May 11, 2022, https://outreach.faith/2022/05/pastors-should-baptize-the-children-of-lgbtq-couples-says-liturgical-theologian/.

9. To learn more about Catholic social teaching on labor and work, see gathered resources on The Catholic Labor Network website, https://catholiclabor.org/. See also collected scriptural passages and excerpts from Catholic social teaching related to the dignity of work and the rights of workers on the USCCB website, https://www.usccb.org/beliefs-and-teachings/what-we-believe/catholic-social-teaching/the-dignity-of-work-and-the-rights-of-workers.

The principle of subsidiarity values decision making and solution finding at the lowest level possible, with the input of those most affected by the matter at hand.

10. Kristjan Archer and Justin McCarthy, "U.S. Catholics Have Backed Same-Sex Marriage Since 2011," *Gallup*, October 23, 2020, https://news.gallup.com/poll/322805/catholics-backed-sex-marriage-2011.aspx.

11. Ibid. Also see Jeff Diamant, "How Catholics Around the World See Same-Sex Marriage," *Pew Research Center* November 2, 2020, https://www.pewresearch.org/fact-tank/2020/11/02/how-catholics-around-the-world-see-same-sex-marriage-homosexuality/.

12. If you are interested in a perspective running counter to this, you might examine the work of Eve Tushnet, who is known for speaking and writing from the perspective of a celibate, lesbian Catholic who embraces the Catholic, traditionalist sexual ethic (limiting sexual activity to heterosexual married couples) and who finds joy and meaning in "same-sex love" rather than same-sex activity. See, for example, Autumn Jones, "'Gay and Catholic': A Q&A with Writer and Speaker Eve Tushnet,'" *The National Catholic Register*, July 12, 2021, https://www.ncregister.com/cna/gay-and-catholic-a-q-a-with-writer-and-speaker-eve-tushnet. Tushnet has written *Gay and Catholic: Accepting My Sexuality, Finding Community, and Living My Faith* (Notre Dame, IN: Ave Maria Press, 2014) and *Tenderness: A Gay Christian's Guide to Unlearning Rejection and Experiencing God's Extravagant Love* (Notre Dame, IN: Ave Maria Press, 2021).

13. Elizabeth Dias, "'It Is Not a Closet. It Is a Cage.' Gay Catholic Priests Speak Out," *New York Times*, February 17, 2019,

https://www.nytimes.com/2019/02/17/us/it-is-not-a-closet-it-is-a-cage-gay-catholic-priests-speak-out.html.

14. Bryan Massingale, "Outspoken 2: Interview Rev. Bryan Massingale," by Ryan Di Corpo and James Martin, *Outreach*, February 28, 2023, https://www.youtube.com/watch?v=lLm0IcsSYkI.

15. Congregation for Catholic Education, "Instruction Concerning the Criteria for the Discernment of Vocations with Regard to Persons with Homosexual Tendencies in View of Their Admission to the Seminary and to Holy Orders," November 2005,

https://www.vatican.va/roman_curia/congregations/ccatheduc/documents/rc_con_ccatheduc_doc_20051104_istruzione_en.html.

Cardinal Tarcisio Bertone, as Vatican Secretary of State, indicated that the policy statement is valid for all seminaries throughout the world.

16. Vincent Pizzuto, "God Has Made It Plain to Them: An Indictment of Rome's Hermeneutic of Homophobia," *Biblical Theology Bulletin* 38, no. 4 (Winter 2008): 181.

17. Ibid.

18. I think about Pope Francis's warning against certain expressions of Christianity in *Evangelii Gaudium*. For example, when "[a] supposed soundness of doctrine or discipline leads . . . to a narcissistic and authoritarian elitism, whereby instead of evangelizing, one analyzes and classifies others, and instead of opening the door to grace, one exhausts his or her energies in inspecting and verifying." He claims that, in such a case, one is not "really concerned about Jesus Christ or others" (sec. 94).

19. John Gehring, "The Scandal of Firing LGBT Catholics," *Commonweal Magazine*, February 16, 2018, https://www.commonwealmagazine.org/scandal-firing-lgbt-catholics.

20. John Gehring provides this framing and quotes Massingale in "The Scandal of Firing LGBT Catholics."

21. *Catechism of the Catholic Church*, #2358.

22. Christopher Vogt, "The Inevitability of Scandal: A Moral and Biblical Analysis of Firing Gay Teachers and Ministers to Avoid Scandal," in *The Bible and Catholic Theological Ethics*, ed. Yiu Sing Lúcás Chan, James F. Keenan, and Ronaldo Zacharias (Maryknoll, NY: Orbis Books, 2017), 152.

23. As the title makes clear, an article by Robert Shrine from February 2022 indicates that "More than 100 church workers have lost their jobs in LGBTQ-related employment disputes that went public in the last decade." You can access it at: https://www.newwaysministry.org/2022/02/18/church-worker-faces-second-firing-from-catholic-institution-over-lgbtq-marriage/.

24. Christopher Vogt, "The Inevitability of Scandal," 152. I'd also note here that firings for the use of reproductive technologies and pregnancy are essentially restricted to women. Further, firing pregnant women in light of Catholic teaching calling for the support of life from conception seems particularly problematic.

25. James Martin, *Building a Bridge: How the Catholic Community and the LGBT Community Can Enter into a Relationship of Respect, Compassion, and Sensitivity, Revised and Expanded Edition* (New York: HarperOne, 2018), 47–48.

26. James Martin, *Building a Bridge*, 49.

27. Editors of *America Magazine*, "How Should the Church Respond When Gay Employees Get Married?" *America Magazine* October 26, 2016, https://www.americamagazine.org/faith/2016/10/25/how-should-church-respond-when-gay-employees-get-married.

28. Here Massingale cites the Congregation for the Doctrine of Faith's *Some Considerations Concerning the Response to Legislative Proposals on the Non-Discrimination of Homosexual Persons*, sec. 11–12. See Bryan Massingale, "Beyond 'Who Am I to Judge?': The *Sensus Fidelium*, LGBT Experience, and Truth-Telling in the Catholic Church," in *Learning from All the Faithful*, ed. Bradford E. Hinze and Peter C. Phan (Eugene, OR: Pickwick Publications, 2016), 172.

29. Editors of *America Magazine*, "How Should the Church Respond?"

30. Vogt, "The Inevitability of Scandal," 154.

31. Ibid.

32. Elizabeth Johnson, *Consider Jesus: Waves of Renewal in Christology* (New York: Crossroad, 1995), 56.

33. Ibid.

34. Ibid.

35. Ibid.

36. Vogt, "The Inevitability of Scandal," 155.

37. Ibid., 156.

38. See, for example, Jesus's encounter with the Canaanite woman in the gospels (Matthew 15 and Mark 7).

Conclusion

SANCTUARY
A Listening and Welcoming Church
"[T]he call to synodality is a call to continuing conversion," stated Cardinal Robert McElroy in a February 2023 address, reflecting on initial reports from synodal consultations across the global Catholic church that began in 2021.[1] In the presentation, he offers commentary on two syntheses that he believes are "critically important for the Church in the United States": one national report created by the US Catholic Bishops, and another working document issued from the synodal office in Rome.[2]

McElroy notes that the synodal process so far reveals "a wide array of joyful realities" experienced in the worldwide church, but also a "series of challenges that the people of God must face if we are to reflect the identity of the Church that is rooted in the compassionate call of Christ and the Second Vatican Council." McElroy proceeds to specify that: "Some of these challenges arise from the reality that a Church which is calling all men and women to find a home in the Catholic community reflects structures and cultures of exclusion that alienate all too many from the Church, or make their journey in the Catholic faith tremendously burdensome." These findings parallel the stories gathered in this book—some joyful, yes, but many lamenting burdens borne within Catholic structures and cultures marked by inhospitality. The Cardinal emphasizes that these painful experiences of alienation and exclusion should prompt the church to conversion. We must do better, working toward a church of inclusion and shared belonging that—as stated above—is more in line with the compassionate call of Christ and the ecclesial vision of Vatican II.

CONCLUSION

Not surprisingly, McElroy explicitly names "members of the LGBT+ community and those who are civilly married but have not been married in the church" among the groups of persons experiencing marginalization. He condemns "heinous acts of exclusion" toward LGBTQ Catholics that continue to contaminate the church, emphasizing that " . . . these exclusions scandalize many Catholics of all ages, regions, and ethnicities." He encourages future synodal conversations to "place great focus upon these practices of exclusion, not only in justice for those who are excluded, but also for the enormously large section of the Catholic community that finds such exclusions unchristlike." He reminds us that LGBTQ persons are deeply wounded by marginalization *and* that their marginalization is a source of scandal for others in the body of Christ.

McElroy's advice to listen to those on the periphery and attend to the scandal of unchristlike exclusion reminds me of something that Tom said during our interview. Tom and his husband Mark are the couple that bring the eucharist to people who are elderly, practice radical hospitality, and strive to live out Henri-Frederic Amiel's call to *be swift to love and make haste to be kind*. Tom said:

> The Judeo-Christian tradition says listen to the people you are scapegoating and don't do it. Don't do that. In a sense, that's to me what the gospels are saying. Jesus is saying no. You don't scapegoat Samaritans. You don't scapegoat women. You don't scapegoat tax collectors and Pharisees. You don't separate yourself from other people. So [scapegoating] is what's at the heart of the *Let's find some class of people that we could say are clearly different from us and are clearly outside of God's will. And let's spend a lot of energy keeping them there* . . . [Lutheran pastor and writer] Nadia Bolz-Weber says 'Whenever you draw a line between yourself and other people, Jesus is on the other side of that line.' To me, that's the positive message . . . Let's not talk about gay people [and other groups we try to scapegoat], Let's talk about whenever we divide, draw a line between ourselves and other people, Jesus is on the other side of that line. It's a more positive way of looking at it. And that's the real message of Christianity, not: *It's okay to be mean to other people and let the church tell you who it's okay to be mean to*. But to say: *It's not okay to be mean to other people*. That's the point.

Conclusion

Of course, we know that official Catholic teaching condemns being mean to others or treating anyone as unworthy of God's loving care. On the contrary, it promotes respect and sensitivity for LGBTQ persons. But Tom suggests that the church's traditionalist sexual ethic nevertheless functions to separate and define as different (and more prone to sin) a whole group of people, framing discrimination against them as "just." Cardinal McElroy highlights the fact that drawing neat lines in order to judge "sinners" and exclude them—from the shared eucharistic table and beyond—scandalizes the faithful. Further, he suggests that the neat lines drawn in traditional Catholic sexual ethics—judging that "all sexual sins are grave matter" (that is, "all sexual sins are so gravely evil that they constitute objectively an action that can sever a believer's relationship with God")—are in need of further discernment. This move to revisit church teaching on intrinsically evil acts is incredibly important.

We've established that current magisterial teaching states that same-sex marriage (and sex between gay and lesbian persons broadly) is gravely evil because it occurs outside the definition of heterosexual-marriage-open-to-procreation, presented by the magisterium as the only context for moral genital activity. Yet McElroy asks: "Does the tradition that all sexual sins are objectively mortal make sense within the universe of Catholic moral teaching?" It's a vitally important question. Wrestling with it, while taking seriously the voices and experiences of LGBTQ persons, including married persons, seems an essential task for the church.

This goes hand in hand with Christopher Vogt's suggestion (noted at the conclusion of chapter 5) that a broader theological understanding of scandal, informed by the New Testament, "should lead us to ask whether the phenomenon of gay men and women promising loving, lifelong commitment to each other should be an occasion for Christians to be scandalized in the very different sense of seeing long-held certainties unexpectedly overturned by the living God."[3] Perhaps we cannot see that the living God is calling us to reassess "long-held certainties" about sexual sin because we are too busy drawing lines and enforcing established borders. Discussions with same-sex, married couples are helping the church to rightly shift its gaze, and this book is a small part of that wider conversation. These couples show us that the church's current *modus operandi*—to distinguish between orientation and activity, to call for loving the person but rejecting the gravely sinful behavior—is not working for the good of so many of God's people. We need both pastoral and doctrinal change. David Gushee argues that pastoral change is essential but not enough because:

> Without doctrinal change, we are still telling LGBTQ kids that their sexuality is just not right, but sinful, broken or disordered in a way that straight kids' sexuality is not. We are still telling them that they can never have an adult sexual relationship that could please God or be blessed by the Church. We are still very likely telling them that they will be treated as second-class Christians when it comes to serving and leading the Church. We are 'welcoming' them, maybe, but not on equal terms with their peers, which is a 'welcome' not many of the rest of us [straight persons] would accept.[4]

Gushee suggests that pastoral progress is clearly necessary and good, but for LGBTQ persons, it's like being offered "cold oatmeal," which is "better than starving but lacks an awful lot."[5]

I argue in this book that the church should expand its definition of sacramental marriage to include same-sex couples. I join many revisionist Christian theologians, Catholic and Protestant, when I reject the notion that these relationships are sinful, let alone a matter of grave sin. On the contrary, the testimony of the couples in my study shows that—far from thwarting potential and cutting people off from God—these relationships lead to virtue, growth in wholeness and authenticity, fullness of life and generativity, and a deepening sense of God's goodness and love. The idea that "there are absolutely no grounds for considering homosexual unions to be in any way similar or even remotely analogous to God's plan for marriage and family" does not stand up to this testimony.[6]

In his address, Cardinal McElroy suggests that "an abstract and deductivist notion of the Christian moral life" seems no longer to serve the people of God well. A more inductive approach—grounded in the experience of everyday, diverse, embodied people—surely serves the church better and moves us to a fuller understanding of what leads to flourishing and what, in contrast, thwarts holiness. In *The Joy of the Gospel*,

Conclusion

Pope Francis affirms that "[a] theology—and not simply a pastoral theology—which is in dialogue with other sciences and human experiences is most important for our discernment on how best to bring the Gospel message to different cultural contexts and groups."[7] An inductive understanding of the Christian moral life asks us to take seriously the *sensus fidei*, an important ecclesial concept affirmed at the Second Vatican Council. While the *sensus fidei* has contested meaning in the theological community, it fundamentally captures that belief that the church has been granted a "sense" or ability to know and receive God's truth as it is revealed through time. As affirmed in *Lumen Gentium*'s second chapter, the *sensus fidei* is "given by the Holy Spirit in baptism to baptized individuals and to the church as a whole."[8] As theologian Orland Rush notes, "[D]ivine revelation, and its accompanying gift of *sensus fidei*, are communicated to, not just the pope and bishops (as if we were some gnostic sect of select *illuminati*), but to the whole People of God . . . (LG 12)."[9]

Affirmation of "a sense of the faithful" implies that the church has something important to learn from the testimonies of LGBTQ persons about how God is at work in their lives, about how they experience sin, and about the conditions that contribute to their wholeness and authenticity. Bryan Massingale points out that "[s]uch testimonies are not doctrinally determinative. But they are indispensable. They become doctrinally significant when these testimonies arouse a deep empathy within the Christian community, such that the *sensus fidei* of the LGBT Christian becomes the *sensus fidelium* of the broader faith community."[10] Recall the work of David Gushee and Luke Timothy Johnson, discussed at the conclusion of chapter 2. These scholars highlight how, throughout history, Christians have come to new interpretations of biblical passages—and in turn changed long-accepted community moral norms—because of transformative encounters with flesh-and-blood persons. The tradition is dynamic. Historically, teachings changed because the sense of the faithful changed. Encounter led to empathy, which led to solidarity and ultimately doctrinal change. And so the Holy Spirit continues to move the church toward the truth today. In Ormond Rush's words, "God continues to surprise us and to provoke us. And the *sensus fidei* is the antenna for sensing those surprises and provocations."[11] Yes.

CONCLUSION

An inductive approach that attends to testimonies of LGBTQ persons cries out for reassessment of a traditionalist sexual ethic that cuts some people off altogether from the possibility of goodness in sexual expression and relationships in line with their embodied truth. Listening to the experiences of LGBTQ persons helps us understand that the application of a traditional sexual ethic too often leads to sinful structures and cultures, resulting in: psychological and spiritual damage to LGBTQ persons, alienated families, broken and polarized church communities, inhospitable and unsafe Catholic institutions, and the bleeding out of so many queer persons and allies from the Catholic church. So very much is at stake.

Cold oatmeal versus a hearty breakfast with hot coffee and a seat at the table seems an apt metaphor for those who take eucharistic practices seriously. I'm reminded of womanist theologian M. Shawn Copeland's powerful words about the connection between the eucharist and solidarity in *Enfleshing Freedom*. She writes:

> In the very act of nourishing our flesh with his flesh, we women and men are made new in Christ, emboldened to surrender position and privilege and power and wealth, to abolish all claims to racial and cultural superiority, to contradict repressive codes of gender formation and sexual orientation. In Christ, there is neither brown nor black, neither red nor white; in Christ, there is neither Creole nor *mestizo*, neither senator nor worker in the *maquiladoras*. In Christ, there is neither male nor female, neither gay/lesbian nor straight, neither heterosexual nor homosexual (after Gal 3:28). We are all transformed in Christ: *we are his very own flesh* . . . If my sister or brother is not at the table, we are not the flesh of Christ. If my sister's mark of sexuality must be obscured, if my brother's mark of race must be disguised, if my sister's mark of culture must be repressed, then we are not the flesh of Christ . . .[12]

We are embodied. We are diverse. All have a place at the table and are responsible to and for one another. Our distinctly marked bodies are transformed in Christ in baptism and eucharist, made new in order to overcome all social hierarchies that divide. Truly, we are called to solidarity—to combat all expressions of racism, sexism, homophobia, economic exploitation, xenophobia—because *Jesus Christ is on the other side of that line.*

In my conversation with Emma and Christina, we discussed what is at stake in conversations about same-sex marriage and the church. You may recall this couple who are raising their daughter, Joy, and who are striving to live with integrity *all of the time* while negotiating being married and working in Catholic institutions. Christina said the greatest benefit of doctrinal change would be: "Wholeness in families. You know, just thinking of all the shame and the hurt and the estrangement people have felt," feeling forced to choose between goods—faith, family, and being in a loving romantic relationship—even believing that "heaven and hell is at stake, that their salvation is at stake . . . that's really evil. So, when there is acceptance and there is inclusion, it's not just *Oh yay, we can all sing kumbaya.* No. [It's a recognition] that freedom and goodness are there for you."

Wholeness. Acceptance. Inclusion. Freedom. Goodness. *It's there for you.* That's marriage at its best. That's family at its best. That's Catholic institutions at their best. That's church at its best. One word that speaks to this "best" is sanctuary. The rich notion of sanctuary points to what marriage, family, workplace, parish, and wider Catholic church community can be *at their best*. Therefore, I'd like to conclude with a brief reflection on sanctuary.

"They shall make a sanctuary for me, that I may dwell in their midst" (Ex 25:8)

Sanctuary is a sacred space, set apart. In a Catholic church, the sanctuary is the part of the church where the main rituals of the liturgy take place—where the Word of God is proclaimed and the eucharist is consecrated. The altar is the focal point of the sanctuary. And in many churches, the sanctuary is where the tabernacle is located. Today's church sanctuary is reminiscent of the Holy of Holies or inner sanctuary of the temple that is described in the Old Testament.[13] In every Catholic church, there is a lamp or candle that burns before the tabernacle as a sign that Christ is present.[14]

Sanctuary is also a consecrated place giving protection to people fleeing from injustice or harm. Sanctuary is a designated place of refuge and safety. "In complex societies, sanctuary exists within tensions around inclusion and exclusion—who is defined as other and who is offered refuge—within cultural, economic, and political structures that change over time."[15] Historically, the practice of sanctuary has "set spaces apart to resist exclusion"—for example, for criminals, runaway slaves, and refugees—"created around the premise that those who are marginalized or persecuted have a place in the community."[16] In her excellent work on contemporary practices of sanctuary, theologian Erin Brigham considers sanctuary from a theological perspective, examining its roots in the Hebrew Bible and early Christian practices and exploring its connections to Catholic social teaching. She suggests that church as sanctuary is a powerful expression of Pope Francis's vision of church as field hospital, in which our priority ought to be enacting mercy and healing the wounded. The Pope says:

> The thing the church most needs today is the ability to heal wounds and to warm the hearts of the faithful; it needs nearness, proximity. I see the church as a field hospital after battle. It is useless to ask a seriously injured person if he has high cholesterol and about the levels of his blood sugars! You have to heal his wounds. Then we can talk about everything else. Heal the wounds, heal the wounds . . . And you have to start from the ground up.[17]

Brigham's ethnographic study focuses on concrete practices of sanctuary in San Francisco, with particular attention to unhoused people and migrants in an environment of profound economic and social inequalities. San Francisco is a meaningful place to study sanctuary practices because it is a city practiced in the art of sanctuary. "Historically and today, the city offers a place of refuge for the LGBTQ community, which some faith leaders have described as sanctuary."[18] Many progressive churches have provided and continue to provide a refuge to queer folks within a wider society that can be hostile to them; they offer radical hospitality within a wider church that too often pushes them to the margins. In chapter 4, we heard stories that illustrate the transformative power of sanctuary in churches where interviewees found enthusiastic welcome and authentic community.

One key point that Brigham emphasizes is that sanctuary involves *shared space* and *shared lives*. Sanctuary is not one-sided but "cocreated by relationships of mutual vulnerability and risk. It is not something the church offers to the migrant [or the LGBTQ] 'other' but rather something that emerges through sharing stories, walking together, and building solidarity gradually through shared life."[19]

Jane and Maggie talked to me about what it means for them to create sanctuary in the church. Maggie said, "I feel like being a married couple in our church, we're creating that space for the church. Every time we go to church together and we're at the sign of peace and we give each other a hug. Or [looking at Jane] when I introduce you to someone. This is my partner Jane. And to say that to another Catholic after mass, having donuts, I feel like we're creating this space for more queer couples to exist. And I'm really proud of that. I'm *really* proud of that." She continued, explaining that before she and Jane were married, she saw herself "as just a gay woman in the church that was marginalized, or didn't exist. So now I'm like: *Oh no. We're here. We're not going anywhere. We're here. This is our church and we're here to contribute to it. In many, many ways.*" Jane nodded in agreement.

"Yeah. I think the word sanctuary comes to mind," Jane said. "We've created a space, and certainly this relationship is a sanctuary for me, and I want it to be a sanctuary for others. So creating a space within our church is all about sanctuary. I think it's always been a dream of mine to be a safe harbor for people, and wanting that to be a model for others." These words are powerful. Jane and Maggie, as a couple, create space for other diverse members of the body of Christ simply by being authentically who they are in the space. The two experience sanctuary in their marriage, and then they become and create sanctuary in the church community. Symbolically, we might say that the light that burns in their marriage-sanctuary illuminates and warms the space for others, who themselves can catch fire—a sign that Christ is present. One-body icons, aflame.

Dan and Jaime, having found a gay-friendly parish, expressed gratitude for the camaraderie they've experienced. When they gather with fellow parishioners, they "find support and realize: we're all dealing with the same stressors, the same issues, and [we're] not alone out there." They told me that for much of their relationship, they were managing "without a roadmap so to speak." Jaime said, "We had little to not much support from the church, sometimes not even from our family." Dan stated that, in contrast, when he was growing up, his parents were a part of a tight community with other couples, part of a "family cluster" that were entwined in each others' lives, with the church facilitating those relationships. He said that the church "played a big role" in establishing those important family connections. Today, while he and Jaime are thankful for a strong LGBTQ community in their parish, they lament that the community consists mostly of unmarried people. Dan indicated that "it would be nice to have more support" as a married couple, from other same-sex married couples. Such a support system—like the one Dan's parents had when he was a child—would make them feel "less lonely" and "less isolated." Dan said, "It's very inspirational when we meet a couple that's been together for decades or whatever—for a long, long time. We're kind of hungry to hear those stories, to learn from them."

Inclusive communities become safe harbors and places for support and growth. When we disallow same-sex marriages, and LGBTQ persons and couples are absent (sometimes having been explicitly expelled) from our church communities and Catholic institutions, we undermine church as sanctuary. We remove possibilities for mutual support, camaraderie, and role modeling that bring relief, healing, and inspiration to vulnerable members of the body of Christ. More directly, when LGBTQ folks are not allowed to be authentically who they are or are absent from the table, in Copeland's words: *we are not the body of Christ*. I think, for example, of Liam and Marty's story: they needed a village of support as they raised their children, but eventually needed to leave their parish to find it; their diverse community of rich-belonging was no longer a safe harbor.

In the conclusion of *Project Holiness*, Julie and I noted how enriched the married couples in our study were by active participation in their parishes. They felt nourished by the eucharist, supported in times of difficulty, motivated to serve others in need within and outside the parish, and inspired by other couples and families to practice fidelity and unconditional love. We suggested that married couples anchor themselves in a church community for all of those reasons—it's tough to live out the married vocation alone. Of course, people can and do find other communities of support; in fact, fewer and fewer Catholics, single or married, are rooted in parish communities. But when the church is at its best, when it is truly sanctuary, it clearly enriches people's lives and moves them toward flourishing, toward friendship with God and others. We saw that some same-sex couples have similar positive experiences of parish life in this book. Yet, stories also show that same-sex couples can be and are harmed by inhospitable Catholic parishes that do not provide full inclusion and belonging, and by the Catholic tradition (specifically its sexual ethics) out of which that inhospitality grows. It's much more complicated for LGBTQ persons and couples, and choices about participation in church communities are fraught.

I hope that the stories gathered in this book, along with stories from other LGBTQ persons, can light a path forward, as long as folks are willing to listen and respond in light of scandalous gospel values. The church can and must practice sanctuary—*being* sanctuary and *creating* sanctuary—in our families, parishes, Catholic institutions, and all of the communities of which we are a part.

Notes

1. Cardinal Robert W. McElroy, "Enlarging Our Tent: The Synodal Imperative Toward a Church of Inclusion and Shared Belonging" (presentation, Bergoglio Lecture Series, Sacred Heart University, Fairfield, CT, February 22, 2023), https://www.sacredheart.edu/media/shu-media/catholic-studies/Cardinal-McElroy-Talk-02-22-23.pdf.

2. Ibid.

3. Christopher Vogt, "The Inevitability of Scandal: A Moral and Biblical Analysis of Firing Gay Teachers and Ministers to Avoid Scandal," in *The Bible and Catholic Theological Ethics*, ed. Yiu Sing Lúcás Chan, James F. Keenan, and Ronaldo Zacharias (Maryknoll, NY: Orbis Books, 2017), 156.

4. David Gushee, *Changing Our Mind* (Canton, MI: Read the Spirit Books, 2017), 171.

5. Ibid.

6. Congregation for the Doctrine of Faith, Considerations Regarding Proposals to Give Legal Recognition to Unions Between Homosexual Persons, June 3, 2003, https://www

.vatican.va/roman_curia/congregations/cfaith/documents/rc_con_cfaith_doc_20030731_homosexual-unions_en.html, sec. 4, quoted by Pope Francis in *Amoris Laetitia*, March 19, 2016, https://www.vatican.va/content/dam/francesco/pdf/apost_exhortations/documents/papa-francesco_esortazione-ap_20160319_amoris-laetitia_en.pdf, sec. 251.

7. Pope Francis, *Evangelii Gaudium*, November 24, 2013, https://www.vatican.va/content/francesco/en/apost_exhortations/documents/papa-francesco_esortazione-ap_20131124_evangelii-gaudium.html, sec. 133.

8. Orland Rush, "The Church as Hermeneutical Community and the Eschatological Function of the *Sensus Fidelium*," in *Learning from All the Faithful*, ed. Bradford E. Hinze and Peter C. Phan (Eugene, OR: Pickwick Publications, 2016), 143.

9. Ibid., 145–46.

For an example from my study, Katie points to the sense of the faithful when she said, "You know, in my struggles with being gay, I know I just kept coming back to the sense of what God wants: good things for me. The sense, if you listen to your life, and if we listen to our lives together . . . why would I say this is wrong?"

10. Bryan Massingale, "Beyond 'Who Am I to Judge?" in *Learning from All the Faithful*, ed. Bradford E. Hinze and Peter C. Phan (Eugene, OR: Pickwick Publications, 2016), 180.

11. Rush, "The Church as Hermeneutical Community," 146.

12. M. Shawn Copeland, *Enfleshing Freedom: Body, Race, and Being* (Minneapolis, MN: Fortress Press, 2010), 82.

13. For a helpful and accessible description of various parts of the church, see D.D. Emmons, "Inside Our Sacred Space," *Our Sunday Visitor*, January 8, 2017, https://www.oursundayvisitor.com/inside-our-sacred-space/.

14. The General Instruction of the Roman Missal in the Catholic Church states; "In accordance with traditional custom, near the tabernacle a special lamp, fueled by oil or wax, should be kept alight to indicate and honor the presence of Christ," (Washington, DC: United States Conference of Catholic Bishops, 2011), https://www.usccb.org/prayer-and-worship/the-mass/general-instruction-of-the-roman-missal, sec. 316.

15. Erin Brigham, *Church as Field Hospital: Toward an Ecclesiology of Sanctuary* (Collegeville, MN: Liturgical Press, 2022), 6–7.

16. Ibid., 34.

17. Antonio Spadaro, S.J., "A Big Heart Open to God: An Interview with Pope Francis," *America*, September 30, 2013, https://www.americamagazine.org/faith/2013/09/30/big-heart-open-god-interview-pope-francis.

18. Brigham, *Church as Field Hospital*, 25.

19. Ibid., 120.

Postscript on Blessings of Same-Sex Unions

On December 18, 2023, the Vatican's Dicastery for the Doctrine of Faith (DDF) issued a Declaration, *Fiducia Supplicans* ("On the Pastoral Meaning of Blessings"), which allows for the blessing of same-sex couples and those in "irregular situations," such as cohabitating, non-married straight couples. With Pope Francis's approval, it marks a shift from the position taken by the Congregation for the Doctrine of Faith in 2021 that blessings of same-sex relationships are not possible because God—and therefore the Church—"does not and cannot bless sin."[1]

In line with Pope Francis's approach broadly, the Declaration takes a pastoral tone, inviting readers to contemplate God's abundant mercy and desire to bless without conditions. It emphasizes that "God never turns away anyone who approaches him! Ultimately, a blessing offers people a means to increase their trust in God. The request for a blessing, thus, expresses and nurtures openness to the transcendence, mercy, and closeness to God in a thousand concrete circumstances of life. . . . It is a seed of the Holy Spirit that must be nurtured, not hindered."[2] At the same time, the Declaration is careful to distinguish between pastoral blessings and liturgical (sacramental) blessings. It reiterates the traditional definition of sacramental marriage as a man and a woman entering into an indissoluble covenant by consent, and repeatedly warns against "confusion" or "scandal" that may be caused by mistakenly equating the blessing of same-sex unions (or other irregular unions) with the Rite of the Sacrament of Matrimony. The DDF asserts that persons in a same-sex union may receive a blessing, but the blessing should be "non-ritualized" and "never be imparted in concurrence with the ceremonies of a civil union, and not even in connection with them. Nor can it be performed with any clothing, gestures, or words that are proper to a wedding."[3]

The Declaration sparked mixed reactions around the globe, from church leaders and lay people alike.[4] Some condemned it as inevitably scandalous, others welcomed it as something to celebrate—a positive development for queer folks and their allies. Still others lamented it as not going far enough, as it does not change magisterial teaching on marriage and suggests that same-sex unions "cannot be compared in any way to marriage."[5] It should be clear by now that I believe not only that the *persons* within same-sex unions should be blessed, but the unions themselves. I've argued—informed by the testimony of the couples in my study—that same-sex marriages can not only rightly be "compared to" but in fact meet the church's description of sacramental marriage as covenantal and generative and would benefit from participation in the official Rite of Matrimony (that is, not just pastoral, but liturgical blessing). Simultaneously, I affirm the Declaration's expansive notion of everyday blessings, its pastoral approach, and the ongoing ecclesial discernment process it represents.

Notes

1. Congregation for the Doctrine of the Faith, *Responsum of the Congregation for the Doctrine of the Faith to a dubium regarding the blessing of the unions of persons of the same sex*, March 15, 2021, https://press.vatican.va/content/salastampa/en/bollettino/pubblico/2021/03/15/210315b.html.

2. Dicastery for the Doctrine of the Faith, *Fiducia Supplicans*, December 18, 2023, https://www.vatican.va/roman_curia/congregations/cfaith/documents/rc_ddf_doc_20231218_fiducia-supplicans_en.html, sec. 33.

3. Ibid., secs. 36 and 39.

4. For an informative discussion of initial reactions to the Declaration, listen to Colleen Dulle, Gerard O'Connell, and Michael O'Loughlin, "Blessings and backlash: A conversation on 'Fiducia Supplicans,'" Inside the Vatican, January 17, 2024, https://www.americamagazine.org/faith/2024/01/17/fiducia-supplicans-reactions-bishops-same-sex-blessings-246971.

5. *Fiducia Supplicans*, sec. 30.

Appendix: About the Participants

BASIC DEMOGRAPHIC INFORMATION

I interviewed twenty-two couples—forty-four people—total. Each participant was surveyed to self-report their demographic data. Twenty interviewees identified as female and twenty-four as male, thus breaking into ten female couples and twelve male couples. Ages of participants ranged from twenty-nine to seventy-nine; the average age was forty-nine and a half years. Thirty-nine interviewees were white (88.6 percent). Nonwhite participants identified as Asian/Pacific Islander (2), Hispanic/Latino (2), or Black/African-American (1). 30.4 percent of the couples have children. On the whole, people in the study were highly educated. All were college graduates; 79.5 percent hold a degree beyond a bachelor's (e.g., professional degree, master's degree, doctorate).

Of the participants, 81.8 percent identified as Catholic, with two listing a dual affiliation (Catholic/Interfaith and Catholic/Episcopalian). Some who identified as Catholic qualified their responses—for example, by writing "Catholic (with nuances)" or "Catholic?" Five people identified as non-Catholic Christian—four as Episcopalian and one as Lutheran (ELCA). Two participants who identified as Episcopalian noted that they were formerly Catholic. Three participants reported no religious affiliation ("none").

ABOUT THE RELATIONSHIPS

Participants were asked how many years they have been together as a couple as well as how long they have been married. Their years together as a couple ranged from three years to thirty-nine years. 81.8 percent had been together for at least ten years, 50 percent for at least fifteen. 36.3 percent of couples had been together twenty-five years or more, with four couples together thirty years or more.

While seemingly straightforward, the question "How many years have you been married?" was complicated for some. Periodically, I got a follow up question as participants filled out the demographic information form, such as "Which date do you want? The church ceremony or the legal marriage?" For example, one couple had a holy union twenty-two years earlier, but had legally married two years prior to our conversation. One couple exchanged private vows in a church decades ago and considered themselves married from that moment of consent, though the marriage was not official either legally or ecclesially; the couple made the marriage legal when they could. Some couples had a civil union when that was all they could do legally, but officially married after Obergefell v. Hodges in 2015. For this reason, it is difficult to provide clear statistics regarding length of marriage that do justice to the experience of these married couples. Based on the self-reported data, years married ranged from two years to twenty-two years, with meaningful qualifications.

A Brief Note

In the introduction I described how I recruited the couples, who resided in six states (California, Illinois, Massachusetts, New York, Pennsylvania, Wisconsin) and Washington, DC. Due to my methodology, what I gathered is not a random sample. I do not claim that these couples represent all same-sex couples who have a meaningful relationship to the Catholic tradition. I recognize the limits of the study and see it as a part of a wider effort to listen. I hope that the interviews in this study can enrich conversations about same-sex marriage from a Catholic perspective and help the church to move toward full inclusion of LGBTQ persons in families, churches, and Catholic institutions.

Bibliography

Alaimo O'Donnell, Angela. "Everyday Sacraments: Final Lessons of Love." *America Magazine*, November 25, 2014. https://www.americamagazine.org/issue/everyday-sacraments.

Archdiocese of Denver. *Guidance for Issues Concerning the Human Person and Sexual Identity*. (Distributed 2022). https://www.documentcloud.org/documents/23218852-guidance-for-issues-concerning-the-human-person-and-sexual-identity.

Archdiocese of Kansas City in Kansas. *Media Statement: Admissions Policies in Catholic Schools in the Archdiocese*. (Distributed 2019). https://www.documentcloud.org/documents/5761141-Archdiocesan-Media-Statement-Regarding-Same-Sex.html.

Archer, Kristjan, and Justin McCarthy. "U.S. Catholics Have Backed Same-Sex Marriage Since 2011." *Gallup*, October 23, 2020. https://news.gallup.com/poll/322805/catholics-backed-sex-marriage-2011.aspx.

Associated Press. "German Bishops Vote in Favor of Blessing Same-Sex Unions in the Catholic Church." *America Magazine*, March 10, 2023. https://www.americamagazine.org/politics-society/2023/03/10/german-church-synod-same-sex-blessings-244883.

Baldovin, S.J., John. "Pastors Should Baptize the Children of LGBTQ+ Couples Says Liturgical Theologian" *Outreach: An LGBTQ Catholic Resource*, May 11, 2022. https://outreach.faith/2022/05/pastors-should-baptize-the-children-of-lgbtq-couples-says-liturgical-theologian/.

Beattie Jung, Patricia. "Christianity and Human Sexual Polymorphism: Are They Compatible?" In *Ethics and Intersex*, edited by Sharon E. Sytsma, 293–310. Dordrecht: Springer, 2006.

Brigham, Erin. *Church as Field Hospital: Toward an Ecclesiology of Sanctuary*. Collegeville, MN: Liturgical Press, 2022.

Brown Douglas, Kelly. "Contested Marriage/Loving Relationship." In *Sexuality and the Sacred: Sources for Theological Reflection, Second Edition*, edited by Kelly Brown Douglas and Marvin M. Ellison, 380–89. Louisville, KY: John Knox Press, 2010.

Cahill, Lisa. "Vatican Dogma v. Margaret Farley's *Just Love*." *Guardian*, June 18, 2012. https://www.theguardian.com/commentisfree/2012/jun/18/vatican-dogma-v-margaret-farley-just-love.

Bibliography

Castelfranco, Sabina. "Pope Francis: Don't Be Afraid to Have Children." *VOA*, January 6, 2022. https://www.voanews.com/a/pope-francis-don-t-be-afraid-to-have-children/6385264.html.

Catholic Labor Network. https://catholiclabor.org/.

Cleghorn, Elinor. *Unwell Women: Misdiagnosis and Myth in a Man-Made World*. New York: Penguin Random House LLC, 2021.

Congregation for Catholic Education. *Instruction Concerning the Criteria for the Discernment of Vocations with Regard to Persons with Homosexual Tendencies in View of Their Admission to the Seminary and to Holy Orders*. November 2005. https://www.vatican.va/roman_curia/congregations/ccatheduc/documents/rc_con_ccatheduc_doc_20051104_istruzione_en.html.

Congregation for the Doctrine of Faith. *Considerations Regarding Proposals to Give Legal Recognition to Unions Between Homosexual Persons*. June 3, 1993. https://www.vatican.va/roman_curia/congregations/cfaith/documents/rc_con_cfaith_doc_20030731_homosexual-unions_en.html.

———. *Letter to the Bishops of the Catholic Church on the Pastoral Care of Homosexual Persons*. October 1, 1986. https://www.vatican.va/roman_curia/congregations/cfaith/documents/rc_con_cfaith_doc_19861001_homosexual-persons_en.html.

———. *Notification on the Book* Just Love: A Framework for Christian Sexual Ethics *by Sr. Margaret A. Farley, R.S.M*. March 14, 2012. https://www.vatican.va/roman_curia/congregations/cfaith/documents/rc_con_cfaith_doc_20120330_nota-farley_en.html.

Coontz, Stephanie. "How to Make Your Marriage Gayer." *New York Times*, February 13, 2020. https://www.nytimes.com/2020/02/13/opinion/sunday/marriage-housework-gender-happiness.html.

Copeland, M. Shawn. *Enfleshing Freedom: Body, Race, and Being*. Minneapolis: Fortress Press, 2010.

Cornwall, Susannah. "Laws 'Needefull in Later to Be Abrogated'*: Intersex and the Sources of Christian Theology." In *Intersex, Theology, and the Bible: Troubling Bodies in Church, Text, and Society*, edited by Susannah Cornwall, 147–71. New York: Palgrave MacMillan, 2015.

———. *Sex and Uncertainty in the Body of Christ*. London: Routledge, 2014.

———. "Transformative Creatures: Theology, Gender Diversity, and Human Identity." *Zygon Journal of Science and Religion* 57, no. 3 (September 2022): 599–615.

Curran, Charles, ed. *Conscience: Readings in Moral Theology No. 14*. New York: Paulist Press, 2004.

Davison, Madeleine. "Memo to the Vatican: Same-Sex Couples Find God's Love in Marriage Too." *National Catholic Reporter*, March 25, 2021. https://www.ncronline.org/news/memo-vatican-same-sex-couples-find-gods-love-marriage-too.

Diamant, Jeff. "How Catholics Around the World See Same-Sex Marriage." *Pew Research Center*, November 2, 2020. https://www.pewresearch.org/fact-tank/2020/11/02/how-catholics-around-the-world-see-same-sex-marriage-homosexuality/.

Bibliography

Dias, Elizabeth. "'It Is Not a Closet. It Is a Cage.' Gay Catholic Priests Speak Out." *New York Times*, February 17, 2019. https://www.nytimes.com/2019/02/17/us/it-is-not-a-closet-it-is-a-cage-gay-catholic-priests-speak-out.html.

Dubus, Andres. "Epilogue: Sacraments." In *Signatures of Grace: Catholic Writers on the Sacraments*, edited by Thomas Grady and Paula Huston, 220–32. Eugene, OR: Wipf & Stock, 2001.

Editors of *America Magazine*. "How Should The Church Respond When Gay Employees Get Married?" *America Magazine*, October 26, 2016. https://www.americamagazine.org/faith/2016/10/25/how-should-church-respond-when-gay-employees-get-married.

Emmons, D.D. "Inside Our Sacred Space." *Our Sunday Visitor*, January 8, 2017. https://www.oursundayvisitor.com/inside-our-sacred-space/.

Farley, Margaret A. *Just Love: A Framework for Christian Sexual Ethics*. London: Continuum, 2006.

Fettro, Marshal Neal, and Wendy D. Manning. "Child Well-Being in Same-Gender-Parent Families: Courts, Media, and Social Science Research." In *Contemporary Parenting and Parenthood: From News Headlines to New Research*, edited by Michelle Y. Janning 283–301. Santa Barbara, CA: Praeger, 2019.

Ford, Craig. "Bishops' Theology Is the True Scandal in Philadelphia Foster Care Case." *National Catholic Reporter*, July 2, 2021. https://www.ncronline.org/news/opinion/us-bishops-theology-true-scandal-philadelphia-foster-care-case.

Francis, Pope. *Amoris Laetitia*. March 19, 2016. https://www.vatican.va/content/dam/francesco/pdf/apost_exhortations/documents/papa-francesco_esortazione-ap_20160319_amoris-laetitia_en.pdf.

———. *Evangelii Gaudium*. November 24, 2013. https://www.vatican.va/content/francesco/en/apost_exhortations/documents/papa-francesco_esortazione-ap_20131124_evangelii-gaudium.html.

———. *Fratelli Tutti*. October 3, 2020. https://www.vatican.va/content/francesco/en/encyclicals/documents/papa-francesco_20201003_enciclica-fratelli-tutti.html, sec. 198.

———. *Gaudete et exultate*. March 19, 2018. https://www.vatican.va/content/francesco/en/apost_exhortations/documents/papa-francesco_esortazione-ap_20180319_gaudete-et-exsultate.html.

Francis, Pope, and Austen Ivereigh. *Let Us Dream: The Path to a Better Future*. New York: Simon & Schuster, 2020.

FSSPX News. "Belgium: The Pope Accepts Blessing of Same-Sex Couples." *FSSPX News Information and Analysis on the Life of the Church*, March 25, 2023. https://fsspx.news/en/news-events/news/belgium-pope-accepts-blessing-same-sex-couples-81151#:~:text=The%20Bishop%20of%20Antwerp%20reaffirmed,of%20the%20German%20Synodal%20Path.

Gaillardetz, Richard R. *A Daring Promise: A Spirituality of Christian Marriage, Revised and Expanded Edition*. Liguori, MO: Liguori/Triumph, 2007.

Gehring, John. "The Scandal of Firing LGBT Catholics." *Commonweal Magazine*, February 16, 2018. https://www.commonwealmagazine.org/scandal-firing-lgbt-catholics.

Gudorf, Christine. "The Erosion of Sexual Dimorphism." In *Sexuality and the Sacred: Sources for Theological Reflection, Second Edition*, edited by Kelly Brown Douglas and Marvin M. Ellison, 141–64. Louisville, KY: John Knox Press, 2010.

Gushee, David. *Changing Our Mind*. Third edition. Canton, MS: David Crumm Media, LLC, 2017.

Hauser, Christine. "Catholic School in Kansas Faces a Revolt for Rejecting a Same-Sex Couple's Child." *New York Times*, March 8, 2019. https://www.nytimes.com/2019/03/08/us/kansas-catholic-school-same-sex-parents.html.

Himes, Michael J. "Finding God in All Things: A Sacramental Worldview and Its Effects." In *Becoming Beholders: Cultivating Sacramental Imagination and Action in College Classrooms*, edited by Karen E. Eifler and Thomas M. Landy, 3–17. Collegeville, MN: Liturgical Press, 2014.

Hogenboom, Melissa. "The Hidden Load: How 'Thinking of Everything' Holds Mums Back." *BBC*, May 18, 2021. https://www.bbc.com/worklife/article/20210518-the-hidden-load-how-thinking-of-everything-holds-mums-back.

John, Paul II. *Catechism of the Catholic Church*. Second edition. Washington, DC: United States Catholic Conference of Catholic Bishops, 2011. https://www.usccb.org/sites/default/files/flipbooks/catechism/.

Johnson, Elizabeth. *Consider Jesus: Waves of Renewal in Christology*. New York: Crossroad, 1995.

———. *She Who Is, The Mystery of God in Feminist Theological Discourse*. New York: Crossroads, 1992.

Johnson, Luke Timothy. "Homosexuality & The Church." *Commonweal*, June 11, 2007. https://www.commonwealmagazine.org/homosexuality-church-0.

———. *The Revelatory Body: Theology as Inductive Art*. Grand Rapids, MI: William B. Eerdmans Publishing Company, 2015.

Jones, Autumn. "'Gay and Catholic': A Q&A with Writer and Speaker Eve Tushnet.'" *The National Catholic Register*, July 12, 2021. https://www.ncregister.com/cna/gay-and-catholic-a-q-a-with-writer-and-speaker-eve-tushnet.

Keenan, James. "Virtue Ethics and Sexual Ethics." *Louvain Studies* 30, no. 3 (Fall 2005): 180–96.

Kirchgaessner, Stephanie. "Pope Francis: Not Having Children Is Selfish." *Guardian*, February 11, 2015. https://www.theguardian.com/world/2015/feb/11/pope-francis-the-choice-to-not-have-children-is-selfish.

Lawler, Michael G. "Faith, Contract, and Sacrament in Christian Marriage: A Theological Approach." In *Christian Marriage and Family*, edited by Michael G. Lawler and William P. Roberts, 38–58. Collegeville, MN: Liturgical Press, 1996.

———. "Marriage and the Sacrament of Marriage." In *Christian Marriage and Family*, edited by Michael G. Lawler and William P. Roberts, 22–37. Collegeville, MN: Liturgical Press, 1996.

Bibliography

———. "Marriage in the Bible." In *Perspectives on Marriage: A Reader*, edited by Kieran Scott and Michael Warren, 7–21. Oxford, UK: Oxford University Press, 2001.

Lawler, Michael G., and Todd A. Salzman. "Human Dignity and Homosexuality in Catholic Teaching: An Anthropological Disconnect between Truth and Love?" *Interdisciplinary Journal for Religion and Transformation in Contemporary Society* 6, no.1 (July 2020): 119–39.

———. *Introduction to Catholic Theological Ethics: Foundations and Applications.* New York: Orbis Books, 2019.

———. "Pope Francis Brings Nuance to Notion of Complementarity." *National Catholic Reporter*, May 29, 2015. https://www.ncronline.org/news/theology/pope-francis-brings-nuance-notion-complementarity.

———. "Quaestio Disputata, Catholic Sexual Ethics: Complementarity and the Truly Human." *Theological Studies* 67 (2006): 625–46.

———. *The Sexual Person: Toward a Renewed Catholic Anthropology.* Washington, DC: Georgetown University Press, 2008.

Liptak, Adam. "Supreme Court Backs Catholic Agency in Case on Gay Rights and Foster Care." *New York Times*, June 17, 2021. https://www.nytimes.com/2021/06/17/us/supreme-court-gay-rights-foster-care.html.

Martin, James. *Building a Bridge: How the Catholic Community and the LGBT Community Can Enter into a Relationship of Respect, Compassion, and Sensitivity*, Revised and Expanded Edition. New York: HarperOne, 2018.

———. "Pedophilia and Homosexuality." *America Magazine*, April 13, 2010. https://www.americamagazine.org/content/all-things/pedophilia-and-homosexuality.

Massingale, Bryan. "Beyond 'Who Am I to Judge?': The *Sensus Fidelium*, LGBT Experience, and Truth-Telling in the Catholic Church." In *Learning from All the Faithful*, edited by Bradford E. Hinze and Peter C. Phan, 170–83. Eugene, OR: Pickwick Publications, 2016.

———. *Outspoken 2: Interview Rev. Bryan Massingale*, interviewed by Ryan Di Corpo and James Martin. Outreach: An LGBTQ Catholic Resource. February 28, 2023. https://www.youtube.com/watch?v=lLm0IcsSYkI.

McCarthy Matzko, David. "Homosexuality and the Practices of Marriage." *Modern Theology* 13, no. 3 (July 1997): 371–97.

McElroy, Robert W. "Enlarging Our Tent: The Synodal Imperative Toward a Church of Inclusion and Shared Belonging." Presentation, Bergoglio Lecture Series, Sacred Heart University, Fairfield, CT. February 22, 2023. https://www.sacredheart.edu/media/shu-media/catholic-studies/Cardinal-McElroy-Talk-02-22-23.pdf.

Merton, Thomas. *Thoughts in Solitude.* New York: Farrar, Straus and Giroux, 1999.

Mescher, Marcus. *The Ethics of Encounter: Christian Neighbor Love as a Practice of Solidarity.* New York: Orbis Books, 2020.

O'Kane, Caitlin. "Pope Francis Says Parents Should Support Gay Children Not Condemn Them." *CBS News*, January 26, 2022. https://www.cbsnews.com/news/pope-francis-says-parents-should-support-gay-children-not-condemn-them/.

O'Loughlin, Michael J. "'It Just Hurts': Catholics React to Vatican Ban on Blessings for Same-Sex Couples." *America Magazine*, March 15, 2021. https://

www.americamagazine.org/faith/2021/03/15/vatican-blessing-same-sex-unions-reactions-pope-francis-240249.

Outreach: An LGBTQ Catholic Resource. *The Outreach Guide to the Bible and Homosexuality*. https://outreach.faith/bible/.

Peterson-Iyer, Karen. *Reenvisioning Sexual Ethics: A Feminist Christian Account*. Washington, DC: Georgetown University Press, 2022.

Pizzuto, Vincent. "God Has Made It Plain to Them: An Indictment of Rome's Hermeneutic of Homophobia." *Biblical Theology Bulletin* 38, no. 4 (Winter 2008): 163–83.

Plante, Thomas G. "No, Homosexuality Is Not a Risk Factor for the Sexual Abuse of Children." *America Magazine*, October 22, 2018. https://www.americamagazine.org/faith/2018/10/22/no-homosexuality-not-risk-factor-sexual-abuse-children.

Pohl, Christine D. *Making Room: Recovering Hospitality as a Christian Tradition*. Grand Rapids, MI: William B. Eerdmans Publishing Company, 1999.

Pullella, Phillip. "Vatican Ruling on Same-Sex Couples Prompts Defiance, Pain, Confusion." *Reuters*, March 17, 2021. https://www.reuters.com/world/europe/vatican-ruling-same-sex-couples-prompts-defiance-pain-confusion-2021-03-17/.

Rush, Orland. "The Church as Hermeneutical Community and the Eschatological Function of the *Sensus Fidelium*." In *Learning from All the Faithful*, edited by Bradford E. Hinze and Peter C. Phan. Eugene, OR: Pickwick Publications, 2016.

Schlegelmilch, Renardo. "Germany's Catholic Church Approved Blessings for Same-Sex Couples. Is This a Revolution?" *National Catholic Reporter*, March 15, 2023. https://www.ncronline.org/opinion/guest-voices/germanys-catholic-church-approved-blessings-same-sex-couples-revolution.

Schneible, Ann. "Pope Francis: Children Have a Right to a Mother and Father." *Catholic News Agency*, November 17, 2014. https://www.catholicnewsagency.com/news/30948/pope-francis-children-have-right-to-a-mother-and-father.

Second Vatican Council. *Gaudium et Spes*. December 7, 1965. https://www.vatican.va/archive/hist_councils/ii_vatican_council/documents/vat-ii_const_19651207_gaudium-et-spes_en.html.

Shrine, Robert. "More Than 100 Church Workers Have Lost Their Jobs in LGBTQ-Related Employment Disputes That Went Public in the Last Decade." New Ways Ministry. February 2022. https://www.newwaysministry.org/2022/02/18/church-worker-faces-second-firing-from-catholic-institution-over-lgbtq-marriage/.

Spadaro, S.J., Antonio. "A Big Heart Open to God: An Interview with Pope Francis." *America*, September 30, 2013. https://www.americamagazine.org/faith/2013/09/30/big-heart-open-god-interview-pope-francis.

Stantz, Julianne. *Braving the Thin Spaces: Celtic Wisdom to Create a Space for Grace*. Chicago: Loyola Press, 2021.

Thomasset, Alain. "The Virtue of Hospitality According to the Bible and the Challenge of Migration." In *The Bible and Catholic Theological Ethics*, edited by Yiu Sing Lúcás Chan, James F. Keenan, and Ronaldo Zacharias, 28–33. Maryknoll, NY: Orbis Books, 2017.

Bibliography

Traina, Cristina. "How Gendered Is Marriage?" In *Sex, Loves and Families: Catholic Perspectives*, edited by Jason King and Julie Hanlon Rubio, 79–90. Collegeville, MN: Liturgical Press Academic, 2020.

The Trevor Project. "Facts About LGBTQ Youth Suicide." December 15, 2021. https://www.thetrevorproject.org/resources/article/facts-about-lgbtq-youth-suicide/.

Tushnet, Eve. *Gay and Catholic: Accepting My Sexuality, Finding Community, and Living My Faith*. Notre Dame, IN: Ave Maria Press, 2014.

———. *Tenderness: A Gay Christian's Guide to Unlearning Rejection and Experiencing God's Extravagant Love*. Notre Dame, IN: Ave Maria Press, 2021.

United States Conference of Catholic Bishops. *Always Our Children*. USCCB Committee on Marriage and Family Life. September 10, 1997. https://www.usccb.org/resources/Always%20Our%20Children.pdf.

———. *Between Man and Woman: Questions and Answers About Marriage and Same-Sex Unions*. 2003. https://www.usccb.org/topics/promotion-defense-marriage/between-man-and-woman-questions-and-answers-about-marriage-and.

———. *The Dignity of Work and The Rights of Workers*. https://www.usccb.org/beliefs-and-teachings/what-we-believe/catholic-social-teaching/the-dignity-of-work-and-the-rights-of-workers.

———. *FAQs on the Meaning of Marriage & Sexual Difference*. USCCB Promotion and Defense of Marriage. https://www.usccb.org/topics/promotion-defense-marriage/faqs-meaning-marriage-sexual-difference.

———. *Marriage: Love and Life in the Divine Plan*. November 17, 2009. https://www.usccb.org/topics/marriage-and-family-life-ministries/marriage-love-and-life-divine-plan.

———. *Ministry to Persons with a Homosexual Inclination: Guidelines for Pastoral Care*. November 14, 2006. https://www.usccb.org/resources/ministry-to-persons-of-homosexual-iInclination_0.pdf.

Vogt, Christopher. "The Inevitability of Scandal: A Moral and Biblical Analysis of Firing Gay Teachers and Ministers to Avoid Scandal." In *The Bible and Catholic Theological Ethics*, edited by Yiu Sing Lúcás Chan, James F. Keenan, and Ronaldo Zacharias, 152–57. Maryknoll, NY: Orbis Books, 2017.

Ward, Nancy. "Pope Francis: Three Key Words: Please, Thank You, Sorry." *JOY Alive in Our Hearts*, May 13, 2015. https://joyalive.net/pope-francis-three-key-words-please-thank-you-sorry/.

Winfield, Nicole. "Pope's 3 Key Words For A Marriage: 'Please, Thanks, Sorry.'" *AP News*, December 26, 2021. https://apnews.com/article/pope-francis-lifestyle-religion-relationships-couples-23c81169982e50c35d1c1fc7bfef8cbc.

Zudrow, Andru. "USCCB Drops Opposition to Catholic Agencies Serving Single LGBTQ Foster Parents." *New Ways Ministry*, July 13, 2022. https://www.newwaysministry.org/2022/07/13/usccb-drops-opposition-to-catholic-agencies-serving-single-lgbtq-foster-parents/.

Index

Always Our Children, 149
Amiel, Henri-Frederic, 182
Amoris Laetitia (Pope Francis), xiv, 2n2, 7n6, 50–51, 52n16, 77n72, 184n6
Archdiocese of Denver, 152n8
Archdiocese of Kansas City, 152n8
Archer, Kristjan, 166nn11–12

Baldovin, John, 159n9
Belgian Catholic bishops, 51n13
biblical interpretation, 56–61, 185; on same-sex activity, 56n24; and scandal 173–176, 183; and the sense of the faithful, 185
binary (two-sex) model of gender. *See* male-female complementarity
blessings of same-sex couples, Catholic Church, 51, postscript, 193–194
Body of Christ, xii-xix, 2, 138, 146, 190. *See also* eucharist
Boyle, Greg, SJ, 47n8
Brigham, Erin, 188–189

Cahill, Lisa, 63n48
Catechism of the Catholic Church, 11n10, 75n66, 170, 172
The Catholic Labor Network, 161n10
Catholic Church teaching: on homosexuality, 62, 170, 183–84; on the ordination of homosexual men, 168–69; on marriage, xiii-xiv, 2, 4–6, 33–34, 50–52, 62; on procreativity, 42, 52, 55, 74–77; on same-sex couples, 2, 50–51, 55, 183–4; on same-sex couple adoption, 76. *See also* disorder; male-female complementarity
Cleghorn, Elinor, 52n17
complementarity. *See* holistic complementarity; male-female complementarity
Congregation for Catholic Education, 168
Congregation for the Doctrine of Faith, xiv, 50; on homosexuality, 5–6, 62; on Farley's sexual ethics, 63n48; on procreation,

Index

42n78; on same-sex couple adoption 76; on same-sex marriage, 50–51, 62, 77n72, 184
conscience, 6–9, 9n9, 92, 129
Coontz, Stephanie, 72
Copeland, M. Shawn, 186n12, 190
Cornwall, Susannah, 59n32, 61–64
covenantal love, 15–16, 18. *See also* sacrament
Curran, Charles, 9n9

Davison, Madeleine, 51n13
Defense of Marriage Act (DOMA), 113
dialogue, xiv, 185
Diamant, Jeff, 166n12
Dias, Elizabeth, 168
Dignity (organization), 31–32, 128–130, 132
discernment, 7–9. *See also* conscience
discrimination (against LGBTQ persons), 121, 138, 155; in Catholic institutions, 150–52, 160–61, 168-173; in Catholic schools, 152n8; and social media, 151, 169; *See also* exclusion in Church communities
disorder, 52–54
Douglas, Kelly B., 59–60, 63

Emmons, D.D., 187n13
encounter. *See* dialogue

eucharist, 11–13, 38, 49–50; 118; 130; 186–187, 190; and eucharistic ministry, 120, 131–135. *See also* Body of Christ
Evangelii Gaudium (Pope Francis), xvn4, 148, 169n19, 170nn20–21, 184–85
exclusion (of LGBTQ persons), in church communities, 117, 132, 134, 144, 149, 152, 158–59, 181-82, 184, 188. *See also* discrimination

families of LGBTQ persons: resources for, 110n8
Family Acceptance Project, 110n8
Farley, Margaret, 53n*e*, 63n48
Fettro, Marshal N, 76n71
fidelity, 1, 10, 12, 16, 18–26, 53
Ford, Craig, 76n69
Fortunate Families, 110n8
Francis (pope): *Amoris Laetitia*, xiv, 2n2, 7n6, 50–51, 52n16, 77n72, 184n6; on church as field hospital, 188; *Evangelii Gaudium*, xvn4, 148, 169n19, 170nn20–21, 184–85; *Fratelli Tutti*, xiv, 150; *Gaudete et Exsultate*, 151; *Let Us Dream*, xixn7, 41, 49; on married life, 18n18; on parenting and children, 55n20, 74n63; on same-sex unions, 33n78; on social media, 151, 169

Index

Fratelli Tutti (Pope Francis), xiv, 150
Fullum, Lisa, 173

Gaillardetz, Richard, 40n5
Gaudete et Exsultate (Pope Francis), 151
Gaudium et Spes (Second Vatican Council), 6–7, 33–34, 75n65
Gehring, John, 178nn20–21
German Catholic bishops, 51n13
Gudorf, Christine, 61n39
Gushee, David, 53–54, 56n24, 57–59, 61, 184–185

Hauser, Christine, 152n8
Himes, Michael, 1
Hogenboom, Melissa, 72n57
holistic complementarity, 63–74. *See also* male-female complementarity
hospitality, virtue of, 47–49, 75, 79n9, 188; in church communities, 134, 138–39, 142–43, 149, 162; and parenting, 34–36, 42, 75. *See also* sanctuary
Humanae Vitae (Pope Paul VI), 74. *See also* procreativity

interpretation, biblical. *See* biblical interpretation
intersexuality. *See* male-female complementarity

Johnson, Elizabeth, 64n53, 174

Johnson, Luke T., 50, 55n21, 56–57, 185
Jung, Patricia Beattie, 61n39

Keenan, James, 18, 40, 53n*e*, 63n48

L'Arche (organization), 14n12, 39
Lawler, Michael, 10n9, 15–16, 52n17, 62–64n53, 76n69
Let Us Dream (Pope Francis), xixn7, 41, 49
Liptak, Adam, 76n69
listening, intentional, xiv-xv, 185
liturgy, wedding, 2, 10–15
Lockman, Darcy, 73
Lumen Gentium (Second Vatican Council), 16, 185

Magisterium, Catholic. *See* Catholic Church teaching
male-female (heterosexual) complementarity, 52, 55–64, 71–73; and interpretations of Genesis, 10, 56nn23–24, 58–61; and intersexuality 61–62; and gender roles, 72–74; in procreativity and parenting, 74–77. *See also* holistic complementarity
Manning, Wendy D., 76n71
Martin, James, SJ, 139n4, 149n4, 171–72
Massingale, Bryan, 139n4, 168n15, 168–69, 170, 172, 185

Matrimony. *See* sacrament of Matrimony
McCarthy, David Matzko, 53
McCarthy, Justin, 166nn11–12
McElroy, Robert, 181–184
mercy, 18, 40, 51, 167, 174, 188; and works of mercy, 51, 136
Merton, Thomas, 17
The Merton Prayer. *See* Merton, Thomas
Mescher, Marcus, xivn2

nature: and sexuality, 62–63

Obergefell (v. Hodges), 126, 166, 194
O'Laughlin, Michael J., 51n13
one body imagery, 10–12, 15–16, 21, 189. *See also* Catholic Church teaching
Outreach (organization), 56n24, 159n9, 168

Peterson-Iyer, Karen, 52n15, 53n*e*, 54n*g*
Pizzuto, Vincent, 169
Plante, Thomas G., 149n4
Pohl, Christine D., 47n9
procreativity. *See* Catholic Church teaching
Pullella, Phillip, 51n13

Rush, Ormond, 185

sacrament, 1, 9–10, 15–17; of baptism, 43; in daily life (ordinary sacraments; quotidian), 1–2; of the eucharist, 11–14, 50; of Matrimony, xv, 2, 10, 12–16, 33–34, 51-2; to one another, xx-xxi, 1–2, 26, 40n5; as outward-facing, xx-xxi, 1–2, 31, 33–34, 38, 41. *See also* Catholic Church teaching; eucharist
Salzman, Todd, 10n9, 62–63, 76n69
sanctuary, 187–191; Church as, 188–191
scandal, 173–176, 182–83, 191
Schlegelmilch, Renardo, 51n13
Second Vatican Council, 6–7, 16, 33–34, 75n65, 181, 185
Senander, Angela, 173
sensus fidei, 185
sexual abuse: and the Catholic Church, 119, 138, 149, 153
Sexual binary. *See* male-female (heterosexual) complementarity
Shepard, Matthew, xi-xii
Shrine, Robert, 171n24
Stantz, Julianne, 101n5
subsidiarity, 161n10
synodality, 181–182; and the Synod on Synodality, xv, 133

thin space, 101
Thomasset, Alain, SJ, 47n9
Traina, Cristina, 52n17, 73–74

Transsssexuality, 61–62, 168
The Trevor Project, xviiin6
Tushnet, Eve, 167n13

United States Conference of Catholic Bishops (USCCB): on the dignity of work, 161n10; on homosexuality, 52–3, 62n45, 149n2; on male-female complementarity, 56n22; on marriage, 52, 55n20, 74–5; on procreation and parenting, 74–77; on Salzman and Lawler, 62n48; on sanctuary spaces, 187n14

Vatican II. *See* Second Vatican Council
Vogt, Christopher, 171, 173–175, 183

wedding. *See* liturgy
work, right to, 161n10

Zodrow, Andru, 76n69

Transsssexuality, 61–62, 168
The Trevor Project, xviiin6
Tushnet, Eve, 167n13

United States Conference of Catholic Bishops (USCCB): on the dignity of work, 161n10; on homosexuality, 52–3, 62n45, 149n2; on male-female complementarity, 56n22; on marriage, 52, 55n20, 74–5; on procreation and parenting, 74–77; on Salzman and Lawler, 62n48; on sanctuary spaces, 187n14

Vatican II. *See* Second Vatican Council
Vogt, Christopher, 171, 173–175, 183

wedding. *See* liturgy
work, right to, 161n10

Zodrow, Andru, 76n69

About the Author

Bridget Burke Ravizza is professor of theology and religious studies at St. Norbert College in De Pere, Wisconsin, currently serving as interim director of the college's Cassandra Voss Center and Norman Miller Center for Peace, Justice & Public Understanding. She holds a doctorate in theological ethics from Boston College, and her work focuses on sexual ethics and the ethics of marriage and family. With Julie Donovan Massey, MDiv, she is coauthor of *Project Holiness: Marriage as a Workshop for Everyday Saints*.

www.ingramcontent.com/pod-product-compliance
Lightning Source LLC
Chambersburg PA
CBHW031619170426
43195CB00036B/743